Ruthless

Ruthless

How Enraged Investors Reclaimed Their Investments and Beat Wall Street

Phil Trupp

WILEY

John Wiley & Sons, Inc.

Published by John Wiley & Sons, Inc., Hoboken, New Jersey.
Published simultaneously in Canada.

For general information on our other products and services or for technical support, please
contact our Customer Care Department within the United States at (800) 762-2974,
outside the United States at (317) 572-3993 or fax (317) 572-4002.

Wiley also publishes its books in a variety of electronic formats. Some content that appears
in print may not be available in electronic books. For more information about Wiley
products, visit our web site at www.wiley.com.

Library of Congress Cataloging-in-Publication Data:

Trupp, Philip Z. (Philip Zber)
    Ruthless : how enraged investors reclaimed their investments and beat Wall Street/
Phil Trupp.
        p.   cm.
    Includes index.
    ISBN 978-0-470-57989-3 (hardback)
        1. Securities fraud—United States.   2. Corporations—Corrupt practices—United
States.   3. Floating rate notes—United States.   I. Title.
    HV6769.T78   2010
    364.16'3—dc22

                                                                    2010018599

Printed in the United States of America
10 9 8 7 6 5 4 3 2 1

To Sandy,
whose love and support
made this book happen

Contents

The auction-rate securities scandal is just one more variation on a reoccurring theme. And that theme is the documented belief of large segments of the financial-services industry that they are above the law, entitled to special privileges, entitled to engage in conflicts of interest, and they have no duty or obligation to average investors.

—*William F. Galvin, secretary of state and chief securities regulator, Commonwealth of Massachusetts*

Author's Note

What Is an Auction-Rate Security?

Y ou may have never heard of auction rate securities (ARS). Until the ARS market crashed on February 13, 2008 most investors were unaware of these niche Wall Street products. They have since become iconic symbols of the biggest financial fraud in modern Wall Street history.

ARS are "debt obligations"—bonds that promise to pay back an investment with interest. They are issued mostly by municipal organizations in need of cheap funding—charities, universities, museums, student loan organizations, hospitals, and the like.

ARS are bonds with fluctuating interest rates. As the "market makers," Wall Street banks underwrote the bonds for the issuers and their brokerages managed the auctions at which they were sold to investors.

Unlike an ordinary U.S. Treasury bond with a fixed interest rate, or yield, the interest rates for ARS were reset at auctions every 7, 28, or 35 days. For example, a student loan ARS might yield 3 percent at one auction and wind up yielding 2 percent at another, depending on how many investors were willing to buy it.

Wall Street banks controlled the auctions and charged handsome fees for doing so. When things were running smoothly, the issuers received long-term financing at short-term rates. And investors received higher yields than plain vanilla money market funds, with no apparent risk to principal if interest rates spiked.

ARS auctions created a unique kind of money market. An ordinary money market is a mix of very short-term U.S. Treasury bonds, cash, and highly liquid securities. ARS, on the other hand, was a money market made up of bonds with long-term maturities of 30 to 40 years. This long-term maturity was the devil in the details which the brokers failed to disclose.

Before the credit crunch and resulting panic that killed off Bear Sterns and Lehman Brothers, ARS investors could sell their securities at auctions with almost no perceived risk—until the market suddenly imploded. That's exactly what happened on February 13, 2008, leaving investors stuck holding bonds no one wanted to buy and no market in which to sell them. The bonds, however, weren't worthless. Investors just couldn't cash them in. If you could afford to wait 30 or 40 years, the original issuer was then obligated to "call" or buy back the bond at full value, or par. After the crash, one of my brokers joked that I'd be proud to hand off my ARS holdings to my grandchildren—a little taste of shtick from "the best and the brightest."

If nothing else, Wall Street is tricky and self-serving. Seldom, if ever, were ARS investors told they were actually buying long-term securities. Instead, the bonds were marketed as "cash equivalents," "cash alternatives," "cash management tools," and "floaters," "same as cash." Investors were told they could get their cash anytime they wanted it—until they couldn't.

These deceptive descriptions of liquidity kept investors feeling secure. The soft sell pitches worked like a charm.

To keep investors' minds off risk, brokers made use of a concealed mix of Wall Street tricks. For example, brokers neglected to reveal little "tells" that hinted something in the ARS market was more risky than investors imagined.

One of those tricks was "incentivization." Bank management pushed brokers to sell ARS by giving them an unexpected reward. When a broker places your cash in an ordinary money market fund, he or she usually makes no commission. But if they lured you into the ARS market—*ka-ching!*—the brokers rang up a commission that was hidden from investors. This little tail was offered because banks knew the market was in trouble and they wanted their brokers to push hard. They wanted to get all the ARS they could off their own balance sheets and into investor portfolios quickly as possible.

"Safety" and "high liquidity" were repeatedly touted by the brokers. It was the typical hard sell using nuanced language. Investors were persuaded that the higher yield of one-half to 1 percent over ordinary money markets was too small to be scary. No big deal. No red flags to signal risk or a Wall Street drive to dump its inventory of ARS bonds. These days, investors have become painfully aware that reaching for yield can be dangerous, even devastating.

Among the other secrets hidden from the investing public—and from some gullible brokers—was that ARS auctions were not fail-safe. Far from it. Failures had occurred as early as 2004. These failures were hushed up like state secrets.

When the market finally collapsed because they weren't producing enough profit for the banks, Wall Street pocketed $336 billion of investors' money and, in effect, told ARS holders, "Tough luck. Sue us!"

HSBC was the first bank to do the right thing. On June 24, 2008, Global Banking News reported the bank would make its investors whole without being threatened by regulators. HSBC clients were lucky. The rest of us would have to fight. It was at this point that my own personal nightmare began.

Introduction

Imagine waking up one morning to discover your life savings have vanished. Your broker is on the phone telling you in a calm, almost indifferent voice that, like it or not, your "cash equivalent" investment, sold to you as ordinary cash, is now frozen, illiquid. Sorry, you can't get your hands on it.

What the trusted broker is careful not to tell you is that you've become part of the biggest alleged fraud in modern Wall Street history, the $336 billion auction-rate securities (ARS) scandal. He's not calling it fraud, of course. More like "temporary illiquidity."

The shock hits hard. When you finally catch your breath you come to a life-altering realization. Surprise! You're broke—or broke enough so that your life and your plans for the future have been significantly altered. But you can relax, it's only a temporary glitch, your broker says. Still, he can't or won't tell you when (or if) you'll ever get your cash back. But he's hopeful, sort of. And when hope runs out, he's evasive, defensive, or absent.

And as days pass into weeks, weeks into months, months into more than a year, you wake up to the grim reality that you're stuck in what Spencer Bachus, the Democratic congressman from Alabama, calls "a financial roach motel." You checked in to the auction-rate securities market believing your broker's reassuring line about "safety" and "liquidity," that auction-rate bonds are "better than Treasuries," and now you can't get out. You're stuck. Your money's illiquid and frozen for who knows how long. Suddenly, Bernard Madoff's $65 billion Ponzi scheme, the one everybody is talking about, looks like chump change. Madoff shrinks to his proper size as a weasel con artist—just another crook. The auction-rate securities collapse, on the other hand, is an *institutional* calamity involving almost every major bank in the Western world. The Savings and Loan crisis of the 1980s and early 1990s, by comparison, fades to a blip on the glaring Wall Street billboard of dirty tricks. When you come to grips with the fact that you are a victim of this gigantic betrayal, your future goes tumbling off a cliff.

Oh, no. You're not going to take it. You reach for help, for solace, for ways to get your money and your life back on track. Within days you find other victims—insurgent, outraged investors—146,500 of them—stuck in the same financial roach motel you're in and unable to get their hands on billions of dollars. A lot of ordinary people, everyday investors, and plenty of seasoned pros at major corporations had no idea they were being set up for what would turn out to be a market failure of such massive proportions. They work with federal and state regulators and with each other on the Internet, to form a take-no-prisoners crusade against the banks and broker-dealers that dumped these toxic assets into your portfolio, knowing all along that when the implosion came, the Wall Street banks and bonus babies had no intention of ever giving your money back.

Armed with digital torches and pitchforks, the victims marched together across the Internet to take on these shameless "fraud meisters." At this writing, this Internet army has gained strategic victories. Through constant and coordinated pressure, and with help from some state attorneys general, we've managed to shake loose nearly $200 billion. That's the good news, although the fight is far from over. Approximately $120 billion to $160 billion remains locked in various Wall Street "roach motels."

Still, the achieved gains are no small victory. The fight has exposed, yet again, a financial industry that lies, cheats, and steals with near impunity. It gets away with these crimes because so many regulators look the other way. The scandal has also shined a spotlight on the cozy

Wall Street–Washington, D.C., nexus. There are no clean hands. The crooks and the cops often have interests in common.

The auction-rate securities rip-off was engineered by the "best and the brightest," those CEOs and Wall Street investment bankers who have given us the greatest financial meltdown since the Great Depression. We haven't solved the problem of greed, and surely the dirty tricks will be served up in heaping portions in the years to come.

On Christmas Eve 2009, for example, Gretchen Morgenson and Louise Story of the *New York Times* reported the details of the double-dealing mortgage scam engineered by one of Wall Street's most prestigious banks. In a news report headed "Banks Bundled Bad Debt, Bet against It and Won," the reporters alleged that Goldman Sachs knowingly bundled and sold junk mortgages then turned around and bet against them, making billions in profits at their clients' expense when the mortgage market collapsed. Responding to the story, Goldman said its securitized time bombs were purchased by "sophisticated" investors who knew exactly what they were doing. Those unfortunate investors had no one to blame but themselves. As to the human misery that blossomed in the wake of the scam, Goldman had little to say.

It was the same rhetoric leveled by Wall Street against auction-rate securities investors: *They should have known better.* Goldman's CEO, Lloyd Blankfein was shocked by the tone of the *Times* story. Why all the fuss? Goldman was "doing God's work," he said. And, yes, the mortgage investors caught flat-footed were sophisticated and knew what they were doing. It's an old line. Maybe those investors should have known better than to trust Wall Street in the first place.

This story is very personal. I was one of those ARS investors who woke up one morning to discover an important chunk of my life savings was no longer available to me. I'd been suckered into believing in the safety of the market, and no one would bet I'd ever get my money back. In fact, my broker wouldn't even talk to me.

Being a victim of financial double-dealing is a life-altering experience. Everything changes. It's mental and emotional rape. Being conned is to play the fool. My ARS experience turned my life upside-down. But it also launched a personal journey that has been one of the most wrenching and rewarding of a long journalistic career. I've been a reporter and columnist for the *Washington Evening Star*, written and ghosted more than a dozen books, been a cocreator of editorial for national magazines, including the *Washingtonian*, and have traveled the world writing for major publications such as *Reader's Digest, Madison Avenue*, Fairchild Publications, and ABC Cap Cities. I have covered virtually every aspect of Washington, from Congress to the White House and the Supreme Court, and am proud to say I was once bawled out by President Lyndon Johnson. I am no stranger to social and economic crime, having risked my life covering mob activity in the trucking industry and the sad state of America's coal mines. My stories have been reprinted in *The Congressional Record* and elsewhere. I have taken good care of my professional toolbox and was prepared to use each of those tools in the battle I was about to wage.

If you are an investor, my story, and those of my fellow victims, may give you a few sleepless nights. If you have a brokerage account—beware. These days I tell people that if you have a broker you may have a problem. And if you're in the shadow of Wall Street, run!

You may not like what you are about to read here. You are in for an unsettling lesson: Wall Street has made betrayal the cost of doing business in the United States, and you are a target. The Street has no shame. No conscience. Many have argued that its double-dealing is a threat to the security of our country. After the financial meltdown of 2008–2009, this argument has gained greater credence and it's left for history to decide. The reverberations have left no pundit behind.

Some of us who faced financial ruin in the ARS scam came close to launching ourselves out of a window. *Ah, but it's only money*, some of you may say. *Aren't you distorting your true humanistic values?* This is what we hear from dreamers and idealists who have never seen their future taken away from them. On one level the idealists are correct. Yes, it's *only* money—food on your table and the roof over your head. If it means so little to you, please allow me to remind you of an old Jack Benny joke:

A holdup man threatens the comedian, "Your money or your life!" he warns. When Benny hesitates, the impatient thug repeats his threat. Benny replies, "I'm thinking, I'm thinking!"

This is America. It is a very cruel place to be broke.

But there is a happy, almost mind-boggling end to this debacle, and it is this: I have learned that *justice* exists in the world. If you fight hard enough, if you demand what's right, if others join your cause, justice can be achieved—even on Wall Street. You may doubt me. But if you stick with my story, I'll prove it's true.

Chapter 1

"Deal With It!"

I believe that banking institutions are more dangerous to our
liberties than standing armies.

—*Thomas Jefferson*

March 2006.

"Take it, Phil, it's free money," my broker said.

Free money? This is a joke, right? Is this some kind of broker
humor? Where's the rim shot? He's never shown much of a penchant
for levity. So I asked with complete sincerity, "Are you kidding?"

"Not a joke," my broker replied, sounding as if my skepticism is
tweaking his sensitive soul. "I'm trying to get you into auction-rate
securities. A *really* good deal," he said in a confidential tone, as if he
were handing me a key to a secret treasure. He went on to explain that
auction-rate securities are "cash equivalents. Completely liquid. Safe as
U.S. Treasury bonds—and with a higher yield."

Cash equivalent? What, exactly, did he mean?

"Like I said, it's just like a money market. You've been trading stocks forever. Don't you get it?"

I'm skeptical. The tricky little catchphrase, "cash equivalent"—it has an odd, not quite tangible ring to it. As far as I'm concerned there's cash, the green "In God We Trust" paper you stuff in your wallet, and *no* real equivalent.

Still skeptical, I ask for a prospectus. This elicits a gruff little chuckle from my broker. His laugh has the indulgent tone of a parent whose toddler asks why the sky is blue.

"Trust me," the broker sighed. He's impatient with my questions.

I hear his cell phone chirping in the background. Seems it is always chirping. The caller must be a VIP, someone with access to my broker's private line.

"Hey, look, I really think I need a prospectus," I persisted. "Do you have one or don't you?"

Now he is annoyed, a bit huffy.

"Yeah, well, I think we do. I'll ask around. It's the size of the Manhattan telephone directory. You up for that kind of reading?"

Long pause. The cell phone is louder now, prodding, as if the gadget is reminding me that its owner has urgent matters to deal with, and that my infantile skepticism, my wanting a prospectus, is getting in the way of him making really big bucks.

"Trust me," the broker repeated, only now he's obviously put out. I half expect him to hit me with something like, *where's the love, man*? "How long have I known you?" he asked. "Have I ever steered you wrong?"

No, not really, and that's because I seldom expect him to rise up like a golden Master of the Universe—a "MOTU," the Polynesian word for a coral atoll or lagoon, typically shark-infested. I have been trading stocks and bonds for decades, in good markets and bad. And throughout this tedious slog through the market I have known only one MOTU. Not the one I'm talking to today. He's merely a hustling salesman, a plain vanilla financial advisor, an FA, an ordinarily well-meaning schlemiel who calls with occasional news of the latest initial public offerings being pushed by his company, A.G. Edwards & Sons. He often puts a sexy spin on those quirky IPOs, for which I pay no fee, though my broker picks up a little undisclosed incentive on the side if he closes the deal. As with his talk of auction-rate securities, he speaks of IPOs in hushed, confidential tones, as if I've been chosen by the gods and am lucky to get my hands on one of those derivative-laden pieces of junk, the vast accumulation of which, on an international scale, eventually delivered us to the "Global Credit Crisis of 2009" and the biggest loss of investor wealth since the Great Depression. But about those auction-rate securities. . . .

"I'm not going to twist your arm," the broker said at last, tiring of my questions. His tone turned slightly hurt, as if he were my dear friend and I was the ingrate. "I can get you a full basis point over anything in money market. Auction-rate securities are completely safe. Completely liquid. Just another form of cash. So—you in or out?" The cell phone is no longer chirping.

"Okay. Do it." It is an act of trust that would come back to haunt me in ways I never could have imagined.

✱ ✱ ✱

9 A.M., February 14, 2008, Valentine's Day

I was seated at my computer, prepared to face a day steering my little stock and bond portfolio through yet another storm of manipulated market short selling on Wall Street. Can't say I was looking forward to it. By now I was sweating marathon days and nights. Deep into microanalysis, I was starting to feel like the obsessive gamblers in the pages of *Fools Die*, Mario Puzo's classic novel of life inside a Las Vegas casino. But I was no gambler. Safety was my byword. This was not a time to take big risks.

After almost eight perilous years of the Bush administration's passion for deregulation, I had grown used to the "market guy's" lack of economic smarts and Wall Street's cocktail of greed and corruption. Short sellers were driving the markets into the pits and the regulatory cops were asleep. The Securities and Exchange Commission (SEC) had long ago faded into the zombie zone. Insatiable Wall Street greed and anarchy had begun to erode the broader stock and bond markets, and they were now seeping into the internals of the larger economy.

I tried not to think too much in macro terms. But caught in a 24/7 news cycle, and as a lifelong newsman, I was addicted to a jumbo diet of daily reading. I voraciously consumed business news and opinion from multiple newspapers and magazines, dozens of Internet news and

financial wire services, videos, and TV shows. I began to think I was
losing it when Jim Cramer of CNBC began to show up in my dreams.

It was clear that an economic storm was brewing. It was more *felt*
than actually *seen* in the daily rush of numbers and news stories. I was
haunted by an unrelenting sense of an enigmatic presence, shadowy
and malign, just waiting to take me and my little portfolio to the wood-
shed. The bears, who eat small retail investors for breakfast, rallied the
short sellers and hedge fund weasels to bet against every company in
sight, especially the banks, and in the process were sucking real value
out of the economy. No one dared say it, but the market swamis were
busy killing capitalism.

Yes, the bears were growling, snarling, gnashing their teeth. Abusive
trading behavior was being fueled, even quietly applauded, at the highest levels of government. President Bush, the cowboy market guy,
assured us "the fundamentals of our economy are sound," even as the
SEC shrugged off Bernie Madoff whistle-blowers and the disturbing
fact that the "too big to fail" investment banks, the so-called I-banks,
had leveraged their bets to unprecedented levels.

The market action was so furious, so often bewildering, that I had
begun to feel like a tightrope walker without a net clutching a copy of
the Old Testament in hopes of a higher intervention.

Who wants to think calamity while being warmed in the memory
of a once-roaring bull market that lasted from 2002 to 2007. Fixating
on the worst might have been the prudent thing to do, up to a point.
But the hardcore rigor of negative thinking is often unsettling, likely
to confuse the detail-oriented small investor like myself, who wallowed
in voluminous research, snapped up stocks on the dips and sold them
on the highs, and whose luck brought home steady double-digit gains.
Plus, nearly a third of all my stock profits were sitting in those super-
safe cash equivalents—those auction-rate securities (ARS). I was okay.
Safe. That's what I kept telling myself.

In retrospect, the smartest move would have been to cash out. Sell
everything. Sock away the gains in safe municipal bonds. Get back to
writing full-time, my real profession. Let the market addiction burn
itself out. Stick to basics. I was thinking retirement—a retirement I had
earned over many years of ups and downs.

I was pondering these options when the phone rang. I could not have known that the calm, paternal voice on the other end of the line was about to turn my life into a living hell.

"We've got a problem." It was my new broker at Wachovia Securities, which had purchased the A.G. Edwards brand. Jim was the savvy guy who had replaced my initial broker, the ARS hustler. His voice was tranquil, devoid of emotion, and I pictured his bulky frame hunched over his Bloomberg Terminal. I imagined he was calling with news of something simple—a computer glitch that had refused to confirm one of my orders. Unlike my first broker, I trusted Jim completely and respected his experience.

"What kind of problem?" I asked.

"It's the auction-rate securities market. It's, uh, well—the auctions are failing."

"Failing?"

"Yeah, well . . ."

"What?"

"Market's frozen," Jim informed me. "For now anyway."

"Frozen! What are you talking about?"

He sucked in his breath and explained the action—or lack of it.

"Not enough bidders out there," he said. "We're getting a lot of auction failures. But the yields are sky high." He explained gleefully that the Port of New York was paying double-digit interest, tax free, to attract new bidders. "Not too shabby," Jim said. "Relax and enjoy it while it lasts."

I pressed for more information.

He explained that liquidity dries up when auctions fail because there aren't enough bidders to make the auctions work properly. Before each auction, ARS investors may sell their holdings, hang on at a specified interest rate, or hold at whatever new rate or dividend is set by the auction. The size of any given auction depends on how many current investors want to sell or hold their so-called cash equivalents at a certain interest rate. What my broker was describing as a liquidity problem had sent bidders heading for the hills, leaving $336 billion in ARS and auction-rate preferred securities in a deep freeze, with an estimated 146,500 investors holding the bag.

"How long is this . . . this freeze going to last?" I wanted to know. Some bonds were paying high penalty interest rates, but what kind of idiot enjoys being informed that he can't get his cash out?

"No telling. Like I said, it's a liquidity thing." The answer was given with a kind of cosmic shrug, an offhand way of saying he had no idea what to expect. When brokers have no answers to pressing questions, you can expect big-time trouble.

The first onset of dizziness hit me like a shot of whiskey. A knot was forming in my gut. I tried to speak but was made temporarily mute by a growing awareness that I was in serious trouble, the kind of awareness that insists on being recognized even when you want it to go away. In those first confusing moments, I felt like a boxer in the ring with an opponent in a fixed fight. The banks were the ringside judges; they held the scorecards, and each one of them had been bribed to score the fight in my opponent's favor.

I had next to no facts on the numbers of bidders at these auctions. I knew the interest and dividends paid out by these suddenly toxic "better than money market" bonds were spiking. This wasn't supposed to happen. How long could this last? As it turned out, my first broker neglected to tell me that many of the ARS bonds were actually long-term debt obligations with maturities of 20, 30, and even 40 years. My ARS, the majority of them, were tied up in 30-year student loan authority bonds—easy to buy but the hardest bonds to sell when the going gets tough. Had I known these bonds carried such long maturities I never would have purchased them.

"Why wasn't I told these are super-long bonds?" I asked, steadying my voice.

Jim hesitated. "I don't know," he said. "Someone should have told you."

"I never received a prospectus. They weren't available . . . presumably."

CNBC's gurus rattled on in the background through my receiver, faint voices making profound statements about the fate of the universe but not a word about an ARS failure. Then I recalled the TV set in Jim's office. It was always on during the trading day.

"Well, I'm a stock guy," he said at last. "I didn't sell you the student loan stuff."

"Stock guy? So what! You locked up plenty of my cash in other auction rates. So I don't get it. You don't know anything, either."

To me, this lame excuse—"I'm a stock guy"—was hardly laughable. By now I was reeling, the second and third invisible whiskey shots were sloshing about in my brain, and not in a good way. Suddenly, the dizzy-woozy disorientation took on a sharp edge of fear.

The majority of my ARS had been sold to me by my former broker. The fact that he was out of my life and working at another brokerage only complicated the situation. Though I didn't know it at the time, among the many things he had neglected to tell me was that if I had moved my account to his current brokerage, along with the student loan bonds I had purchased, there would be no hope at all of redeeming my cash. This was another fact that had never been explained to me until much later, when the crisis began to peak. That first broker purchased my student loan ARS at A.G. Edwards. When he moved to another brokerage he wanted to take my account with him. I refused. He was indignant as only a broker can be, taking on the mantel of the violated, trusted friend. He apparently didn't realize that moving ARS from one brokerage to another doomed the investor.

That initial ARS investment and the others that followed had been described as "safe, cash-equivalent" securities. It had been a word game and I had fallen for it. That Triple A-rated Missouri State Student Loan Authority bond (on the surface, what could be more worthy or benign to a socially conscious investor?) he sold to me was, he swore, "completely liquid" and better than any money market fund I could find. Now this investment, along with other ARS I had purchased for my account, looked like worthless junk. Not that the market failure was my former broker's fault, Jim, my savvy, new stock guy assured me. He assumed an innocent bystander posture, indicating a certain innocence or perhaps embarrassing ignorance. Was I supposed to swallow the belief that all this had occurred overnight; that as an insider, my broker had never gotten word of troubles in the ARS market? And what he did not tell me, and perhaps did not know, was that Wachovia and the rest of the United States' banks and broker-dealers had no intention of ever giving the money back without a fight.

"You need to understand about the liquidity issue," Jim repeated, his words wedging into the grim silence of my shock. "This probably won't last forever." I shouldn't worry too much, he said reassuringly. "Sooner or later, Wall Street always comes up with a fix."

"Fix? What kind of fix? And when? And, by the way, please don't keep hammering on *illiquidity*. I get it already!"

By now I wanted a real shot of booze, something to jolt me into a Hemingway-like posture of bravery, exuding the steely courage the novelist presumably displayed at hearing the first sounds of a lion in the bush. I pressed Jim hard. I insisted on getting answers. What kind of fix was he talking about? Yet I knew instinctively it was a pointless question and a sure sign of my own rising panic. It was silly of me to expect him to play the prophet and come up with firm answers about the future.

"Can't say when we'll get a handle on it," he replied, still calm, still reassuring. Did he know how weak he sounded? Did it matter?

Oh no! I was getting the old cosmic shrug again. Now the grim impulse of the initial shock turned decidedly nasty. The conversation was spinning in circles.

"But you *vouched* for the damned bonds," I insisted. "You made a point of it, said the auction rates were completely *safe*, just another kind of money market—a *better* money market." I waited for Jim's response. All that came back was the sound of his breathing and the chatter of CNBC. "Say something, *damn it!*"

"I've said about all I *can* say. Besides, I'm not supposed to talk about it."

"What?"

"We've been told not to discuss it with clients. Anyway, I don't have much detail. Even if I could talk, I wouldn't know what to say. Not now. Maybe later."

I couldn't believe it. *Didn't* believe it. Wouldn't allow myself to believe it. My brain was in negation mode, retreating and attacking at the same time. It suddenly occurred to me that as a reporter I'd covered many life-altering stories. In the course of a 40-year-long career I'd been attacked by real life pirates; risked my life living and working in a government habitat on the sea floor; been a boxer who knew when it was time to quit; survived a holdup at gun point; was threatened by New Jersey gangsters; once found myself surrounded by sharks in mid-ocean; and, perhaps riskiest of all, I'd been a seat-of-the-pants day trader who, of necessity, did business with all manner of Wall Street creeps.

But this ARS thing was different. I couldn't get my hands on my money, and an arbitrary cone of silence had been imposed on an entire industry. I was livid, dangerously angry; my sense of restraint was spilling away. I could handle all the challenges I'd faced in the past—the sharks, gangsters, gunmen. I had been lucky to maintain control of these situations and had lived to tell about them. But this—this *freeze*, this *silent treatment*—Jim was handing me felt like an act of a malevolent god, a personal economic Katrina that ripped into my reality and threatened my future plans and everything I had worked for. How could this have happened?

Suddenly, a passage from Nassim Nicholas Taleb's book, *The Black Swan*, floated into memory: "Our blindness with respect to randomness, particularly large deviations. . . ." Yes, what you don't or can't see is the thing that will take you down the hardest. *The Black Swan* was pecking at my brains, pummeling the synapses that transmit thought and reason. *You're on the cusp of going broke. You're going broke. . . .*

"Look," Jim's voice crept in, sounding very distant, like a hushed stream of wind on the far side of a distant canyon. "You're going to have to deal with it until we get a handle on the situation."

"Deal with it? What are you, crazy?" I went after him hard about his outlandish silent treatment, the I-can't-talk-about-it mantra. "You're a fucking coward," I said. "You're just following orders, and to hell with your clients. How does it make you feel?" Long silence. "Afraid to talk? I thought you were better than that."

"It's a bad market," he said softly, unwilling to be rattled. "Very ugly."

"You think I don't know that?"

His gratuitous comment was an understatement in a market that served up gut-churning swings and gyrations that had all but killed off old-fashioned buy-and-hold investing, Warren Buffett style. Gone was faith that good companies are immune to destruction by hedge fund manipulation and artificial bubbles. It was no longer possible to make reliable judgments based on economic fundamentals. I had never imagined that *ordinary cash* could be so compromised by market manipulators. Stock prices were constantly manipulated. A healthy company like IBM, despite its great sales and tons of cash, could be crippled by collusive short sellers. But cash? No, I couldn't grasp it. I didn't need my broker to tell me the market of 2008 was in shambles. Who other than the darkest of *Black Swan* devotees imagined that Wall Street was preparing to shut down its own financial gears and become a ward of the state— and at the same time strip you of your cash safety net?

Few outsiders could have foreseen the catastrophic global calamity engineered by Wall Street's wrecking machine. Jim's refusal to discuss the ARS market collapse made it all too clear that the best and the brightest were greedy beyond anything Hollywood had written into the character of Gordon Gekko, the antihero of the film *Wall Street*. In early 2008, when my ARS investments suddenly went into hiding, few had even dreamed a $750-plus-billion taxpayer bailout would be needed to keep the nation's free market banking industry from top- pling over a cliff.

I continued to push Jim, desperately trying to get a grip on the situation.

"How can you *not* discuss this? I'm your client. You sold auction- rate securities to me. Plenty of them. Your predecessor told me, 'Take it, it's free money.' It was a lie. Pure bullshit. And now you can't dis- cuss it? You're dumping your professional responsibility?"

"Well, *I* wasn't the guy who said it was free money. That was your *other* broker. And he's gone."

"Neither one of you ever came up with a prospectus. Do you even have one? 'You'd never understand it.' That's the line I got. Well, did you read it?"

"Maybe I can get one."

"Maybe? How fucking reassuring. Like that's going to fix things! How come you never even hinted at the possibility of auction fail- ures? And the other one—Mr. Know-It-All—he's ducked into a fox- hole. You sold me other ARS. Both of you pushed yield. And you *made* money pushing them. You didn't know I knew that. It's your little secret, right? By the way," I hissed, "do you have any ARS in your own portfolio?"

Another long pause. "Nope, like I said, I'm a stock guy."

He launched into a gratuitous, if belated, history lesson, explaining that the ARS market had been around for more than two decades and it had always functioned smoothly. He didn't know what he was talking about. I learned too late there had been failed auctions in the past. And I would learn much, much more. Perhaps the most sickening part of my learning curve was that the industry had engaged in a cover-up of a scripted heist.

"Be reasonable," Jim pleaded. "Nobody could have predicted this." He sounded desperate. I wonder if, in my anger, I sounded as pathetic as he did.

"You *must* have had some warning—*that's who*! You should have known. Isn't that your job? Quit ducking behind bullshit," I shouted. "You can't just shut me down. That little ethic you're supposed to follow—that little thing called trust—whatever happened to it?"

"Sorry. You can keep talking, but I can't. I'm not supposed to talk about it."

I wanted information, not excuses. I had made a fair number of commissions for this broker. He owed me. I looked at my hands. They were shaking. Was it rage or fear? When your life is abruptly altered none of the old responses make sense. *Sorry, Mr. Trupp. You're condition is terminal. Sorry, Mr. Trupp, you're broke but there's a chance McDonald's is looking for burger-flippers. Maybe it's just a nightmare. None of this is really happening.*

In retrospect, I suppose I should have been better prepared for the shock. Years earlier, when I first began what amounted to amateur day-trading through a Merrill Lynch branch in Sarasota, Florida, I had come face-to-face with a whole new set of emotions. I'd go from days of virginal profit-rich euphoria to *Texas Chain Saw Massacre*-style fear and loathing. When the bear was busy tearing the limbs off of small investors like me, I'd bolt awake in the middle of the night soaked in sweat brought on by nightmares in which the world's stock exchanges had crumbled and the U.S. government had defaulted on its bonds. *Ruin—it's the darkness at the heart of every serious investor.* These are the horrors of the novice. The ARS shock had the power to fling me back to thoughts of ruin, shame, destruction of hope. We live in hope and die in despair, and illiquid money is nothing but despair. I heard the whirring chain, and unlike my early trading days and sweaty nights, this time it was for real. It is one thing to lose money betting on a stock, it is quite another to be robbed of it, to be fleeced by a Wall Street banking cabal that was beginning to tear itself apart after years of insane risk-taking and malfeasance.

"Look, it's a temporary thing," Jim repeated. "Nothing's forever." He was trying to be a good guy. But between the lines it was clear that he had no firm grasp of the situation. For a moment I actually felt sorry for him. "You get it, right? The markets are hung up. We'll fix it," he said with a kind of clerical unctuousness. He promised to do his best to get my money back. He'd make sure Wachovia's bond desk took care of me. By now, however, his assurances were meaningless. I wanted my cash and I wanted it *now*.

Before I could fling a pent up volley of epithets at him I was muffled from within by a sense of encroaching darkness. I don't know how else to describe it. It was a fear-driven blindness of the psyche. And fury. Plenty of fury. Though I didn't realize it at the time, fury—guided and multiplied—would become my best ally.

I glanced out the window at the stark winter trees crooked against a graying sky. I had always loved winter. Now I felt no love of anything. My wider world was slipping away against that threatening gray sky.

"Do you know what this does to my plans, my life?" I persisted, desperate to undo the tangle of confusion and perhaps prod solid information out of Jim. *Oh, no, you're slipping into a pity trip. Stay mad. Really mad.*

That 30-year maturity on those bonds was beginning to feel like a jail sentence—for life! Silently, patiently, I counted 10 seconds off my watch, sucked in my breath, and tried my best to slow the fist that was pounding inside my chest.

"You sound pretty damned glib," I said, sarcastically. "Like it's nothing. Like it's what you said—a glitch."

Maybe deep down I really did hope Jim was unconcerned. I secretly wanted him to shrug off the news as a mere anomaly that would soon pass and allow me to go on living a normal life. On the verge of panic you are likely to tell yourself all kinds of lies. *All will be put right again . . . Stop it! You're buying into the lie. Stay mad! Fight, goddamn it!*

Politicians like to say genocide is a political problem. Yet on that grim February morning, the Day of Valentines and flowers and gushy love, I was face-to-face with a unique and unexpected paradigm: a form of economic genocide that would take down tens of thousands of innocent investors. A new Ice Age cometh. Clearly Al Gore had it all wrong.

"Relax," Jim pleaded in his easy-going-shit-happens monotone. "The auctions, we'll get 'em back on track."

"Give me a projection. When will they start up?"

"Who knows? Soon. Maybe."

"You say you don't know. You say you didn't see it coming, so don't pretend you see it getting fixed."

"Hey, I don't have a crystal ball."

Safe, Triple-A rated, better than Treasuries, completely liquid. The old sales pitch was running through my head like a sonic loop.

I recalled Hemingway's admonition that every writer needs a foolproof "shit detector." Well, I am a writer, and somehow in the day-to-day shock and awe of the stock market my shit detector had unexpectedly crashed. In the wake of the ARS debacle, my shit detector whirred back to life. I was going to get my money back—or else!

The pressure of the phone against my ear was starting to numb the side of my face. I wanted to scream and curse, wanted to make so much noise and raise so much hell that the reality would go away and allow me to reach the wintery open space of the real world beyond my window. My life was out there—my truth about a respect for security, of rewarded success, love of family, love of freedom. "*Free money!*" How could I have entertained such an idiotic idea?

By now I had slipped over an invisible line. For the foreseeable future I was part of what would become ever-disturbing headline news. Soon the financial writers would be calling the ARS collapse the greatest attempted theft in the history of the world—a $360 billion rip-off that would make the Savings and Loan crisis of the 1980s look like a commonplace street mugging.

Shock, anger, betrayal—the first stages of denial—had me pinned down. Slowly, slowly, a kind of gut-shot motion was clutching at me.

"Try to compartmentalize," Jim suggested. "Deal with it. You aren't the only one who's stuck. It's going to be fine, eventually." Fat chance. My youngest grandchild would be 40 years old by the time the student loan bond matured and got called. Me, I'd be 100!

"Eventually" is a mighty long time. Jim was trying to put a better face on what appeared to be a mass mugging, but he was failing. His hollow reassurances, telling me I wasn't the only one stuck in the mess, merely added to the mix of fury and confusion. It's like telling prisoners they're not alone. *Cheer up. You've got plenty of cellmates. Misery adores company, right?* I doubt jailors get much applause with that line.

"Please don't ever say *eventually* again," I told him. "If you do, I promise you're going to regret it."

More silence on the far end of the line. Out of nowhere a couplet from a Ming Dynasty poem popped into my head: "There are no mutton dumplings for you/No use getting worked up about them."

Very profound. I am not a Ming philosopher. As I mentioned previously, I had made a fair amount in commissions for this broker. Now, in the face of what appeared to be a disaster, he was too business-as-usual, too banal in informing me that my soon-to-be retirement had become merely a distant if not entirely absurd dream; that years of work and thrift, my cautious decision to negotiate the bear traps of the financial markets had come to nothing.

Like the odor of swamp gas, the faint stench of fraud wafted through the telephone line.

"Damn it!" I said, "Do you have any idea how depressing, how humiliating this is?"

Again there was the flickering sound of talking heads from CNBC in the background. Phones rang in adjoining offices at Wachovia. Random scratching sounds filtered through the earpiece.

"Like I said, I can't discuss it," Jim sighed, sick of my ranting. "We're not getting anywhere. I'm sorry, Phil."

Sorry doesn't get you much. *Sorry* isn't an excuse, let alone an explanation. It's crap. A cop-out. It's the Abominable Wall Street Frankenstein handing you your "YOYO" notice—the smirking announcement that says, "Too bad, sucker, You're On Your Own!"

I placed the phone back in its cradle, watched the little red light blinking on the handset, leaned back in my swivel chair, the one my wife Sandy had given me as a birthday present. My body sunk into the cushions like fluid dead weight.

* * *

It was a long time before I was able to lift myself out of the chair, and when at last I did, I was overwhelmed by a passion to fling that lovely gifted red swivel chair out of the window and follow straight behind it two stories below onto the brick patio.

No, no. You can't do it. You have to fight. Besides, two stories isn't enough height to finish you off; and Sandy, your long-suffering wife, will be forced to spend the rest of your savings on medical expenses because of your miserable—and shocking—cowardice.

I didn't know it at the time, but this was the first sign of what would eventually become uncontrollable urges to suicide, a temporary primal urge that would morph into a compulsion.

At this moment of despair, I decided salvation depended on going back to my roots. Words would be my weapon. I turned to the written word and the competitive world of journalism. I rose up professionally as a reporter in the Watergate era, a time when media still believed in holding elected leaders accountable. I would return to those Watergate days of investigative, bare knuckles journalism. I would use words to get my money back—words that in the end might result in justice for all ARS victims.

My model would be Upton Sinclair's *The Jungle*. Sinclair exposed the meatpacking industry run by the old robber barons. He revealed their corruption and disregard for any form of life, human or animal. To my way of thinking, the killing floors of the Chicago meat packing plants were not so far away from the standard model of the New York Stock Exchange or the Wall Street banks. Sinclair demonstrated that unfettered capitalism and idol worship of the marketplace as some kind of all-knowing, self-correcting godhead was a philosophy that reduced the whole of society to an object of exploitation. He exposed a cruelty that few except those blood-soaked workers on the killing floors could have imagined.

Wall Street is no less bloody. No less soulless. The ARS debacle was an indicator of much worse to come. As an investor, I was intellectually aware of this unfortunate truth, but I couldn't admit it, couldn't allow myself to codify it when times were good and my cash looked safe. We had yet to "bust the buck" or bring the entire economy to its knees.

Yet when suddenly herded into the ARS fraud I became just another inconsequential nobody prodded down the financial cattle

chute with a one-way ticket to futility. The reality of the killing floor
came to the surface. I imagined the force of those big CO_2-powered
nail guns used to stun unwitting cattle.

I made up my mind that I was in a battle to the end. The contours
of the fight were as yet unclear. Wall Street had conspired with its brokerages to steal billions of investor dollars via an obscure market that
was made to seem safe as Grandma's passbook savings account—and
they intended to get away with it. No way was I going to cave to this
takedown.

There would be frightening, life-altering blows to my body and
mind between Valentine's Day 2008 and the end of the fight. "Deal
with it," I had been told. Oh, yes. I would deal with it all right,
though at the moment I wasn't sure how.

My instinct was to storm Jim's office and demand my money
back. Now! I had read *The Godfather*; it was Wall Street's quintessential business model. Still, I couldn't move. I wanted to scream that
illiquidity was nothing but slick jive talk from Wachovia, which on
that fateful day was the fourth largest bank in the United States. It
had the distinction of having written hundreds of millions of dollars
worth of junk mortgage paper, and its president, G. Kennedy "Kenny
Boy" Thompson, was forced to resign and yet managed to sail unim-
peded to the golf tee with a multimillion dollar golden parachute.
His departure came in the wake of Wachovia having been caught
allegedly laundering drug money, according to an April 2008 front-
page story in the *Wall Street Journal*. (Two years later, in a March 15,
2010, story, the *Journal* reported that Wachovia was in talks to settle the drug money charges leveled by the U.S. Justice Department.)
In 2005, Wachovia, among other big name banks, was caught up in
a scam to betray its elderly depositors by passing out private information to Internet scammers. The story was reported May 23, 2005,
by *Information Week* and ConsumerAffairs.com. And now it was the
bank's trusty brokers who were incentivized to push ARS paper into
their clients' portfolios while ignoring—certainly not *warning* about—
problems and auction failures all the way back to 2004. I wanted to
trash Jim's office, take a crowbar to the newly redecorated reception
area—if only I could find strength to defy gravity and lift myself out
of my chair.

At some rational level beneath my rage I understood that violence wouldn't win. I'd wind up holding a one-way ticket to the gray bar hotel.

Frozen money . . . frozen money. My entire being was in revolt. I could see the abyss. In a red haze of tangled emotions I stumbled out of my office and poured myself a full glass of vodka.

It was not yet 10 o'clock in the morning.

Chapter 2

The "Back Nine"

We are at the beginning of a great populist rebellion against those who showed no self-restraint when it came to lining their pockets. The entitlement mentality arose from an inflated sense of their own value and how much smarter they are than anyone else.

—*E.J. Dionne Jr.*

My wife Sandy took the news with typical calm. No fusillade of gut-wrenching questions. She certainly was entitled to ask anything she wanted. It was, after all, *our* money and *our* problem.

We huddled on the sofa. I tried to explain the situation, although I really didn't know what had happened, or why. It's bad enough having to admit to your trusting wife that a big chunk of savings has mysteriously vanished, but it's another thing to tell her that your hard-saved, after-tax stash of our future, dollars crucial to retirement, had become "illiquid." My ignorance and humiliation made me feel like a double loser on a big bet. But this wasn't about big bets. It was a supposedly safe cash investment based on trust.

I refreshed Sandy's memory. I had temporarily parked a substantial amount of cash in auction-rate securities—cash to be used to help fund our retirement. Much of it came from stock market profits. My broker assured me ARS were completely safe investments, a great place to park cash with a higher-than-market yield.

Now the money was illiquid. The word "worthless" haunted me. I was furious with myself, dangerously angry at Jim, and I was rabid at the very thought of my initial broker who placed a large chunk of cash in a bond issued by the Missouri State Higher Education Student Loan Authority (MOHELA). Still, it was important to remain superficially cool. I had to think through the situation and reassure Sandy that, somehow, it would work out and we'd get our cash back.

I looked at Sandy wondering how this out-of-the-blue shock might affect her. Her expression hadn't changed much. A hint of concern fanned out at the corners of her eyes and lips, but she remained calm, and I could tell her mind was busy working on what small bits of information I had gotten from Jim.

"Jim won't talk?" asked Sandy. "What about the other one?" I had two brokers, Jim and his protégé, Victor. "This is a major deal. Why the silent treatment?"

"Called Victor. Got the same treatment. No talking. No asking. No nothing. I guess the lawyers have started to swarm."

We stared at each other. The sound of traffic on Nebraska Avenue, near our home in upper northwest Washington, D.C., seemed nosier than usual. It was the jumbled sound of worldly indifference.

Sandy gave me an incredulous look. Did she believe I was concealing a dark secret? Something I was afraid to tell her? Did she suspect I might have blown all that cash on one of Jim Cramer's crash-and-burn stock tips? Or was I floundering for a plausible cover-your-ass excuse?

But Sandy knew I was risk-averse. I didn't make emotional decisions. I had been trading stocks a long time, was characteristically skeptical, and carefully researched the value of any Wall Street product. I knew Wall Street was a bad, crime-ridden neighborhood, and I had the scars to prove it. Years ago, I had shown weakness for the Big Bet. No longer. Auction-rate securities were sold as boring and safe—"same as cash," according to my brokers, whose silence I now viewed as cowardice and betrayal.

"Come on," Sandy persisted, punctuating the traffic noise. "Jim must have given you *something*."

I shook my head. "No."

"Is that legal? It's *our* money! I mean, can he—they—*really* do that? How does all that cash vanish into thin air? Who's got the money?"

Good question. Too bad there was no answer. I must have looked like the poster boy for personal deflation.

"It's going to be fine," she said with a reassuring smile.

"Sure," I replied. "Somehow, some way, we're going to get our money back." I stood and paced the living room like a caged animal, still furious and trying to keep it inside. I didn't feel nearly as brave as my words.

What I knew for sure was that brokers have responsibilities to their clients. For starters, they have an obligation to understand the products they sell. Due diligence and truth-telling are supposed to go with the territory, along with an obligation to suggest suitable investments. If a client is close to or at retirement (and I was deliciously close) a broker can get into serious trouble if he stuffs a portfolio with junk assets. I knew several people who had been slammed by less than suitable investments. One soon-to-retire friend had allowed himself to be talked into betting on metals futures. His "specialist broker" leveraged his holdings 70-to-1. Within 45 days, my friend's retirement had melted down into a pool of despair. With characteristic gallows humor, he quipped he would soon be applying for a job at Kmart. Now I was thinking along similar lines.

I wasn't surprised that my friend's metals portfolio blew up in his face. Metals brokers are a cagey breed. They talk like treasure hunters, and they have been known to vanish without a trace, leaving their clients wondering if they'd been had by landlocked pirates. On the other hand, ordinary stockbrokers tend to be more grunt-like. While many are on the level of used car salesmen, others are big talkers—tricky talkers. A handful actually know what they're talking about. But mostly they plod along, push what their managers tell them to, and stay connected to their clients who supply the mother's milk of commissions.

Still, the grunt types have a duty to be objective and to answer reasonable questions. They're not supposed to ignore inquiries or talk garbled Street Speak. They assume their clients are greedy, unsophisticated dolts whose grip on the world of finance is tenuous and based mostly on bromides. Sadly, the typical investor wants to believe a broker puts his client's interests first. This is an industry-wide fiction, but this doesn't stop many unfortunate investors from buying into the myth.

Was I any wiser? There I was, the die-hard skeptic, decades of trading to fall back on, hanging out in space without a clue as to why I couldn't get my hands on our cash. *Sorry, your whole life has changed. No further comment will be forthcoming!* So much for experience. As for trust, how could I ever have assumed it was more than just a word?

✳ ✳ ✳

Valentine's Day was the beginning of many sleepless nights. My head was a jumble of what-ifs. I felt like the aging character in Philip Roth's novel *Everyman*, each second passing with excruciating empty longing. The simple everyday activities that once had given my daily routine color and animation were being consumed by the dark pool of inexplicable loss.

Somewhere around two o'clock in the morning that first night, I slipped quietly out of bed, negotiated the winding, unlit staircase, and clicked on the television in the living room. Our new flat screen TV had been snatched up at a bargain price at Radio Shack. Now the bargain struck me as an extravagance. Maybe we could unload it on Craig's List.

I flipped to the Military Channel: A rerun of *Hitler's Bodyguard* flared onto the screen. Perfect. The grainy black-and-white images reflected my mood. I had grown up during World War II with food rationing stamps and unrelenting anxiety. Would my father return from the war? Were the Germans really invading Baltimore and heading up East Pratt Street? Well, I wouldn't let them touch my Victory Garden! It took Jim's cryptic telephone call to bring me back to those hardscrabble boyhood days in East Baltimore. As I watched Hitler and his jack-booted goons goose-step across the screen, I was reminded once again what it means to confront an uncertain future. I switched off the TV, crawled back into bed, and spent the rest of the night in a toss-and-turn stupor.

Being something of an insomniac didn't help. My mind wandered over the physical and psychic challenges of years past. It was a way of trying to muscle-up for a new opponent—an opponent that just happened to be the fourth largest bank in the United States crawling with high-priced corporate lawyers; an opponent whose factual omissions amounted to deception. And this opponent was not Wachovia alone, but every major bank and broker-dealer in the Western world. Institutional fraud—Wall Street's eternal modus operandi. With so much power in their corner, is it any wonder that those who scripted the multibillion dollar ARS scam believed they were home free? That they would never be forced to give back a penny of it? Wall Street believed it could pull it off and never break a sweat.

I promised myself that night that I'd find a way to break through. I wasn't going down without a fight. I would find a way to crack the code of silence and get the answers I was looking for.

✳ ✳ ✳

The next morning, I drove Sandy to her office in downtown Washington. She was scheduled for a nine o'clock meeting with her staff at Planned TV Arts. Only half-listening to what she was saying, all I could think of was, *where's the money?*

Until now, I had never been conned. Or if I had been conned in the past, I was blissfully unaware of it. Like Madoff's unfortunate true believers who were hit with a powerful blow a year later, I was struck by an opaque disbelief, a kind of financial North Korea.

A panicky brain is not your friend; it is entirely irrational. The very idea that Jim had betrayed me was just too crazy. There was so much I didn't know, so much I wanted not to believe. For a brief moment, I pictured him seated at his nondescript desk. It was a familiar, even comforting image: a big, bulky man wearing a quirky New York Yankees fan shirt, always with his wry been-there-done-that air about him. I admit it. I liked the guy.

When my first broker departed in 2006 (much to my relief), Jim had approached me about handling my account. At the time, Edwards had been purchased by Wachovia Securities. It was a disappointing development, so much so that I was on the verge of digging around for a new broker-dealer—a mating game or act of faith on a level with finding a spouse. Wachovia had endured too many scandals for my taste. Wachovia CEO G. Kennedy "Kenny Boy" Thompson had recently been fired. After 32 years of checkered service, he strolled comfortably to his golden golf tee soaked in money—not bad for a guy who nearly wrecked the bank with an ill-timed purchase of Golden West Financial Corp.'s portfolio of bad-to-the-bone interest-only mortgages. His replacement, Robert K. Steel, came to the job with a little too much *White Fang* attitude and the Alpha Man swagger of the Goldman Sachs alum. His cozy association with the deregulation-crazed George W. Bush did not thrill me. Steel remained with Wachovia for less than a year. By December 2008, he had engineered a merger with Wells Fargo Bank, causing a flurry of questions from Washington regulators.

I had no idea how big or how ugly the ARS crash really was. In trying to deal with the second day of having my life turned upside-down, I was seeking direction, coping with shock, hoping to steady my mind. The full scale of the market implosion would come later.

I dropped Sandy off at her office and headed up Connecticut Avenue. It was a grey winter day. The crowds moved like automatons along the avenue. Everyone appeared bloodless. The heater in the car was turned on full blast, but it failed to warm me. Everything beyond the windshield seemed distant; surreal.

I turned on the car radio. Right-wing election babble. I couldn't concentrate on the excited words pouring through the speakers. These political talking points had nothing to do with me. The real world was fading away. I kept going back to Jim's role in the ARS mystery. He was aware of my concerns over his new corporate parent. He had persuaded me to take the long view, stick to the knitting. I trusted him, liked him. That A.G. Edwards had become Wachovia Securities wouldn't matter, he said. I wanted to believe him. Keep working with him. Nothing would change except the corporate logo, he said. Plus, he would add a second broker to my account—a smart, young backup guy. "Talented, very sharp," Jim enthused over his protégé, Victor. I was flattered at the prospect of having two brokers on my side. But on this bitter winter morning, driving home in a half-trance, two brokers seemed to add up to double trouble.

"I'm a stock guy, you're a stock guy," Jim suggested at one of our early meetings. He said it quietly, with a touch of brotherly assurance.

How ironic, I thought, to be stuck with frozen bonds. Wall Street is a product-making machine, and it is interested only in the fees it makes for selling mostly toxic products. We had gotten used to the heads-we-win, tails-you-lose mentality and found ways around it. But this was 2008. The full mind-numbing recklessness of Wall Street had yet to make screaming headlines or evoke populist outrage. And few realized the ARS calamity was an indicator of a white-collar crime tsunami so devious, so greed-sickened that it would bring the entire developed world to the brink of another Great Depression.

* * *

The unknown has a way of neatly excising one's self-confidence. My moods swung between agoraphobia and spasms of anger. At times, I was so close to losing control that Sandy would back away from me. I punished myself for having accepted Jim's sales pitch. I recalled being flattered by his offer to take my account and save me the trouble of picking through the weeds in search of a new and suitable broker. *Was Jim just another used car salesman? Another portfolio churner?* Had my journalistic skepticism softened with age? The very thought made me cringe.

Unlike my departed broker, the eager client-gatherer who was the first to place the bulk of my cash into the toxic auction-rate securities pit, Jim had a reputation as the hardest working guy in town. I had good reason to trust him. After all, I had been aiming to find a way to work with him. The only thing getting in the way was an old Edwards company policy against client broker-hopping. I suppose this was meant to be a corporate promise of across-the-board talent, a tacit way of letting clients know they were safe with any broker in the house.

"We're about the same age," Jim laughed when I decided to sign on with him. "We're on the back nine," he winked. "Let's do this right."

The back nine . . . what a pleasant way to acknowledge one's mortality and approaching retirement. With our combined experience we stood a chance of making excellent gains in the market as we headed toward that Great Clubhouse in the Sky.

The frustration of dealing with my former broker stuck with me like a persistent hangover. I was sick of hangovers, past and present. Before making the commitment, I checked Jim's record with the Financial Industry Regulatory Authority (FINRA), an industry-funded organization charged with, among other things, keeping brokers honest. Later, I would discover that FINRA was just another Wall Street hoax, but we'll get to that later. If there had been complaints about him, it would show up on FINRA's web site. Jim came up clean. At the same time, I asked around about him with a few of his associates. Again, no complaints, no problems. "Not many like him these days," a woman in her 60s told me.

Before signing on, I decided to visit Jim at his office to get a feel for the way he organized things. You can tell a lot about a broker that way. An office that looks like it was decorated for $1 million screams self-absorbed con man. What I hoped to find was an actual workplace—not an art and antiques gallery.

Jim's office was located on a busy corner in upper northwest Washington. The office was a 10-minute drive from my home. I parked in the garage of the office building amid the BMWs, Jaguars, and various iterations of Mercedes-Benz. My 2006 Honda Civic seemed a little dowdy in such opulent company.

A perky young woman in the reception area of the office was warm and professional. I was offered a comfortable seat and coffee in a paper cup. I was informed that Jim was on the phone; he was expecting me and wouldn't be long. In one corner of the reception area was a small TV set. CNBC talking heads were speaking like Old Testament scholars about copper futures. "Prophets," I muttered. Shills looking for believers. Oh, Nostradamus, will Exxon break $100?

"Mr. Trupp," the receptionist called, breaking into my internalized cynicism. "You may go in now."

The first thing I noticed when I walked into Jim's unpretentious office was a calendar featuring a photo of a grinning President George W. Bush, beneath which was the word COUNTDOWN in bold, black letters. Could it be? Was Jim a "Bushie"? If so, I was out of there! Interview ended!

"What's this?" I said, motioning to the calendar.

Jim chuckled. "Oh, *that*." He rolled his eyes. "My daughter gave it to me." He laughed in a way that suggested we might share politics in common. As it happens, I hate politics. I'm a wonk, a policy guy, and registered Independent.

I gave Jim a quizzical look. "Oh, for a moment I thought—"

"No way." he said. "Guy's a jerk." We shared a big yuk.

Did he disown our cowboy president for my benefit? Or did he actually believe that our laissez-faire head of state was the kind of scholarly person who knew what laissez-faire actually meant? These may seem like idle or even silly questions. After all, we're talking money here, not philosophy. Still, you're better off really understanding your broker, knowing what he's about and how he thinks, because all of this is going to make a difference in your dealings with him and your ability to sleep at night.

Jim invited me to run a few items through his Bloomberg Terminal, an unusually friendly gesture. I stood up, leaned over his desk, and peered at the flashing video screens. Allowing a client to get near a Bloomberg Terminal is a sign of respect on the part of any broker, since the unwashed schlemiel, the typical retail investor, can neither afford a Bloomberg Terminal nor perform a mind-meld with its complexities.

Jim's gesture, offered so easily, was starting to overcome my customary suspicion. My former broker had allowed me to tinker with his Bloomberg Terminal—but he did so with a sense of surprise (he didn't believe I could operate the computer). It took about two minutes before his surprise morphed into pique.

"Wish I had one of these babies," I said.

"It's pretty handy," replied Jim.

We spoke about the structure of my portfolio—actually mine and Sandy's, which I managed. A half-hour later I left Jim's office. The CNBC channel was still on in the reception area. Noise. Nothing but noise and a hell of a lot of shilling!

The next day I phoned Jim.

"Okay," I said. "Let's do business."

✳ ✳ ✳

That pleasant, easy-going visit seemed ages ago. Faced with financial calamity, all that good ol' boy bonding faded to ancient history, a fossilized relic of a former life. Still, the memory of that first visit to Jim's office lingered. It was as if I was still searching for something I may have missed—a subtle quirk, a look, a turn of phrase that would have revealed him as just another company man walking the company line. And the company line appeared to be a trap: If something goes terribly,

terribly wrong, those supposedly valued clients are to be handled as potentially litigious spoilers who will slow the relentless gears of the Wall Street product-making machine.

In the first few days following the auction-rate securities freeze, I must have called Jim every hour in the vain hope of finding signs of a thaw—green shoots. Jim still wasn't saying squat. Victor was even worse.

"If you call again on this, I'll have to hang up," Victor threatened with perfectly modulated snippiness. It occurred to me that here was a person who'd never missed a meal and who'd never been in a fight that wasn't stopped. He had no idea what I had in store for him in the months ahead.

According to Jim, all the other brokers were surrounded by a cone of silence handed down by Wachovia's head office. I should have expected it. Wall Street's culture is essentially sociopathic. Every disaster from the Great Depression to the Savings and Loan scandal (and more recently, the Madoff affair) had given the public a depressing inside view of a financial Bedlam stacked against the investor. In the past, most investors tried to avoid examining too closely the inner workings of the beast. But as the great 2008 meltdown unfolded, they would be forced to confront the reality of massive greed and stupidity.

The rumbling of a crash had become more audible since the summer of 2007 when the Dow had begun to peak at 14,000. With the ARS scandal swirling about like a storm in the making, much of the industry was engaged in a massive cover-up of insider trading, collusive short selling, and the making of phony bubbles. It is pertinent to note that Wall Street, so perilously removed from Main Street, still believed that cover-ups would succeed in a 24/7 news cycle. In the days to come, I would take every advantage of this mistaken belief.

Wall Street's lack of ethics was the antithesis of the old A.G. Edwards brand. The company had never, to my knowledge, been the object of a scandal. Good old AGE: Always Good Ethics! Not your typical cold caller chophouse. I resented the silent treatment, the lack of good information. Jim and Victor apparently were walking the company line. I *hated* it! For all the good they were doing me now, these two brokers may as well have been wrapped head-to-toe in duct tape. I was tempted to storm the office, throw furniture out the window, call the police, the FBI—any law enforcement agency, because what was happening was an outright crime, plain theft, and I wanted justice. I wanted my money. And deep down I wanted something else: truth— maybe the rarest commodity in the self-aggrandizing, deceitful world of Wall Street.

The following ARS complaint against Merrill Lynch by Massachusetts securities regulators, dated July 31, 2008, summarized how clients were manipulated and lied to:

> This administrative complaint . . . charges the firm with separate counts of fraud and dishonest and unethical conduct for creating and implementing a sales and marketing scheme which significantly misstated not only the nature of auction-rate securities, but also the overall stability of the auction market, resulting in thousands of investors being abandoned with illiquid investments. . . . Particularly egregious was the manner in which Merrill Lynch co-opted its supposedly independent Research Department to assist in sales efforts geared towards reducing its inventory of ARS. . . . First, it allowed Sales and Trading [desks] to directly request and advocate for written research to be published, endorsing the safety and high quality of nearly all types of ARS and recommending investors buy ARS. . . . Further, when Sales and Trading, including Auction Desk personnel, did not agree with the tone or context of a published research piece, Merrill Lynch managers permitted Sales and Trading to insist the published report be replaced with a more friendly sales piece.

When the ARS scam became public, Merrill Lynch wasn't the only outfit accused of lying. Regulators would be in for a busy time. They would show that the carnage was immediate and universal. The loss of $336 billion is equal to about 2 percent of U.S. gross annual product. That's enough money to fund the departments of Agriculture, Education, Energy, Housing and Urban Development, Transportation, and the biggest bureaucracy in the history of mankind, the Department of Homeland Security. If these stolen funds had been placed in the private sector, millions of jobs might have been created or saved.

* * *

It was getting more painful to meet Sandy's green-eyed, questioning gaze. "Anything new?" she'd ask. I did my best not to sound weak or confused. But I had no more information than I did on Day One. Nearly a week had passed and I was still in shock.

"This doesn't seem right, not at all," she insisted. "We have to do *something*."

Then, for a moment, I lost it. "I don't know anything. I don't have any ammo."

She knew how frustrated I was. "Aren't you the one who said let's wait and see?"

I got up and paced around the living room. I headed into another room and poured a drink. I had never been a big drinker, though now there was a psycho-medicinal urge that would become a more insidious part of the drama over time.

I slid into the kitchen feeling a little woozy. My world, my future, was turning slowly, slowly, tilting toward an abyss, the magnitude of which I could not have imagined at the time.

Back in the living room I flopped down next to Sandy.

"Maybe it's time to lawyer-up," I said.

"I'm not so sure."

"Are you kidding?"

"Maybe it's just a glitch, like Jim said."

I placed my glass on the coffee table. "*Glitch?*" Such understatement.

"You can always hire a lawyer. Honestly, I have a feeling it's going to work itself out."

Sandy persisted in asking gentle questions. She was well-intentioned, but her calmness merely underlined my frustration. There was so much I didn't know. Maybe there was fear in knowing. Who really wants to know the worst? Was I experiencing the classic denial syndrome?

After a while, I calmed down, or tried to. I would adopt her wait-and-see position. Tough it out. It was a galling decision, though I knew I'd eventually make a great deal of noise, maybe get myself in deep trouble. It has been a practice of mine to face, dead-on, the very elements most troubling in my life, regardless of consequences.

By the time I got to the bottom of my drink, I had convinced myself that Jim might break ranks and do the right thing and start talking. Like my first broker, Jim had purchased thousands of dollars in auction-rate securities for my account. He obviously knew something I didn't. What was it? Was he hiding the facts for a good reason—to keep me from going over the edge? *No! There is no good reason to clam up.* My always critical inner voice yelled at me: *Well, of course he's probably hiding something! Don't be stupid! Trust no one!* There was a flash of anger piercing my subterranean fear and denial. *Hold on,* I told myself. *Don't start acting like a chump. The crisis is brand new. Anything can happen.*

✳ ✳ ✳

I slipped on my running shoes and took off jogging toward Rock Creek Park. My head began to clear. Landscape in motion, the sun and clouds moving over and around the trees had a soothing power. Cars passed on both sides of the narrow two-lane roadway. My breathing steadied. I began to calculate the options: the tactics, means, and methods journalists use to get the answers buried beneath layers of obfuscation.

I turned off the roadway and started up a steep hillside. The sense of climbing gave over to a keen urgency. Knowing no one would hear, I shouted, "There are no secrets!" I knew this from practical experience. Three-quarters of any secret is a lie cloaked in a myth. A noisy, persistent reporter can find out just about anything. When, for example, I covered NASA as a reporter for Fairchild Publications and ABC Capital Cities, I would go to my sources inside the Russian embassy to get the information NASA had classified as confidential. "No secrets!" I repeated when I reached the top of the hill.

Bent over and breathing hard in the shade of century-old oaks and pines, I heard the sounds of unseen creatures alive in the bush. I experienced a welcome sense of power. Below me, on the shoulder of the narrow roadway, a young man and a woman ran side by side, graceful as dancers. They seemed blissful, two youthful bodies moving in sweet, erotic unison, as if freed from doubt.

I watched until they disappeared around a bend. I made my way down the hill, careful not to slip on the layers of wet leaves. Running had cleared my head and I was kicking myself for having been weak and too emotional. I jogged past the Carnegie Mellon campus—yet another vault of secrets—and sprinted back to the house. I switched on to the computer, got the browser working, and googled auction-rate securites.

I needed information, and plenty of it.

✷ ✷ ✷

It was there on the Internet. Google pages encompassing many developing stories, blogs, and commentaries. Because I had never received an ARS prospectus, and because I had been trusting, I hadn't gone to the trouble of conducting an Internet search. "Just like cash" was a line I bought with only minor hesitation.

I had been trading stocks and bonds for decades. I took pains in my research. Developed analytical skills. I *never* bought anything I couldn't understand. Stupidly, I had let my guard down in buying into the seemingly innocuous ARS pitch. I trusted. Big mistake! During the dot-com bubble of the 1990s, I was a scrupulous and often cynical buyer. Of course, most dot-com offerings were junk. Many seasoned traders understood this. The impossibly high price-earnings ratios and beta numbers assigned to these so-called "killer" stocks were laughable. The dot-com bubble was a psychological game with almost no fundamental underpinnings. However, it wasn't an outright con; those would-be dot-comers had mostly good intentions, and some very fine products emerged. Still, a savvy trader had to exercise a little of P.T. Barnum's philosophy, toss in rudimentary short-technical analysis, and voila!— there was money to be made on what amounted to promises of a new Industrial Revolution, digital style. ARS wasn't like the dot-com binge. The bonds were supposed to be good as cash. No ups or downs. Their face value remained constant. On reflection, I realized the soft sales pitch, my reaching for extra yield—these softened my skeptical nature and led to trouble.

So imagine my embarrassment gazing at a computer screen filled with unsettling ARS data—more than I could possibly absorb in a week and all of it new. I realized that trusting promises of safety, liquidity ("these babies are just like Treasuries," my first broker had enthused) had made me no less gullible than the dot-com believers who had their heads handed to them when the bubble burst.

Dot-comers may have been dreamers, but most were not liars. On the other hand, the hype surrounding sales of ARS and ARPS (auction-rate preferred securities) came with massive omissions. The promise of safety neglected the fragility of the auction process and avoided any mention of the fact that failures had occurred. Bottom line: ARS and ARPS offered no security.

One of the very first stories I found online was from *CFO* magazine. An article by Stephen Taub dated February 13, 2008, carried a scary headline: "Is Your 'Cash' in Danger? Auction-rate securities, which thousands of companies report as a cash equivalent on balance sheets, may be imperiled." The article verified much of what I already knew: The auction rate market had come to a screeching halt. Companies that listed ARS on their balance sheets as cash were in for a sickening jolt. The article said Citigroup had told the Associated Press that nearly $6 billion of mostly municipal debt auctions had failed. Citigroup was lead underwriter for most of those sales.

Yet the overall market, I learned, was much bigger than I imagined. Auction failures were piling up exponentially. In fact, by the end of February 2008, more than 80 percent of ARS auctions were failing. No one had whispered a word of this to me or any other investor I knew.

At last, I was beginning to grasp the dim edges of the wider calamity. Various reports estimated about $200 billion in auction-rate bonds were at risk; the figure would rapidly grow beyond $300 billion and trap more than 146,500 investors. Half of it was corporate and municipal debt; the other half belonged ordinary investors, the oft-dissed "retail investor" who was allowed into the ARS market with a $25,000 ante.

Unlike my brokers, dozens of Internet sites agreed on a definition of auction-rate securities. After the market crash, the FINRA web site provided a simple explanation: Auction-rate securities, it said, were long-term bonds and preferred stocks that acted like short-term instruments because of rapid-fire resets of their interest rates—the resets coming every 7, 28, 35, or 49 days. The rates are reset by a Dutch auction. They combined the higher interest rates of long bonds with the presumed easy accessibility of short-term loans. And because investors could buy or sell ARS instruments at frequent auctions, the securities took on a false glow of liquidity. The phrase "cash equivalents" was liberally used by brokers to create the illusion of ARS as just another kind of money market with more appealing yields.

The word "bond" never came up in my transactions with Jim, Victor, or my first broker. Risk was treated as just another four-letter epithet that had no place in the auction market.

And that's where investors got off track. We were living in an illusory world that had yet to bust the buck or witness runs on the banks. Cash was cash, right? Where's the risk?

Like so many other investors, I assumed that cash was full faith and credit stuff, green government-backed notes. Bulletproof. Now, too late, arrived the epiphany. Cash takes many shapes and forms, not all of them easy to identify. Cash equivalent is one of those fuzzy areas. I accepted the definition based on trust, a certainty growing out of my experience in the financial markets, a belief that I knew what I was buying. It was an optimism linked to having been reasonably successful using certain skill sets. Psychologist Roy Baumeister calls this brand of self-confidence an "optimal margin of illusion," a cocksureness that might be applied to the entire galaxy of Wall Street.

In late February 2008, Baumeister's principle seemed written in red ink across my forehead. I would look in the mirror and see a reflection of the arrogant image of Bear Sterns CEO Jimmy Cayne, whose talent as a bridge player deluded him into believing he was a genius at all other games, like running a bank. I wondered how Jimmy Cayne felt when he woke up one morning and found that his genius had led Bear Sterns off a cliff.

Was I any smarter than Jimmy Cayne? Bitterly, I recalled my own cool reaction to Nouriel Roubini's 2006 lecture to the International Monetary Fund. "Dr. Doom" was characteristically gloomy, warning his audience that a catastrophic fiscal crisis was brewing. He predicted that a housing bust was on the way and that speculative "oil shock" would be a precursor to the most painful recession in 60 years. Nobody wanted to hear this, let alone believe it. Like economist Anirvan Banerji, who attended that fateful lecture, I was unconvinced. Banerji was later quoted in a *New York Times* magazine article by Stephen Mihm dated August 15, 2008. Mihm dismissed Roubini, noting that he didn't use mathematical models and that Dr. Doom was a career naysayer. I wondered how Banerji felt about his remarks now.

I also had read Nassim Nicholas Teleb's *The Black Swan: The Impact of the Highly Improbable*, published only a year before the ARS crisis. Teleb's book was basically a work of philosophy, although his online homepage explained that he used the example of banks as a "particularly worrisome case of epistemic arrogance." Virtually the entire economic establishment had dismissed the predictions of Roubini and Teleb because of the optimal margin of illusion—and (cold comfort) I was no less misguided than any other doubter.

* * *

Ten days into the crisis, some of the initial shock began to fade. In its place came outrage—the kind that can get you into trouble. I thought of it as predetermined counterpunching. I had used this technique as a college student driving a taxi to make ends meet. One night a holdup man put a gun to the back of my head. It was past midnight, the streets were empty. Fortunately, a police station was only two blocks away. I simply put pedal to the metal and drove to the police parking lot. No way was this guy going to blow me away with the taxi flying down the street at 60 miles an hour. At the police parking lot the gunman took off running. Years later, threatened by seagoing muggers, I fired a flare shell into the hull of a pirate vessel in the British Virgin Islands. Pirates aren't so tough when they find their boat sinking miles from the nearest land. And before that, as a reporter investigating a trucking scandal on the East Coast, I was threatened by Tony Soprano types. In the end, I wrote my stories, won small awards for them, and was told (in strictest confidence) what might have happened to former Teamsters boss Jimmy Hoffa.

I pondered the physical and psychic challenges of the past as training for my new opponent—an opponent unlike any other I had encountered: a major bank with a nasty reputation flanked by ruthless corporate attorneys. It was an institutional juggernaut I had trusted and that, in turn, had gamed me and casually ripped me off without explanation or excuses.

How do you beat people like that? With so much power going for them, no wonder they were able to script a multibillion-dollar scam. Such a con goes beyond hubris, beyond the arrogance of ordinary street thugs. It was stealth robbery based on a perverse delusion of invincibility. Wachovia and all the other mega banks figured they could pull off the heist without getting sweat stains on their Brioni suits. I had to figure a way to change all that.

Yet surprisingly, it was Sandy who started the heavy push-back.

"Where's our money?" she demanded. "Who's got it? It's *our* money!"

Sandy had been on the wait-and-see track. Why the sudden change of direction?

"We can't let these bastards get away with it," she growled. It's financial rape." Now she was pushing with the persistence of the mythical Sisyphus, a tragic figure invented by the Greeks, fated to push a boulder up an endless mountain to atone for the foibles of human-kind. Only Sandy was not tragic, and if the stone was to be pushed to the mountaintop, it would be dumped with bad intentions on the heads of Wachovia executives or anyone else who believed they could get away with robbing us of our future.

Chapter 3

A Sweet Deal—Until It's Not!

By rescuing the financial system without reforming it, Washington has done nothing to protect us from a new crisis, and, in fact, has made another crisis more likely.

—Paul Krugman

In those first grim days after February 2008, I had no immediate grasp of the magnitude of the meltdown. There was confusion and misinformation at every level. Was the ARS market blowout confined to a few sectors or was it a much deeper systemic problem? Had the entire auction-rate market imploded? I had yet to confirm that virtually every bank and brokerage in the United States was involved, as well as foreign banks such as UBS, Credit Suisse, and Deutsche Bank.

The media wasn't jumping on the story—not yet. This was puzzling. How could such a seemingly major economic event stay off the front pages? Mainstream headlines were focused on Iraq, Scooter Libby, clouds over the Cheney vice presidency, and "change we can believe in." The collapse of the Republicans in the election cycle and reemergence of the Democrats gobbled up much op-ed space. The business pages of the *Washington Post* and the *New York Times* were busy picking through the confusing "credit crisis." The Dow and other market indexes were dropping. A mortgage meltdown was under way. Yet the ARS scandal was just beginning to creep into print on tiny, mouse-like feet.

Even now, as I write this in August 2009, none of the major TV networks have run an ARS expose. Where's *60 Minutes* when you need it? Not a peep on the radio. Even National Public Radio appears to have missed the story. One of the financial arms of General Electric's broadcasting empire, NBC's market show, CNBC, had gingerly taken on the subject and then dropped it. CNBC provides a forum for financial shills and attractive commentators like Maria Bartiromo and Erin Burnett. The network certainly isn't in the business of hurting its corporate boosters, especially the banking sector.

Consumer groups had begun dipping into the ARS trauma by the end of February, and an ambitious-sounding consumer advocate in Washington, D.C., leaped into the arena. A tough-talking outfit calling itself "Americas [sic] Watchdog," described the ARS meltdown as the "single worst case of fraud in Wall Street history." It was a provocative phrase that would take hold, and last, once the story got some traction. I had no way of confirming that the Watchdog had it right. I had seen plenty of scandals on Wall Street, although none had directly impacted my family's future.

The unfolding scandal was indeed huge. The Watchdog group's seemingly hyperbolic language quickly became the phrase du jour. It was dead-on, catchy, and frightening. The Watchdog bit the banks hard and barked menacingly: "If you sell an investment product as a cash equivalent, it had better be a cash equivalent or we will come after you," the Watchdog web site growled. ARS victims were incited "to get off the fence and fight." It was too early for a fight, however; the situation was confused, with investors still in shock. A kind of fog of war had them baffled and off balance.

I telephoned the Watchdog seeking an interview. Unfortunately, I got the distinct impression that this consumer organization had too many irons in the fire—environmental pollution, mesothelioma, and so forth—to slow down for one aggrieved reporter looking for answers to a very personal problem. Aside from making tough statements online, I couldn't determine whether the group was just flinging words about or taking tangible action.

"ARS? Oh, yeah," groaned one of the Watchdog's consumer advocates when I called in late February 2008. "What a rip," he said. "We're flooded with calls."

The group's spokesman promised to get back to me, but he never did. I gave up on calling him.

Blogs were just beginning to run with the bad news. In those early days, when all was confusion and misinformation, not a lot of substance was available. Bits and pieces had yet to coalesce into a three-dimensional picture. The Internet was gradually piling up stories, opinion pieces, and scattered reports, yet it was hard to get a firm grasp.

Not many people had ever heard of auction-rate securities or auction-rate preferred securities. This was a far-flung outpost of the credit markets, unknown to most investors, let alone to the general public, whose window into the world of finance pretty much consisted of checking out 401(k) accounts, what was left of them. ARS investors were considered insiders, the sophisticated crowd who should have known they were messing with tricky financial debt instruments. True, about half the ARS investors were seasoned pros. The rest were ordinary investors with a little extra cash looking for a slightly fatter interest bang for their bucks. The Wall Street product machine that constructed the bonds automatically, and for legal purposes, assumed that retail investors were as diligent, as smart, and as nimble as the money managers who ran hedge and pension funds. That was the inside joke, and Wall Street knew it. For many thousands of investors, however, it was a tragedy, because it was this obvious false assumption that allowed Wall Street to roll, fleece, and con the small players. Wall Street recoils at the idea of warning investors in plain language that many of its products are subject to that four-letter word: risk. The bigger the risk, the more obfuscation the market makers throw at it.

The first detailed news I found online was from SmartMoney.com. Entitled, "The Troubles of Auction Rate Preferred Shares," the article by James B. Stewart echoed much of my own outrage. Dated February 28, 2008, Stewart told of being stonewalled by his broker at Merrill Lynch:

> Last year, when some money market funds turned out to hold some mortgage-backed securities and faced a liquidity crisis, their sponsors stepped in and redeemed the shares at face value. This seemed the only decent course, not to mention a good long-term investment in customer loyalty. But when I asked my broker at Merrill Lynch if it would do the same for owners of these money market equivalents, the answer was no.

I checked out BlackRock's web site. The company said, "We do not see any issues with the financial health or fundamentals or these funds as a result of the failed auctions."

Really? A huge market implodes and BlackRock, which promised to continue monitoring the disaster, tells its clients that it's merely a glitch! BlackRock's advice in the face of a growing credit crisis was simple: We should all take a deep breath and relax.

What I learned that awful day in February 2008 was that seismic shifts were at work behind the scenes, the result of which would live up to Americas Watchdog's indictment. It's hard to imagine a volcano blowing its stack and wiping out whole populations in secret, yet this is what was happening all across the financial spectrum. Only a few people knew the truth of what was going on in the ARS netherworld.

I was determined to find out what they knew that I didn't.

✳ ✳ ✳

Traffic on Connecticut Avenue was stop and go as I drove Sandy to work on a dreary Monday morning in early March. Sandy was talking about some work-related matter. The car radio was reporting the usual news, weather, and sports—none of which mattered to me. *Where's the ARS story? It's an economic bombshell! Why isn't anyone reporting it? Someone should be shouting protests.*

I told Sandy about finding Americas Watchdog online and the brief conversation I had had with someone in its Washington office.

"That's good," Sandy said. "Stick with them. Maybe they can help."

I drifted away. Americas Watchdog provided a shadow of hope, a bit of cheerleading. In a state of anxiety, any positive signs appear 10 times bigger than the reality. In the back of my mind I kept wondering how an organization that didn't spell its name properly was going to do us much good.

Given my state of mind on that bone-chilling day in February when I got the news from Jim, I never could have imagined that soon enough I would become one of the central players in the crisis. Two percent of GDP. Vanished. It was a huge event. It seemed crazy on that morning that I'd somehow muster the resources to dig into the heart of the ARS scam. I was aware that if you really want to take on Wall Street you must be willing to get down in the mud. Both of you will get filthy, but Wall Street actually will enjoy it.

"We're trying to get her on *Fox & Friends*," Sandy was saying as we headed down Connecticut Avenue. Her words cut into my internal narrative. "It's looking good for the Pundit Panel," she said.

"Hmmm." I glanced at the faces of the drivers passing in adjacent traffic lanes. They seemed so happy. So self-absorbed and carefree. And there was Sandy, my best friend in the world, seated next to me, doing her best to take my mind off all that frozen cash, the two of us cruising together in a crush of traffic; and yet I felt isolated, like a miserable castaway.

On the drive home, I stopped and picked up a day-old *New York Times*. There it was, a headline on the business page, big and black as my mood: "Fair Game: As Good as Cash, Until It's Not." I gritted my teeth as I read the March 9, 2008, lead by financial reporter Gretchen Morgenson:

> Investors across the nation are finding themselves in Wall Street's version of the Hotel California: They have checked into an investment they can never leave.

An investment they can never leave? I will likely live with that sentence for the rest of my life. Morgenson's clever reference to the 1976 hit song by the Eagles hit hard. "Hotel California" was a song about insanity, loss of innocence, the collapse of the American Dream into a welter of materialism and decadence. I wondered if the Eagles knew they had been fortune-tellers, prophets predicting the fate of Wall Street and the country at the hands of out-of-control risk-takers. As for ordinary investors, they were prisoners of their own misguided trust. *Yes, exactly. I should have listened to my gut back when my first broker booked me into a room at the financial Hotel California.* Blood rushed to my face. I wanted to toss the newspaper into the street, but I couldn't stop reading. It was ghoulish.

Morgenson's article continued:

> The investments, which Wall Street peddled as cash equivalent, are known as auction-rate notes. They're debt instruments carrying rates that reset regularly, usually every week, after auctions overseen by the brokerage firms that originally sold them. They have long-term maturities or, in fact, no maturity dates at all.
>
> But because the notes routinely traded at auctions, Wall Street convinced investors they were just as good as cold, hard cash.
>
> Lo and behold, the $330 billion market for auction-rate notes ground to a halt in mid-February when bids for the securities disappeared. Investors who thought they could sell their holdings easily are now stuck with them. It turns out that the only thing really just as good as cash is, well, cash.

Back home, the *Times* balled up in my fist, I called Jim.

"What kind of secret do you think you're keeping?" I asked. "Story's in the *Times*."

"Then you know about as much as I do," he replied, voice dust-dry.

The official silence had by now morphed from unethical to ruthless, and I told him so. I was determined to find out everything I could, and I was determined not to roll over and play nice. Been there, done that a few months earlier when Jim invited me to a lecture by the economist Jeremy Siegel of the Wharton Business School. Siegel was accompanied at the lecture by a self-described "innovator" from a purveyor of exchange-traded funds (ETF). Siegel was the much-admired brains of the duo. The ETF guy was the business end.

Jim had invited some of his most active clients to this rubber-chicken affair. When Siegel's lecture ended, it was question-and-answer time. I pressed him for answers to one of my most aggravating questions. Why had he been among those economists who persuaded the Bush administration to suspend the up-tick rule, a safety net passed in the 1930s to keep short sellers from crushing the markets? The shorts—especially the banks—were at it again, swarming like blood-starved vampires determined to profit by sucking every ounce of value out of equities. Siegel brushed me off. He gave me a wishy-washy answer about how computers work and how the fractional value of arithmetic numbers nullified any advantage the shorts might have. I almost laughed. It was gobbledygook. And he was dead wrong. I looked over at Jim. His expression said it all, so I shut up. That was then. But no more. No way. No more Mister Nice Guy.

"I understand your frustration," said Jim, his voice on the other end of the phone sounding like a spring-loaded trap. "You're ticked. But I can't—"

"Can't what? Jesus! It's all over." I took a deep breath. "Talk to me, damn it!"

"I'm really sorry," Jim replied. "I can't. But you're getting a penalty [interest] rate while you're waiting for the market to ease."

That much was true. Some ARS issuers were paying a penalty interest rate of nearly 20 percent. Unfortunately I was holding a Missouri Student Loan Authority bond. Before long, the interest rate on the MOHELA bond would drop to near zero. The Port of New York, one of the hardest hit by penalty yields, bought back its bonds to avoid having to pony up those killer rates.

Surely I wasn't the only client twisting the arm of his broker in the pursuit of answers. Jim had a substantial client book built up over many years. A great many of those clients had by now been ringing his phone off the hook. Jim let me know he was spending lots of time on the phone with his angry ARS investors, all of whom were in a world of confusion and hurt, and whose outrage was stoked by a profound sense of betrayal.

Did I detect in Jim's voice a note of remorse? Embarrassment? Or was it raw desperation? Maybe all those outraged ARS investors, whose business Jim had handled over the years, were getting in the way of business as usual. I had no way of assessing where Jim stood in all this. He could not have guessed that nearly two years later, the Financial Industry Regulatory Authority (FINRA) of Washington, D.C., and New York would move to hang a permanent scarlet letter around the neck of every broker who sold ARS. Ironically, FINRA, the so-called self-regulatory organization (SRO), would soon be exposed as one of the central players in the ARS bait-and-switch. Still, had Jim foreseen a potential FINRA demerit hanging over his head, perhaps he would have been a little more forthcoming.

"I have calls to make," he said, annoyed.

"What a shock. They wouldn't have anything to do with auction rates, would they?"

He did not appreciate my sarcasm. "If you need the money right away, we can arrange a margin loan. It's about 7 percent or thereabouts."

This struck me as particularly ludicrous. Not only was Wachovia sitting on my money and flatly refusing to tell me why I couldn't have it back, but now the company was all too eager to make money on my misfortune. Unlike other victims I would later meet along the way, ordinary people whose life savings were frozen, I was lucky enough to have other money to live on, plus Sandy had a full-time job. I had been writing books and articles and creating publications since 1962, though Sandy often enough reminded me, "Hey, there's nothing like a *steady* paycheck." Amen to that.

With her words in my head, I slammed the receiver down. I was now beyond ordinary angst. I had slipped into the bitter realm of contempt. I didn't want to feel contempt for Jim or for Victor, either. But I was locked in the passion of the situation. There were only cops and robbers.

Toward the end of March, I found some details and gained a bit more perspective on the ARS market implosion. The *Wall Street Journal* confirmed the worst fears. The newspaper declared that the ARS market had "virtually collapsed." Yet, it was still too early to assess the full damage—both direct and collateral.

"How much money are we talking about here—total?" Sandy wanted to know. It was still too early to answer her question. I knew how much we had locked up, but the global picture remained unclear.

The Internet reports that were coming in were too fresh and too vague to draw firm conclusions about the wider scenario. The amount of frozen ARS swung wildly from $100 billion to $330 billion to $1 trillion. Weeks passed before more accurate reports arrived from the *New York Times* and the *Washington Post*. The figures most used ranged between $300 billion and $336 billion.

"You're the writer," Sandy said one evening over dinner. "If you had to write about this situation, you know, so anyone could understand it, what would you say?"

I had to think hard about that one. In the middle of the night, my angst-driven brain found an answer.

"I'd tell them Wall Street has punched a big hole in the economy," I told her the following day. "They've ruined lives. Robbed us of jobs. They don't care and neither do the cops."

Sandy blinked. "And that's just the start," she said.

She was right. The scandal would in time expose more than we could have imagined in those early days. We would discover a side of Wall Street and official Washington that would further polarize the political economy and poison the well of political discourse.

∗ ∗ ∗

I kept notes. Reams of notes. It was important to learn everything I could about the auction market and why it went so terribly wrong. I discovered that a year earlier, in January 2007, banks that sold ARS stumbled on liquidity problems. Subprime lending was the tip of the spear of the so-called credit crisis. The auction markets no longer attracted enough buyers without the banks and brokerages jumping in to support the auctions. Wall Street was seized by a hushed-up panic. I wondered why I had never been informed that a crisis was building. Later, I realized I was thinking with the wrong side of my brain. Banks almost never inform the public of troubles unless they're looking for a bailout. Why should they worry about auction failures when they had a perfectly good way to solve the problem by dumping their own ARS on unsuspecting investors?

The accounting firm Deloitte & Touche had given early warning to institutional ARS clients (the corporate *machers* as opposed to the retail investors) that the ARS market was showing cracks, according to D&T's January 10, 2008, Alert 08-2, "Auction Rate Securities Warrant Scrutiny for Impairment." D&T went on to add that "many issuances of [ARS] have been adversely affected by turmoil in the credit markets; thus, their current fair value is at a discount, sometimes substantial, from par value." The firm added that as far back as 2005, the Financial Accounting Standards Board (FASB) had questioned the use of auction-rate paper as cash equivalents. These disturbing facts were generally hidden from the investing public. ARS paper was losing face value, yet the brokerages, including Wachovia, continued to list the par value on monthly statements.

The big players rushed to sell before the crash, apparently acting on inside information. Investment banks holding ARS paper were taking hits on their balance sheets. They had made a conscious and very quiet decision to quit propping up the auction markets. At the same time, what appeared to be an orchestrated decision had been reached by the market makers to stop buying back ARS from their clients. All of this was kept under wraps, even after mid-February, when the crisis went public.

Why did the markets shut down all at once? Did Wall Street reach an agreement in secret? Was this conspiracy, collusion, or coincidence? Goldman Sachs, Merrill Lynch, Lehman Brothers, Bank of America, Wells Fargo, Wachovia, UBS, Citigroup, Fidelity, Morgan Stanley, Deutsche Bank, and others had simultaneously pulled the plug without a word of warning. Investors holding ARS were taking the hit, but it was a major windfall to the banks holding the cash.

Seven months after Gretchen Morgenson's article appeared in the *Times*, Senator Max Baucus, the Montana democrat who chairs the Finance Committee, came up with his own version of "Hotel California"—a description more graphic and more appropriate to Wall Street culture: "It [the ARS freeze] was almost like a roach motel," he said at a September 18, 2008, hearing of the House Financial Services Committee. "A financial roach motel. They [investors] could get in but they couldn't get out."

✳ ✳ ✳

There had never been anything like it in Wall Street's checkered history. We had lived with the expected frauds and con games, the endless greedy mini-Madoffs, and the unscrupulous tricks and sleights of hand most investors grudgingly accepted as the cost of doing business with a subculture whose ethics would make Tony Soprano's crew blush. But the ARS debacle was the whopper—the great white whale of frauds, swallowing the earlier Savings and Loan scandal as if it were a school of plankton.

There was less than cold comfort in knowing I wasn't the only one stuck with frozen cash. Dozens of big, money-soaked investors also had been slammed. Earthlink was stuck with $60 million; Palm, $75 million; Intuit, $328 million; Monster Worldwide, $357 million. The list went on and on. The longer the list, the smaller I felt. Still, I was more concerned with the fate of the retail investors who accounted for half of all ARS victims.

I made up my mind to push back hard. I would be ruthless. This was the only frame of mind that made sense to me in a fight such as this one. Wall Street bankers are ruthless. It's the only business model they understand. We'd receive vivid proof of their ruthlessness during the multibillion dollar taxpayer bailout orgy of 2008 and 2009. Wall Street made a clear threat: Without this outrageous tax infusion, they were prepared to pocket their bonuses and shut down the vital flow of lending and bring the economy to the edge of ruin. To go all out against them was a matter of hitting back street-fighting style, and all the while making a big noise in the form of words that would reach thousands of readers on the Internet and in print.

I had to quit squawking and find an outlet. Or many outlets. It was important to gain an audience willing to raise hell. Willing to use ruthlessness as a defensive tactic. But first I had to find the proper venue.

Becoming so painfully intimate with Wall Street was distasteful to me. I was always content to do business at a discreet distance. I had no reason to get down in the mud. Now I had to interact directly with persons who, in my perverted point-of-view, were a kind of a mutant species driven by hubris, entitlement, and arrogance and wildly turned on by their big "G Spot"—greed. F. Scott Fitzgerald was fascinated by those he considered rich, those idle patrons of the arts who have long since been forgotten but whose spawn now run hedge funds. Fitzgerald was in paradise hanging out with the swell money crowd on the French Riviera in the 1920s. He had never learned that southern France was a sunny place for shady characters. "The rich are different," he once told a skeptical Ernest Hemingway. However, Fitzgerald's rich crowd of yesteryear has become today's superwealthy, who long ago departed this reality for an alternate universe. Today's Wall Street barons patronize the arts with cash purchases. But unlike the patrons of the 1920s, the new crowd views art as symbols of success. The new super rich need no country, no president, and no government. Theirs is a suffocating inner world of "I've got mine and that's all that counts." I got as far away from this crowd as possible—a refugee from a land of the soulless.

It would be painful to reenter. There was no way I could get into this tussle alone, and so I began searching the Internet for other ARS victims, as well as other disenchanted refugees. This fight would require a team effort. Words and force of numbers would be primary weapons. I was determined to round up as many investors as I could find on the Internet and elsewhere. Together we stood a chance of forcing the regulators to do their jobs.

Thus began a firm decision to undertake what would become the fight of a lifetime.

But first I wanted to seek the advice of my closest and most perceptive financial gurus.

* * *

High among them is Harwood S. Nichols, senior vice president of a regional banking firm and one of the most sophisticated analysts and economic historians I have ever known. I met him in 1982, when he worked as a portfolio manager at the now defunct Mercantile Safe Deposit and Trust Company. I have conducted business with him at several banks over the years. He had never once steered me wrong. Harwood had an amazing grasp of detail, depth of experience, and formidable common sense. More important, he had gained my respect not only for his smarts, but also for his decency—the latter being virtually unknown in the fleecing shops along lower Manhattan.

Harwood, whose friends call him Nick, was one of a very small number of financial people I could count on to be a truth teller.

I phoned him at his office. He groaned when I told him about my ARS problem.

"Well, if it's any consolation, you sure as hell aren't alone," he said. "Plenty of very smart people are trying to squeeze through a mighty small door."

We decided to meet for brunch at the InterContinental Hotel near his office in downtown Baltimore. It was a nostalgic setting for me, seemingly far from my immediate gloom. The hotel dining room overlooked the city's Inner Harbor, a few blocks from where I had spent my World War II childhood. It was a real working harbor in those days, and it had enlivened my lifelong fascination with the sea. I recalled hulking warships limping in from around the globe headed for repairs at the Sparrows Point dry docks. As a boy I had spent days on end hanging out on the piers among the sailors and workmen who had arrived from the wars in faraway places with names I had never heard of.

I scanned the slick, new harbor. Its mortal war-driven, oil-blackened surface had been magically transformed into an idyllic setting for trendy shops and cafes—a watery suburbia in midtown. The unending stream of wounded warships I had witnessed with awe as a boy had been replaced by sleek white hulls and the bright sails of sporting boats. They dotted the waters like restless children, unmindful of long ago conflicts. These fiberglass trophies were the frivolous playthings of a more prosperous and somewhat more peaceful generation; they had taken over and given the harbor fresh, innocent face.

Harwood strode across the room with characteristic steadiness. He was 67 years old and handled himself like a much younger man. He had a solid presence that covered a modest (and moderate) personality, a vestige of his combat experience in Vietnam. He was devoid of arrogance and maintained an Irishman's appreciation for the absurd and the written word (his 1988 book, *Money Sense: The Parents Guide to Teaching Children About Money*, is among the very best of its genre). As a moderate Republican, he favored the building of new city parks, decent and progressive public schools, and responsible health care. I have often wondered how a man of his sensibilities ever came to the world of finance.

"So, you're going to raise hell," he grinned. "Good luck."

"I just want my money back."

"You're not thinking of hiring a lawyer, I hope."

"It's occurred to me. You know somebody who's really good?"

Harwood leaned across the table. "First of all, your bond isn't worthless," he said in a half whisper. "It's paying some interest. It's got a call date. It's 30 years from now, I know. But liquidity will begin to flow at some point. You're not going to have to wait it out all those years."

"Easy to say."

"All I'm saying is the bond has value. Besides, I'd hate to see you impoverish yourself with lawyers."

Because my MOHELA bond matured in 30 years, my children and grandchildren would be the eventual beneficiaries of that now-frozen cash. My plans for retirement had become a bad joke, I insisted. Harwood nodded. He was used to wild economic swings and disappointed investors.

Harwood related some of the ARS problems he'd heard of. A developer had purchased a large tract of property near the waterfront, had architectural designs drawn up, and had signed contracts with construction companies, only to have the entire project come to a screeching halt. The development money was tied up in ARS. "Millions," Harwood said.

He told me of other investors, many of them on the corporate side, whose plans had been placed on indefinite hold: college money delayed, medical procedures postponed, mortgage money frozen, tax bills that couldn't be paid, houses that had to be sold to pay Uncle Sam. Listening to Harwood's list of ARS stories got me thinking that a problem of this magnitude might draw a response from the feds who were sure to be pressed by corporate and institutional investors—political contributors who represent the life's blood of Congress.

"Maybe the government will step in," I suggested.

"Anything's possible, of course. But don't count on getting bailed out."

We could not have guessed that a few months after our meeting in Baltimore the Bush administration would move to bail out the entire banking sector, with exceptions, to the tune of nearly $800 billion in taxpayer dollars. Lots of that money went for bonuses and executive compensation. None of it would be used to make ARS victims whole.

Harwood in his scholarly way gave me a thumbnail history of the auction-rate market.

"It was a sweet deal," he explained. "The issuers got their money, the banks got paid for holding the auctions, and the investors pulled down a little extra interest. But you know how it is. There were fuckups."

Harwood informed me that the Securities and Exchange Commission had issued a cease and desist order against 15 firms in 2006. The banks were caught manipulating the auctions and misstating information concerning risks. This shell game was played out between January 2003 and June 2004.

"The banks were under no obligation to guarantee against failed auctions," Harwood added. "Investors just weren't made aware of the liquidity and credit risks. No one was explaining it to them."

"So this 'completely safe' line of crap has been pitched for years?"

"Unfortunately, which is why I never wanted anything to do with it."

"Was it the same cast of characters?"

"Yeah, it always is."

Hardwood said it was common knowledge that the major banks had made a decision not to act as bidders of last resort in the auction market, and they weren't about to make their intentions known. If true, as later proved to be the case, this amounted to a violation of the Securities Act of 1933—misstatements, omissions, the carte blanche of obfuscating sins. No risk continued to be the mantra. Meanwhile, all efforts were to be focused on getting ARS off the balance sheets and into investor portfolios.

Before the ARS crash, financial intermediaries had lost the ability to borrow short-term, which had been the usual practice to finance long-term assets. Harwood explained that these long-term assets, such as stocks, bonds, and securitized mortgages, lost value and caused normal lenders to freeze up and run to the short-term Treasury market. At this point, the then-obscure phenomenon known as the credit crisis was building steam. Details of the crisis were opaque. You had to be on the inside to grasp the implications.

The ARS market relied on a very liquid short-term cash environment and, while investors were in the dark, the credit crisis had infected the market the way a digital virus shuts down a computer.

"The market failed," Harwood explained, "because there were no buyers for those who wanted to redeem. And the supposed backup buyer—usually the underwriter—was completely tapped out."

"But the underwriters made a pledge to investors," I said. "They couldn't have been more reassuring."

"They couldn't live up to it," Harwood replied. He then issued a blanket indictment. When transactions get too complex, the lawyers and the legislators usually step in and set up protocols so that all parties can feel comfortable with the mechanics of a transaction.

"What I believe happened in the ARS crisis is that all parties failed in their responsibilities, namely the buyers, the sellers, and the legislators."

"But the sellers *should* have known. They sure get paid enough," I said, speaking of the sizeable fees paid to the banks for managing the auction market.

"I'll admit the possibility of a market failure was always there," Harwood said. "But what about guys like you who got into the ARS business? The higher yield was a clear indicator that a higher risk existed."

I felt a sudden flush of embarrassment. Harwood was right. Reaching for yield has its inherent risks. But the extra yield was negligible, just slightly above money market for Treasury rates.

"Okay, mea culpa," I said. "But I questioned this from day one," I shot back. "I couldn't get a prospectus. No one I know has ever seen one. My broker swore these lousy ARS things were safer than Treasuries. 'Take it, it's free money.' That was his pitch. 'Trust me.' It was the usual crap. He dismissed any possibility of risk. In fact, I don't recall that he ever used the word."

"I can't speak for anyone else," Harwood shrugged. "Still, I want to be completely clear. I didn't sell ARS and I don't own them. And let's not discount the fact that both sellers and buyers bear some responsibility. There's plenty of baggage out there."

It was a bit painful to admit, but he had made a telling point. Investors in their greed (or perhaps need) to get higher yields than were available on safe money market funds incurred the risk brokers swore didn't exist; and in the end, they got slammed. ARS salesmen, in their rush to make commissions, and pushed by their managers, misrepresented the bonds as being safer than they were. I felt foolish. I trusted someone who was either blind or a huckster.

"I had no idea the brokers were making commissions on ARS," I said.

"Well, they were—25, maybe 50 basis points."

"Didn't the fact that they were making commissions on ARS, and no commissions on money market cash, tell them something was up, that this particular market was different? The push to sell should have clued them in that problems in the market were getting serious. But they never mentioned it, and I can't get a peep out of my brokers."

"Maybe." Harwood paused, looked out over the sunny harbor below. "So here we are in a tough situation. The legislators, the regulators, are stuck once again with a market that wasn't transparent, and where the rules and protocols put unsophisticated savers at risk. So now comes more oversight and regulation. It goes around, it comes around."

"That's Wall Street's concern," I said. "I just want my money and an honest explanation."

Hardwood shook his head. "Given the current environment, it's hard to imagine any underwritings in the near future. As for a broader explanation, you'll need to keep digging."

"So I'm stuck."

Harwood's unflinching stare answered the question. It was now clear I'd have to figure out a way to fight—and not just with words, but with the collective anger of everyone I could enlist in the cause. It was a tall order.

Chapter 4

"I Have No Dreams"

The most essential gift . . . is a built-in, shockproof shit detector.
> —*George Plimpton: "An Interview with Ernest Hemingway,"* The Paris Review, *Spring, 1958*

As February's shock faded and the snows of winter visited the East Coast, Sandy insisted that I get out of the house, away from the computer, the telephones, and the streams of Internet blog sites.

I was glued to the computer and finding my way deeper into the fight. It was obsessive. In a strange sort of way the ARS scandal was a little like the pack behavior I had noticed while working on a movie project a few years earlier. When I had finished writing the story, the wolves appeared out of nowhere demanding byline and screen credits. Their method of assault, like that of the ARS sellers, was to grab the money and run. I was forced to threaten legal action to protect my interests from being swallowed whole. The ARS scam reminded me of

Samuel Goldwyn's classic remark that Hollywood isn't just about the money—it's about *all* the money. But unlike the Hollywood money changers, the Wall Street scammers were a lot less charming and infinitely more devious.

Wall Street creates a lack of transparency for obvious reasons. The business of making money out of thin air requires what syndicated columnist Michael Kinsley calls "transparent obfuscation." This is another way of saying that transparency and truth (facts) mean little if no one understands how to put the two together. Here's some language from a credit default swap, those mysterious, unregulated derivatives that have caused so much financial misery:

> The parties may elect in respect of two or more Transactions that a net amount will be determined in respect of such Transactions, regardless of whether such amounts are payable in respect of the same Transaction.

Got that? It's taken from the 2002 Master Agreement of the International Swap and Derivatives Association.

With swaps-talk as background, I knew that a search to unravel the jargon of the ARS crash would prove to be a maddening slog.

Of the many brokers and analysts I have dealt with, I trusted only two of them. One of these trusted advisors had examined the inside game that was being played out in the ARS arena. He called it "the big ugly," and here's what he revealed:

- Individual brokers had incentive to push ARS to their clients, both at the retail and commercial levels. They collected fees, or "tails" for selling ARS. There was no apparent tail associated with placing cash in money market accounts. Brokers were advised to keep this tail well-hidden between their legs and to avoid discussing the intricacies of the ARS market.
- The banks and brokerages manipulated the auction process, submitting orders to buy or sell shares for their own accounts, a practice that gave the market a superficial look of liquidity. In 2004, the SEC investigated these practices. Two years later, the agency ordered broker-dealers to disclose what was going on to investors and to stop manipulating the market. The SEC order was largely ignored.

- ARS were highly profitable for the broker-dealers. A killing was being made in fees from the issuers amounting to hundreds of millions of dollars. Issuers were paying big fees to the banks and brokerages to keep the auctions going.
- Certain broker-dealers were allegedly using inside information to buy and sell ARS for their own accounts. These allegations would eventually find their way into class-action suits and complaints by state securities regulators.
- "The dealers were misrepresenting ARS," one source said. "They told clients it was good as cash. It wasn't." The National Securities Dealers Association, as well as the Financial Accounting Standards Board warned that ARS are risky, long-term debt, dependent on the broker-dealers to prop up the market. They were liquid only at the time of sale.
- The broker-dealers maintained a phony appearance of liquidity. Insiders knew when the banks decided to quit supporting the auctions, the market would go into cardiac arrest. They didn't tell clients that their access to cash depended entirely on the perpetuation of what amounted to an artificially viable market.

This wasn't the end of my search for what my confidant had called the big ugly. I later discovered that the auctions were failing as early as 2004. It was at this point that brokers were being pushed by their supervisors to off-load in-house shares of ARS into client portfolios. The banks knew what was coming. By early 2008, more than 87 percent of the auctions had failed.

Did this failure happen on cue? Was it scripted? Does a 20-year-old market just suddenly fall apart? And what did an ARS investor need to do to get his or her money back?

I made another phone call to a trusted source.

"Right now," he said in a low voice, "the mantra is, you want your money back, hire a lawyer and take a chance on arbitration."

I told him we were considering such a move. Like most other investors, I had signed a binding arbitration agreement when I went to Wachovia as a client. It was standard procedure. Unfortunately I knew very little about the inner workings of Wall Street's official form of justice.

"Oh, right. You do know that arbitration is stacked against you," my source warned.

He was right. I'd be facing a panel of three inquisitors. There would be someone from the industry, most likely a broker–dealer. The two public members would also have industry ties. One of them would act as an industry mouthpiece, unsympathetic to my position, and with every motivation to favor Wachovia's position. This individual would be there to defend what amounts to an institutional point of view and almost certainly would not give credence to the claim that the ARS debacle was a case of institutional misconduct.

It would cost $1,800 just to file for FINRA arbitration, and FINRA was a creature of Wall Street, financed by the banks. It was a slick SRO, another self-regulating organization stacked against investors. The sham was that FINRA, slipping the word "regulatory" into its title, fooled any number of investors into believing it was somehow connected to the federal regulatory apparatus. The ruse worked pretty well. In any confrontation, the FINRA panel would argue that I should have done more research, regardless of how the bonds were misrepresented by the broker. Everyone knew the drill. After all, I was automatically presumed to be a sophisticated investor with a long track record. The chances of my winning in arbitration were slim to none.

I literally hated the thought of facing yet another Wall Street scam: the farce of FINRA arbitration. But going legal required taking the risk.

Okay, I told myself, *if that's the game, so be it.* At the same time, it occurred to me that I might get lucky, find a way to change the dynamics. If I dug deep enough, raised enough hell in a public forum, I might find a way to level the playing field. And then came the crazy notion that if I could somehow manage to focus enough heat on FINRA itself and its slanted arbitration process, popular outrage might cause a restructuring of the entire system. It was a big order and I decided to make this one of my goals. I jotted it down in a little green notebook of goals I kept on my desk: Find a way to get rid of mandatory arbitration agreements when signing up for a brokerage account. It would be tough going, but I was determined to work all the angles. I could not have imagined that two years later Democrats in

Congress would include this very idea in its financial regulatory reform proposal.

I told Sandy what I was thinking.

She said, "Just get our money back."

"Sure, first things first."

Still, I couldn't let go of the idea of taking a swipe at arbitration's anti-consumer quicksand pit.

* * *

Most people—that is, most rational people—max out on obsessive behavior and eventually fall back into familiar modes of behavior. This typically occurs after experiencing life-altering situations. We shout; we despair; we curse fate; and, ultimately, we find a more balanced mind-set. Yet the ARS trap pushed my limits. How do you get back to normal when normal—the old, comfortable mode you have fashioned over time—is no longer available? How do you pick up the pieces when you can no longer find them? What's the fallback position? As long as that ARS money was out of my reach, my world was upside down. No new normal existed; no cozy niche on the standard bell curve was available. I decided to strip the concept out of my thinking. Too much thinking and second-guessing was making me a little crazy.

The more I discovered about the ARS heist, its audacity and its level of deception, the more intense I became in my research and in my determination to find an outlet—a voice. Not just any voice. It would be a writer's voice—action expressed in order to make a point, to gain allies. This is my way of extracting truth from opinion and undisciplined emotion. I wasn't interested in writing pretty phrases. The words needed rough edges. That part would come easy. There is a particular wasp's nest of outrage that comes from weeding through the toxic lairs of modern finance.

"You can't make this stuff up," I told a friend. "And if you try to, the reader will shrug it off."

A fraud of such magnitude doesn't just happen. It isn't a random event, like an automobile crack-up. There has to be continuity, a predetermined format, and a choreographed dance routine. I wanted to know who wrote it. Who was directing it?

"Sounds like conspiracy theory," my friend Rod said to me at the local gym.

"Well, it wasn't an accident," I replied.

I was also aware that a few brokers were doing the right thing, as HSBC had done. There was a story online about an investor who owned $100,000 in auction paper. He complained to his broker, who agreed that owning it was not what the client or the broker wanted. In an act of uncommon fairness, the broker used his own money, not his firm's, to buy back half of his client's ARS. The broker plunked down $50,000. The cash appeared a few days later in his client's checking account. Such acts of charity and fairness are rare in financial circles, but they do exist in small doses.

I was hatching a plan of investigation to be followed by a campaign of pressure against the banks and regulators. This still-vague concept of information-gathering was rapidly taking shape. The standard editorial outlets I had grown used to in my professional career—the old-fashioned world of print, as well as radio and TV media—were paying little if any attention to the ARS mess. It was easy to understand their reluctance. Those standard-bearers of public information were beholden to the Wall Street empire and its gatekeepers. Given this reality, where would all this dark, encircling energy lead me? Answer: the alternative media, the blogosphere—virgin territory for me. I was aware that the blogosphere was yet to be a disciplined forum. But its arc, its power to leap over the usual information roadblocks, was amazing. And the audience reach was both massive and universal.

Yes, Sandy and I had finally agreed to find an attorney. There was some comfort in this decision, and in Sandy's growing vehemence. "Where's the money?" she kept asking. "All that money—it just disappears? Not a chance. We're taking it back." Her tough attitude was an inspiration.

Of course I wanted the money. But I wanted more. My obsessive personality demanded that I hit back. Sure, hand over the cash, but don't think you can do this to me and then slink away into anonymity. I wanted this fraud up in lights in Times Square. How sweet, how just it would be to expose the reptilian soul of Wall Street. And along with these more anger-drive obsessions, I also wanted to help other investors. "Never Again" seemed a reasonable (if overused) working title for the strategy that would eventually take shape. Which is to say, going legal made sense as standard procedure. Yet, I was determined to take it to another, more intimate level. The aftershock of the rip-off was getting more personal by the day.

Sandy's outrage continued to soothe me. She knew just how to tune it, how to nuance her anger so that it relieved me, temporarily, of my own rage. It allowed me to take a psychic break, a time out from the nagging angst. That was the good part, though I admit the scandal was always on my mind even in those quiet times.

Not so good and deeply frustrating was my inability to get a solid handle on the genesis of the ARS breakdown. I wanted to know everything about this horror movie that had caused so many howls of pain and fear. It was going to be like an episode of the TV series *Criminal Minds*, a drama built on pretzel logic. The metrics of finance aren't terribly complex or difficult to comprehend once you get the hang of it. What happens on the surface of the markets is pretty straightforward stuff; it doesn't require superhuman brainpower. That's Wall Street hype, the notion that they're always the smartest people in the room. Often they're the shrewdest, but truly big minds don't push the world to the brink of disaster. That takes a special talent that has yet to be defined.

Wall Street creates products. The products make money for Wall Street, not for you. It's the action stirring below the surface—the collusive behavior, the machinations of the so-called secret banking systems, "dark pools" of money, the manipulation of commodities, the off-balance-sheet numbers, the currencies—that leave investors in a state of confusion. It's this sleight of hand action that allows the financial services machine to fleece its "honored" clients. It's the old gangland trick: The one who plans to take you down greets you with a bouquet of flowers, a big smile, and a tender kiss on the cheek.

I believed we could find justice. Admittedly, seeking justice on Wall Street is a little naïve, I suppose, like hoping you've been sufficiently saintly to be allowed into heaven. Still, the obsessive part of my brain believed in justice. I'd seen it as a journalist. And as foreman of a criminal grand jury in D.C., I'd witnessed good people receiving deserved rewards. In one of our many cases, for example, two supercilious wiseguys were accused of murder. They walked into the jury chamber with such arrogance and disdain that they managed to turn off the grand jury members, most of whom were retirees sick of listening to the lies of child molesters and murderers. They were insulted by the demeanor of these two defendants, and they voted to indict. I voted an "ignoramus" (the inglorious legal term grand jurors use to say a prosecutor hasn't nailed his case). Nasty and arrogant as these suspects may have appeared, the prosecutor hadn't shown probable cause for a murder rap. The accused walked out of the jury room looking like they owned the place. About a month later, someone else came forward and confessed to the murder. The two posturing assholes, the arrogant innocents, got justice.

But what about Wall Street? Was there a stitch of honor or objectivity one could count on? We have made a habit of granting Wall Street special privileges, a status reserved for those best and brightest to create and share prosperity. I wanted with all my heart to believe that justice was more than a word or an abstract concept, even on Wall Street. Justice is an ethical and judicial construct written into law. I took comfort in this belief, and, at the same time, I had my fingers crossed in hopes that I wasn't being delusional expecting anything like honesty from the banks.

"Bankers—they're an unevolved species. Shame Darwin didn't study capitalism," I blurted out during one of my rants.

"Yep, if Darwin had studied economics, we'd have a chance to survive in a better way," Sandy replied.

✳ ✳ ✳

Now that we had made a decision to go legal, Sandy kept insisting that I take a step back from the blogosphere searching. We had to find the right attorney—an attack dog who knew the securities industry and its ways, and who understood how to play the gotcha game. But this didn't mean I was going to let down. No. I was determined to take on the ARS rip-off in my own way, although I would have laughed at anyone who said I'd eventually find myself a part— at times, at the center—of an army of tough, rowdy, pissed-off allies whose money, like my own, had been put in the deep freeze and denied to us. This crew would be a version of Hell's Angels without the tattoos.

One freezing late March morning I received an e-mail from a Houston-based law firm. Shepherd Smith Edwards & Kantas was trolling for ARS victims willing to take a chance on a class-action battle. I knew a class-action complaint, even a successful one, would net pennies on the dollar for the plaintiffs. In the end, the only real winners would be the lawyers.

Out of curiosity I called the phone number on the computer screen and spoke with one of the firm's attorneys, Sam Edwards. He asked a few questions. How much money did I have at stake? Which banks or brokerages had I dealt with? How long had I been active in the market?

"I'll be straight with you," Sam told me. "You are what they call in the arbitration trade a 'sophisticated investor.' They'll say you should have known better, should have done more research." He was confirming what I already suspected.

"I do plenty of research," I replied. "But my broker made ARS sound so benign—just another money market. Cash."

There was a pause. Did I hear Sam let out a sigh of resignation?

"Hard to believe," Sam said at last. "A guy with your experience getting anywhere *near* Wall Street."

He suggested an alternative: Hire an independent advisor, perhaps a trusted accountant with a broker's license. "Wall Street is utterly corrupt," he said. "I can't believe you haven't figured that out yet." His tone suggested mild hectoring, as if to say, "There goes another sucker thinking he's more canny than the professional hoodwinkers."

I was grateful to Sam for his advice. It was good advice from a smart, experienced attorney. Sam was, however, in the stew of post-scam regret. His was after-the-fact wisdom. The hindsight would have come in handy at the beginning of 2008. Now, hearing Sam's unvarnished disgust for Wall Street culture, all I had was local color. Sam headed up class-action cases and I had decided to go it on my own.

* * *

I had been making lists of names, e-mail addresses, and phone numbers from the growing ranks of ARS victims who were going public and looking for advice and retribution via the Internet. Nearly all the information I had gathered came from online sources. Most of the victims fell into three distinct camps: very angry; very depressed; very angry and very depressed. Add another variable: more than a few investors were spoiling for a brawl. The brawlers would, in the end, be the most effective soldiers. Like the rest of us, they were humiliated. They had been taken for fools. No amount of excuse-making about a credit crisis and liquidity squeezes would heal the insult. Imagine a mugger assaulting you on the street. As he stuffs your money, credit cards, and jewelry into his pockets, he then says, "I wouldn't be doing this if you hadn't been dumb enough to walk down this street in the first place. Hope you'll understand."

Is this too much of a metaphorical stretch? No, the brawlers would insist. The banks used every trick in the book to steal ARS money, and for an excuse they were blaming the theft on the crisis they had created by over-the-top risk-taking. They were even blaming investors. We were the greedy ones, they said. We hadn't done our due diligence. We deserved to take the hit.

I have followed this crisis from the beginning, and I have yet to hear a single apology from Wall Street or from the politicians and regulators in Washington. Former SEC Chairman Christopher Cox, whose passivity enabled the auction-rate debacle, remained stoic. He was one of the good old market guys.

Me, I liked the brawlers.

Yeah, the voice inside whispered. You'll be in good company with the take-no-prisoners types. You're angry and humiliated. But somehow you're going to tell a Wall Street tale of deceit and corruption that may make a difference to others.

∗ ∗ ∗

The tale wouldn't be confined to my own struggle. I wanted to do what the late author Studs Terkel had done and allow other voices to join in.

One of the first stories I picked up online was that of an 81-year-old man suffering with lung cancer. Most of his money was stuck in illiquid auction-rate preferred securities. He had placed his cash there because his broker had convinced him the auction market was safer than U.S. Treasury bonds. "Uh, preferred bonds my ass. What a joke," he growled in a weak, rumbling voice. "I'm dying. Damned near broke. I got a wife. Medical bills I'll never be able to pay. I'm going out busted. *Preferred*. Jesus!"

I asked if I could name him if I was lucky enough to someday get the opportunity to write the history of the ARS scandal. "Hell no," he replied. "I don't want people feeling sorry me. Don't fancy talking to my wife and kids about it, either."

I knew his refusal came from deep down. He was ashamed of having been conned by his stockbroker, an event similar to being conned by a used car salesman or a really sleazy hooker.

There were many victims whose situations made my own mess look relatively manageable. That message came home to me every day over the Internet and also through an increasing volume of telephone calls from ARS victims who had found my phone number online.

I ramped up my story-gathering by going on an all-out comment-writing campaign on various Internet blogs. My favorite sites were the *New York Times'* DealBook and Seeking Alpha. These well-read sites brought in plenty of feedback.

There were dozens of other sites, such as Investment News, The Motley Fool, and TheStreet.com. Hundreds of sites. Most of them were pro-industry. Many were outlets for ranters and apocalyptic prophets. Others were hyping products, like bulletproof Forex software and other fantastic formulae for making huge profits. There was a whole universe of sales pitches by unscrupulous fund managers who, for a price, promised outrageous profits.

At a time when the New York Stock Exchange was tanking badly, I stumbled across a site called Death Cross Trader. It was a snarling bear fund managed by Zach Scheidt. His particular bloodlust aimed to short sell equities and profit off Wall Street's biggest failures. Scheidt was selling his very own inventive trading system that would suck the life out of stocks with uncanny accuracy. Just what we needed in a time of distress! It was disheartening to find so many super-bear schemes that promised huge returns by taking on the role of Dracula. Death Cross Trader mocked the bulls, said they deserved to be rolled. You could almost hear the rattling of bones in the background.

I continued to search and make use of every reasonable web site to shout out to ARS investors. I wanted to learn the details of their stories, and I let them know I was planning to someday write a book about the fiasco—a mystery and a crime I would eventually try to solve. I let it be known I was in the early evidence gathering stages.

I began creating a master list of names and anecdotes. It was a little like gathering up bits of kryptonite to use as weapons in a larger battle that was rumbling like a pounding echo over the horizon. I wrote so many comments on so many blogs that Google began to pick them up and carry them under my name. Such irony. The accomplishments of my other, earlier life, my history as a writer, explorer, musician, NOAA aquanaut, slowly gave way to my commentaries on everything from the ARS scandal to the uptick rule to the role of regulation in a financial industry gone wild.

I had no hesitation listing my name, e-mail, and phone number at the end of these commentaries. Privacy was not my ally in this crusade. The personal information I left behind on these sites was my digital business card. Opening up, becoming easily accessible, put me in touch with an ever-growing community of ARS investors armed with their own digital torches and pitchforks—a community of outrage more than ready to burn down the oligarchic banking system that had created so much misery while propping itself up at public expense.

The stories flowed in sometimes alarming volume. One day nearly two dozen outraged e-mailers wound up in my in-box. There was a woman in her late 70s fighting cancer (there were many cancer cases and mostly elderly investors). She couldn't afford to pay for her medications. Most of her savings were locked up in auction-rate preferred securities. These so-called ARPS were similar to ARS in that they were sold at frequent auctions and were in reality 20- and 30-year bonds boxed in closed-end funds. ARPS were popular with investors at or near retirement. They were pitched as ultra-conservative. As it turned out, they were toxic bombs primed to explode.

A 55-year-old woman from Seattle wrote: "For the first time in my life I am homeless." The cash she needed to make a down payment on a home was frozen by her bank, which she named as Wells Fargo. (In 2009, the bank faced a complaint by California Attorney General Jerry Brown for allegedly misrepresenting ARS and ARPS.)

I asked the Seattle correspondent if I could use her name in a story. "Oh, heavens, no!" she exclaimed. "I'm so embarrassed. You just can't imagine." I told her I certainly could imagine how she felt; after all,

I was struggling with a level of embarrassment that I couldn't bring myself to discuss with friends or our own grown children.

"I worked my whole life," the woman told me. "Always had a roof over my head." She sold the house she had been living in for many years. It had been a nice, comfortable place, modest, although it was becoming difficult to keep up with repairs. The woman was at a stage of life where it was necessary to downsize and take a little cash out of her equity to live on. She placed the proceeds of the sale with Wells Fargo, she told me.

"My broker said he had this great, real safe way to park my money while I looked for a new home," she explained. "He was real nice about it. Said it was lots better than money market. I knew this broker. I trusted him. So I took his advice." I could hear her breathing (or was it suppressed sobbing?) on the other end of the line. "If it weren't for a few friends," she went on, "I'd be homeless. I'm so ashamed."

I received many such messages. The following was typical: "Not only are my husband and I under great stress, my trust in this country's financial institutions has been permanently destroyed." This e-mail arrived in 2008, in the pre-bailout months, pre-Madoff, a time when the trust and optimism that had once tempted record numbers of investors into the markets was beginning to crash and burn.

The scale of what would soon become a tsunami of disillusionment had yet to sweep away what was left of the United States' almost (forgive me) childlike trust in banks and brokerages. A TV journalist once asked economist Paul Krugman how bad the economy was likely to get under the guidance of former President George W. Bush and Treasury Secretary Hank Paulson. Krugman, always comically pessimistic, said if he answered truthfully, holding nothing back, a panic would ensue. We'd horde all the canned goods we could get our hands on and head for a cave somewhere in the Ozarks.

From the tone of the e-mails that were starting to pile up in my office, one would assume Krugman was being a bit too optimistic.

* * *

In order to keep up with the volume of e-mails, I made weekly visits to Office Depot. I bought reams of paper (I kept on file copies of hundreds of e-mails). I was running through ink cartridges at a record pace. My foray into investigative financial journalism, I could tell, was going to be mildly expensive. I still didn't know it would turn into a full-time job.

I was committed. There was no way I could stop. The obsession had set in deep. The best reporters and detectives are driven by such impulses. I was willing to do whatever it took to gain ground, to find a way and a means to make a difference for others, to force the hand of regulators, and to get my own cash back. At times, the weight of this ambition seemed absurd—more than a little foolish. Who was I to duke it out with a financial cabal that had the ability to bury me with legal fees and physical threats? I knew Wall Street has its own hit squad. It can attack in lots of ways. Hits don't always come from the barrel of a gun. It didn't take long to find chilling stories of intimidation, especially aimed at insiders and whistle-blowers. No one is immune when the Street decides to shut you up. My job was to find a gutsy whistle-blower, someone like Harry Markopolos, the gentleman who later busted Bernie Madoff after his complaints had been ignored by the SEC and FINRA.

James B. Stewart, a *Wall Street Journal* reporter, is an example of one of the countless savvy people who became a victim of the scam. Several months into the implosion he confessed: "As regular readers know, I was among the victims. . . . I've heard from hundreds of others [ARS victims]. Wall Street's reaction was to offer to lend investors their own money—using our other assets as collateral and charging us market rates. It was insult on top of injury."

✳ ✳ ✳

Blues/folk singer Joni Mitchell's ballad, "Amelia," speaks of "comfort in melancholy." Indeed, we know it's all too true. Melancholy allows you to sink into your own hurt, to find an ironically warm comfort zone that allows you to ache without regret. I am sure Freud would agree. It's called feeling sorry for yourself in a safe kind of way that defies outside ridicule.

I was too often tempted to take that route, although I knew it was a dead end. The voice in my head screamed, *Be a mensch!* And I shouted back, *Okay, I'm doing my best!*

Sandy and I might have lived the rest of our lives in modest comfort, even without our ARS cash. We'd need to be frugal, cut out travel and a few other luxuries we had earned from hard work, saving, and investing—the all-American formula to gain what passes for success. But without that locked-away cash I would never know a sense of inner peace. I would always be the guy who was conned out of his future plans, the schmuck who should have known better. Life isn't fair. Right! And so what! Old truisms are like worn-out blankets: They're real, they're serviceable, but they don't give you much warmth.

By the end of March, all my determination suddenly and unexpectedly morphed into a curse, the very opposite of what I hoped to accomplish. It hit me especially hard one day at the gym. I was in the pool warming up for a two-mile swim. It was supposed to be a pleasant cool-down after six rounds of boxing with young men less than half my age. I have to say it wasn't really all-out boxing with them. Our workouts were more like gentle sparring. Real boxing, even at the amateur level, is a bloody business—no country for older men. During the sparring session, I pulled my punches. I couldn't even jab properly. I ducked and danced and spent most of my energy protecting myself against my students' attempts to deck me. The last thing I wanted to do was take out my gloom on innocent, shiny-faced students.

Later, standing in a swimming lap lane, no other swimmers in sight (the lifeguard was probably upstairs flirting with the trainers) Joni Mitchell's lyrical ennui hit me. My arms and shoulders ached from blocking punches. I squatted in the swim lane until the water reached my chin. How easy it would be to sink, I thought. Sink below the surface and breathe. Breathe deeply. All the madness and the anger will slip away.

I stood straight up. Alarmed by my own thoughts, I slapped the water with my palms. *Stupid, stupid, stupid! How dare you even think such things? You, the family elder, with grown children and growing grandchildren—and Sandy. Fuck it! Get a grip and hang up the boxing gloves and everything else and fight to get your money back. That's your business now. So be all business!*

* * *

The following e-mail arrived from southern California. It was sent to me by the son of an ARS victim who was writing to me because his dad was too ill, and apparently too despondent, to handle the aggravation of writing to a stranger whose name kept popping up on financial blogs. I received permission to reproduce the e-mail, but only after promising not to reveal names:

> My father . . . helped [create] a company in southern California back in the 1970s and served as vice president. After 35 years, the company was sold. . . . He took the check from the sale of the company to Wells Fargo Bank. He told them his main priorities were first and foremost safety, followed by liquidity. My father knew he would have to withdraw a large amount of money in a matter of months to pay taxes. The financial advisor (at Wells Fargo) recommended auction-rate preferred securities, telling my father they were safe and liquid. When my father went back to withdraw the money to pay his taxes he was told he could not have his money. My father was forced to sell other assets, pay taxes late, and pay penalties for late payment. . . . His money is still frozen. My mother says that all the dreams she had for what they would do when the company was sold are now gone.
>
> "I have no dreams," she says.

A successful businessman works for decades to build a company, a career, a life, a planned retirement. Now the rewards of a lifetime of work are denied to him. This gentleman was no bonus baby. He wasn't making a living using other peoples' money to take crazy risks and invent toxic products. He took the risks of an honest businessman during a lifetime of hard work to create substantial products. Real things. He made sacrifices and hoped for a generally carefree retirement. In this story, I would later discover why the mainstream press had only touched lightly on Wall Street's ARS con.

* * *

I was in New York on business and looking forward to a face-to-face meeting with one of the hardest-working reporters in the business media, Daisy Maxey of the *Wall Street Journal/Dow Jones News Wire*. We had communicated via e-mail and telephone. I was eager to spend time with her. We shared much in common. We were journalists, we were covering the auction-rate scandal, and we were avid scuba divers. In truth, I would have preferred trading dive stories with her instead of digging through financial scandals.

"ARS is seen as a rich man's problem," explained Daisy as we shared breakfast at the Manhattan Diner on Broadway. "They're mostly well-to-do people" she said. "Their problems don't resonate with your average reader."

"That's odd. ARS people aren't exactly in a league with Bill Gates. This rich man stuff is a misconception."

Daisy picked at her scrambled eggs. I sipped my coffee. I suppose she knew I was studying her. Fair skin, youthful, unfussy blonde hair, hazel eyes that every day looked into the unblinking, steely gazes of the financial elite, those who bought Washington on the cheap and who handed out obscene bonuses paid for by their shareholders (later by the taxpayers). I had put in seven years at Fairchild Publications and ABC Cap Cities. And, like Daisy, I had to deal with these greedy elites, gatekeepers, and other entrenched interests. I was fair in my reporting, but I seldom liked the people I had to deal with. Daisy had an edge: She was young and charming—qualities that enhanced her ability to soften up the self-absorbed savants.

Elitism in any form has been a road bump for journalists ever since the First Amendment. Daisy was making it more-or-less official. There was a media bias toward ARS investors, she suggested. Because they had a little money to invest, most consumers of mainstream media weren't sympathetic to ARS investors. Gretchen Morgenson of the *Times* had given subtle hints of this built-in bias, though she never said so directly in print. Daisy revealed a social sense and tapped into the human side, as did Morgenson, and understood that with the coming of the financial meltdown ordinary Americans were demanding answers and demanding clawbacks of those outrageous bonuses being handed out for wrecking the economy.

I had complained to Daisy that there was a glaring paucity of news coverage of the ARS story by the mainstream media. To find out what was going on it was necessary to read the specialty publications like the *Wall Street Journal*, the *Financial Times*, *Forbes*, and *Barron's*. And even these outlets were not invading the inner sanctums of the elites who had perpetrated the fraud.

Bloomberg News was an exception. Still, not even Bloomberg could compete with the blogosphere. On the Internet there were no gatekeepers to contend with. Everything was free for the taking. No cows were sacred. There were no stylebooks or fear of advertiser blowback. If you wanted to unearth the details of a scandal, uncensored, nothing competed with the Internet.

"I think you're right," said Daisy. "But do you think there's enough clout there to make a difference?"

A good question. I pointed to the fact that all the major news outlets had online presence. And there were pure online creatures that had significant influence and audiences. For example, there was *The Daily Kos, Huffington Post, Slate, The Drudge Report*. Each had its point of view—"a conflict center." The most important issues of the day were being hashed out online. Digital journalists and opinion makers were putting pressure on the elites and the established media.

"No conflict, no drama," replied Daisy.

"No conflict, no change," I replied. "The online crowd isn't like the older breed of protesters. They saw millions march in the streets against the war in Iraq—all for naught. I want to get investors excited, get them organized to fight back in more specific ways. A hunger strike on Wall Street will surely get some attention."

If you really wanted to get inside the auction-rate battle, go online, I told Daisy. Of course she already knew that. On the Web, the mass of ARS news breached like a whale in an ocean of white-collar crime stories. It seemed to me that the business pages of most metropolitan dailies read like crime reports. But for various reasons these smaller crimes crowded out the more massive ARS story.

"Do you believe print editors are snobs? Gatekeepers?" I asked. "Do they view anyone with enough money to ante up $25,000 for a single bond to be too wealthy, too removed from Middle America, to be seen as sympathetic?"

"It's not the editors," Daisy said. "What you're talking about, well, it goes back to editorial points of view."

The mainstream press outlets such as the *Washington Post, Los Angeles Times*, and the Great Gray Lady, the *New York Times*, had protested the scandal. But these outlets weren't having much impact.

I wasn't comfortable with the idea that my favorite newspapers took such modest positions.

Daisy and I ordered another round of coffee. We entertained the notion that wealth is often greeted by scorn or envy. It's as if making lots of honest dollars has no moral high ground and can't be defended. Wealth, even honest wealth, is forever suspect. It's America's quiet conundrum. Is it possible that wealth, by its very nature, is viewed as being just a little anti-American? Or did this seeming contradiction of values have its roots in contempt for Wall Street and suspicion of corporate America? Both are held in low esteem in the broad American psyche, even though we crow about our financial power. But I believe we're closet hypocrites when it comes to making money. Americans like to wave the flag and salute what they perceive to be free enterprise and capitalism. Yet opinion polls don't reveal our shadowy suspicions of these very same means of enrichment.

"It's unfair," I said to Daisy. "There are decent people who work very hard, take risks, and with luck they become successful. Does their success deserve the crime suffered at the hands of those brokers they trusted? Theft is what it is."

"I agree with you," said Daisy. "It's all a perception thing."

"A very good friend of mine in California believes there's going to be a populist rebellion. They're not going to march with placards. They're going to invade the homes of these Wall Street types in Greenwich and take back the ill-gotten loot."

Daisy laughed. "What a thought."

She politely listened to my rudimentary activism. To succeed, the underlying cause had to be repeated over and over again until it can no longer be dismissed. ARS had to become part of the mainstream vocabulary. Editorial and political positions had to be established and maintained.

"Not easy," Daisy remarked. "But doable."

She agreed media was the necessary driver of any cause. In his excellent book on basic political strategy, *Taking on the System*, Markos Moulitsas Zuniga, creator of the powerful web site *The Daily Kos*, makes a telling point: "Without the media, little can be accomplished."

"Here's the way I want to proceed," I said. I explained that I'd find a new media outlet or create one if I had to—and I'd find like-minded individuals who would engage in a pressure campaign against the federal and state regulators. I couldn't do it alone. I'd try to become part of a central online clearinghouse for ARS victims and write exclusive news for that audience. The stories might be picked up by other Internet bloggers and even mainstream writers. We'd force the hands of the gate-keepers, get them to listen and eventually force the regulators to act.

Daisy had made the point that the Internet, despite its consider-able power to reach a worldwide audience, still isn't strong enough on its own.

"You need to get those conventional editorial gatekeepers on your side," she said.

"We'll become too visible and vocal to be ignored."

Then Daisy threw a twister: "Is there an issue, any issue, that blog-gers took away from the mainstream or forced the mainstream to act?"

I had an immediate answer. "Yeah, Bush's gift to Wall Street—privatizing Social Security. The bloggers killed it. Writers like Brad DeLong and Devon Black and good old Huffpo." I laughed, not a jolly laugh. "Can you imagine where we'd be today if that half-assed scheme had actually been approved? And keep in mind that the Democrats were talking compromise."

I thought for a moment. "Look at what those Netroots, the Web, did for Obama. It's a dynamite medium if you understand how to use it. The stupid Social Security giveaway, the Obama campaign—the main-stream glommed on to them because of the political clout of the Web."

"Do you think the ARS story will have a happy ending?" Daisy asked, pushing at the edges of what she may have viewed as my overly idealistic strategy.

"Everybody wants a happy ending. We want resolution. We want our money back. Yeah, a happy ending isn't so crazy."

"Life isn't fiction."

"Woody Allen once said, 'If you want a happy ending, go to Hollywood.' Sometimes I think that's what's most attractive about it. Hollywood gives you what real life can't. We're always looking for the happy ending, and if it's not there, we just keep on rooting for it."

We parted that morning agreeing on fundamental principles. We promised to stay in touch.

I was jubilant. I had made a powerful ally.

Chapter 5

Bill Meets Mohela

We can't trust the banks to help boost the economy. The invisible hand of the marketplace is in the taxpayers' pocket.
    —*Representative Dennis Kucinich (D., OH)*

A few weeks later, at a party in Reston, Virginia, I was delighted to see an old acquaintance, a much-respected Washington attorney, Peter Panaretes. A few years earlier, Peter had graciously introduced me to a Chinese consultant for help on an illustrated novel I was writing about the life of an ancient Chinese calligrapher. Aside from mutual respect, my friendship with Peter was based on a love of music. I knew Peter had blue chip financial bona fides, although we seldom had reason to discuss Wall Street. I enjoyed his wit, his love of travel (the Italian Dolomites, especially), and his fondness for the arts—a trait rare among financial types, unless you include the fetish of collecting masterpieces as badges of success.

What I most admired about Peter was his lack of pretension, his Mark Twain-ish sense of humor, and his love of classic jazz. These traits marked him as being a cool guy. Cool has its limits, of course. As the afternoon wore on, I got a surprise dose of reality. I was in the market for a lawyer and, for the first time, asked Peter to tell me about his legal practice. As it turned out, he was in the business of defending banks and brokerages. This out-of-the-blue revelation was about as unexpected as a missed chord by Aretha Franklin. I was hoping Peter might consider defending our claim against Wachovia. Perception being what it is, I assumed he was a defender of the little guy.

"I thought you knew," Peter said, responding to my surprise and stocking up on little chicken wedges spiced with dill in a creamy sauce. "Yeah, I work for the *other* side," he said.

"You mean the *dark* side," I said. He was in no position to help us.

Though I was always set to pounce on anyone who defended Wall Street, there was nothing to be gained by launching into a diatribe against an admirer of Louis Armstrong. Yet inside of me the little voice protested against him: *How can you, of all people, have anything to do with these conniving crooks?* It just didn't fit what I knew of Peter. I was tempted to launch into a rant (I was still spoiling for a fight). But it would have been rude to sound off. Who was I to berate Peter's choice of a profession? And, besides, who makes a scene at a garden party? Answer: someone who has been robbed by shady characters.

Our hostess, a former president of the American News Women's Club, introduced the party's big attraction. There was applause as she and a troop of Irish River Dancers whirled into action; they were a much needed distraction. The precision of the dance had a kind lulling, hypnotic effect. For the moment, our ARS troubles faded. But not for long.

I turned to Peter. "How do you stand those . . . *people*?" I asked. "The financial types, I mean—the bonus babies?"

Peter laughed. "They're just people," he said. "They're *different* because of the business they're in. But they have their problems, like anyone else."

I did my best to submerge my anger in the beat of the dancers. They performed at a blistering tempo. No matter how hard I tried, I couldn't tame my emotions. Again I turned to my friend Peter.

"Okay, but really, how do you *deal* with them?" I pressed. "Those self-aggrandizing bastards think they're above it all."

"It's mostly damage control," Peter said. "That's what we do. We try to keep them out of trouble. Usually they don't listen." He took another bite of his salad. "Say, these potatoes are darned good," he said, scooping another portion into his mouth.

"Damage control—it's not working all that well, is it?" The words just slipped out. It was an inappropriate remark, totally out of place. "I'm sorry," I said defensively. "I came out here to relax. Now I'm right back where I started."

Peter sighed and turned his attention to the dancers.

His remark about damage control would turn out to be the understatement of the year. If Peter sensed that the country was heading for an event resembling the Great Depression, he didn't let on. Dire warnings were floating about, but few in Washington were taking them seriously, at least not in public. I was convinced that all the damage control in the world wouldn't be enough to deter Wall Street's headlong plunge into the pits, pulling the rest of us in with them. The ARS scam was the beginning—the *tell*. Only a few super-bears were waving red flags and pointing at black swans. Larry Kudlow, CNBC's zealous and nattily dressed "free market capitalist," was still pimping for his "Goldilocks Market." Kudlow's optimism was method-acting and a sure sign that trouble lay ahead.

"Well, you're no help," I groused, interrupting Peter's focus on the dancers. "You know, I'm on the other side. I've got big troubles."

"Troubles? What sort of troubles?"

I told him about our ARS situation. "I was hoping you'd be able to help us. But you're on the other side. It's not personal. I'm a little out of joint."

Peter groaned in the same way my accountant groaned when he discovered ARS in my portfolio. "Holy shit! You're gonna wind up in arbitration!" he exclaimed. "How did you wind up with this crap?"

Peter shook his head. "Gee, I'm sorry," he said. "Wish I could help. What exactly is going on?"

Apparently he hadn't heard much detail about the ARS debacle, or if he did know, he wasn't letting on. I told him how the bonds were sold deceptively, as cash equivalents, and so forth. I laid into my brokers. "They damned well knew what they were doing—making money on the deal and off-loading their in-house inventories."

I must have said a few other things, too, personal things, bitter comments that may have stung Peter. He was stoic. He didn't flinch. He didn't wince. Instead he smiled gently. He'd heard it all before. He was in the business of defending Wall Street. I bit my lip. No point ranting. I returned to the buffet and loaded up on bow-tie pasta and poured another slosh of vodka into my glass. Out of the corner of my eye I could see Peter snapping his fingers to the beat of the dancers. It was selfish to press a friend who has done nothing to bring about the dilemma and who had been so helpful and gracious in the past.

"Sorry to be so self-indulgent," I said by way of apology.

Peter shrugged. "I wish I could help. But professionally my hands are tied."

There was no use in babbling on. I had already said too much. It was crazy to risk a good friendship.

I told him Sandy and I were in search of an attorney to represent our ARS case, someone experienced in arbitration. "Somebody with a mouthful of canines," I grinned.

"Well, I might be able to get you started," Peter said. He leaned back and allowed the twangy sound of the music and the tap-tapping of the dancers' feet to wash over him. When the dancing ended and the applause faded, he scribbled the name of one of his partners on his business card. "Give him a call. Mention my name."

The next day I called his partner, mentioned Peter, and laid out the problem. Did he know of a good defense attorney?

"Let me give it some thought," he replied.

The next day I called again. The partner suggested the services of a Baltimore-based legal firm, Tydings & Rosenberg, and a young attorney working there named Bill Heyman. I called him and arranged a meeting.

* * *

Our introduction to Bill Heyman was set to take place at a conference room in downtown Washington. It was early July. The office air-conditioning was working overtime against the city's swampy summer heat.

"You sure he knows where we are?" Sandy asked.

Heyman knew exactly where the conference room was located. Though his offices were located in Baltimore, Heyman spent some of his working time in Washington fighting arbitration cases at FINRA. It takes unnatural perseverance and a strong stomach to go head-to-head, day in and day out, with industry lawyers in a financial bull ring in which the plaintiffs act the part of the hapless bull attacked by picadors, matadors, and other tormenters. I couldn't help wondering if the industry panelists viewed arbitration as a blood sport.

"Arbitration—it's such a stacked deck," I said. It just slipped out. It was the wrong attitude at the wrong time, and I immediately regretted it.

Sandy was alarmed. "Stacked deck? Like how?"

I had done some cursory research but had refrained from discussing it with her. It made little sense to dampen her positive attitude. The statistics were just too gloomy. Besides, what was the point of dumping the stats on Sandy? It would be like running the cheerleaders off the field on the day of the big game. Still, she deserved to know the facts.

"You're going to get the details from Heyman," I said. "May as well get a jump on it."

Thus began a recitation of the dreary facts. The win rate for consumers in arbitration had slipped from 53 percent in 2001 to 36 percent in 2007, according to the Securities Arbitration Commentator, a Maplewood, New Jersey group that tracks award percentages. Even if you do win, the expected return is somewhere between 22 and 38 cents on the dollar. No matter the decision, the industry walks away with at least the majority of your dollars.

Sandy gave me a dark look. "You sure we should be doing this?"

"It's our only option for now. You sign on with a brokerage, you automatically agree to binding arbitration."

"You'd be better off in Vegas." For the first time, Sandy was visibly exasperated. "I mean, it sounds like heads they win, tails we lose. You're going up against the crooks that are defended by crooks in a court paid for by the crooks. Didn't you say so yourself? You said the banks support FINRA."

"Never said it was fair. Anyway, let's hear what Heyman has to say."

Sandy reached across the table and snatched an apple tart off the deli plate she had purchased earlier. She nibbled at it in silence. It was obvious what she was thinking; she was running our odds. I could feel the heat coming off of her. Suddenly the room seemed too big, too airless. The flat screen TV mounted on the wall appeared to be strangely menacing, as if it were a direct conduit to defeat or an artifact out of Orwell's *1984*. Big Brother was not only watching, he was going to rob us for our own good—this in line with the twisted logic of Wall Street.

I had written a list of attack points to gear up for this meeting with Heyman. Among them was an assault on the kangaroo court of arbitration. I couldn't change the system, although at a certain point along the curve I was determined to give it a try. FINRA's version of arbitration was just another cog in the machinery of institutional misconduct. It seemed all wrong that arbitration takes on issues of fraud, deception, and outright theft and tries to justify them. It would be best to let the courts handle these cases. If Wall Street lost its protective shield of arbitration, it would be forced to defend criminal and civil charges in court. Such a move might prevent at least some of the ongoing criminality. Indeed, the notion of turning the tables, of tossing the wolves to the courts was a fantasy, but that didn't mean it was impossible. *Get your money back and go after FINRA later,* I had written at the bottom of my yellow legal pad. *Find the weakness and exploit it.*

Poor Sandy had put up with so much grief from me. She stood fast and strong. I tried to imagine what a loner faces in a situation like this. There were thousands of elderly people out there holding frozen ARS and wondering what to do next. Many of them were on their own, and more than a few were pretty much adrift like the blind physician who had contacted me via the Internet and later by phone. Here was a woman in her late 50s, not only blind but also disabled and bedridden. Virtually all her savings were frozen. Essentially broke and unable to work, she was living with a friend who looked after her. I just couldn't get her out of my mind.

I was eager to get this woman's story in print. The physician, however, was afraid to speak out and tell her story on the record. She said she had filed for arbitration and had received ominous calls from her broker angrily insisting she knew exactly what she was buying when she purchased her auction bonds, understood the all risks, and had only herself to blame.

"You're trying to make a fool out of me," her broker raged at her.

Lawyers from the brokerage firm descended upon her like lice. The physician said they foisted a snowstorm of documents on her, all of which she said had to be read and signed. "But I can't see," she pleaded. "What do they want me to do?" In the end, she couldn't afford to hire an attorney and was forced to defend herself.

I tried hard to get her to tell her story on the Web or elsewhere. I would have passed it on to contacts at the *Wall Street Journal* and the *Washington Post*. A tale of such ruthlessness, such callousness, might have brought down the entire farce of the ARS scam, along with the cynical Kabuki dance of FINRA arbitration. I passed my contact information to Daisy Maxey, hoping she might pry the story out of her. Nothing worked.

At this writing, the physician has gone through her arbitration. She might have come away with a few pennies on the dollar. The outreach to Daisy Maxey was naïve, a hope that a woman-to-woman encounter might work and turn the physician's situation into a publishable story. It did not. We have heard nothing from her since our initial contacts. Her phone is disconnected.

✳ ✳ ✳

I kept checking my watch. It was a few minutes before noon. I tried to picture Bill Heyman in my mind's eye. We were expecting something of a cliché: a tough-talking older man, someone out of the Jack London School of Central Casting who might pick up on my activist frame of mind. I had dragged myself from self-pity to fighting shape—cold-hearted and radical all at once, and I wanted Heyman to sharpen the attack.

The 40-something attorney who showed up precisely on time appeared almost too small, too modest for the over-sized conference room. He certainly did not fit the preconceived image of an attack dog. In his dark blue suit, dark necktie, and expensive-looking shoes, he gave the appearance of someone a little too polite, a little too sensitive to be taking on a crew of financial swamies.

We shook hands. I introduced him to Sandy. He offered a soft, quick grip, as if his hand possessed a shyness of its own.

"It's good to meet you," he said, quietly. "I hope I can help out."

I had informed him of our problem during our initial phone conversation. We were not the first people to come to him with ARS on the brain; it was his past experience with the situation that sold us.

Sandy offered him a place at the head of the conference table. He settled into the seat, smiling wanly. "Okay, let's see what we've got," he said.

I placed my files and other documents between us. He gazed with curious abstraction at the stack of letters to and from Wachovia officials (including correspondence with interim CEO Lanty L. Smith). Our entire financial life was spread out on the conference table: reams of securities statements; my complaints to FINRA and the SEC; copies of our checking accounts and bank statements; and a copy of the buy-order of the contested ARS from its issuer, MOHELA. The panel of arbitrators would review this material looking for evidence of sophistication—"an excuse to say you should have known better," as Heyman put it. An attorney friend had warned us earlier that if all the financial statements added up to seven figures, "our sophistication" would be an automatic presumption. I mentioned this to Heyman.

"He's right," Heyman nodded.

"Seven figures doesn't mean you can't be conned," I said.

Heyman removed his jacket and began his inspection of our papers.

Included in this pile of documents was a copy of an auditor's report alleging that MOHELA, forced by subpoena to open its books well in advance of its bond having been sold to me, was using investors' money in less than prudent ways. When the regulators weren't looking, MOHELA officers apparently treated themselves to the perks familiar to the likes of hedge fund managers.

"I see you've been doing your homework," Heyman said. His voice was soft. His eyes scanned the documents through rimless glasses. "That's good," he said. "We'll need everything. All your papers. All your notes."

"I'm a writer, Mr. Heyman. I'm liable to have too many notes." I reeled off a list of the Missouri auditor's complaints against MOHELA's business practices. "How could any broker sell this piece of junk to me? Where the hell is there even a hint of due diligence? This outfit— MOHELA—is flying a skull and cross bones—and my broker's saying, 'Take it, Phil, it's free money.'"

"He said that?"

"Yes, yes, and *yes*! You can't make up stuff like that."

Heyman grinned. Perhaps he'd heard it before and was mulling the irony of hearing it again. Our predicament wasn't new to him.

"I understand your concern," he said, almost in a whisper as if to cool my temper. "By the way, call me Bill. And you're Phil and Sandy, right?" We nodded. Best to do away with the formalities. "Did you discuss MOHELA with your broker?"

"Yes, I did. He described it as a student loan outfit. Moody's Triple-A rated. Seemed fairly benign. He made it sound as if it was guaranteed by the State of Missouri. But, honestly, he couldn't have done any real homework. The background in the auditor's report, that would have been an obvious turn-off."

Heyman picked up the report and skimmed it.

"I doubt anyone at Wachovia knew about it," he said. "What started you looking into it?"

I explained that after the shock of the market meltdown, I wanted to know everything I could about this particular student loan agency. Higher education: at the time, it seemed a perfectly worthy cause, an ethical investment like other ARS paper issued by hospitals, municipalities, universities, the Metropolitan Museum. Why shouldn't MOHELA be legit? Foolishly, I assumed my broker had done his homework. I had no idea MOHELA was under investigation by the state. The true story came out only after the market froze and I contacted Missouri State Auditor Susan Montee. She put me in touch with the auditor in charge of the investigation. His office sent a copy of the disturbing October 2007 report.

"It was a shocker," I told Heyman. "For a relatively small operation, handing out $350 million in loans over six years, MOHELA was dishing big bonuses to its top five executives."

"What else did the auditor tell you?"

"Plenty," I said. I felt my face turning red. I gave Heyman a thumbnail briefing, a MOHELA fact sheet taken from my interview with the auditor:

The organization had allegedly raised salaries willy-nilly. Perks included 480 hours of leave time for executives. Three of the five top executives turned leave time into cash at a cost of more than $200,000. MOHELA was generous with personal allowances: $146,000 in auto allowances had been doled out. The fab-five executives received life insurance policies with premiums of $50,000 annually, with coverage totaling $800,000 to $1.7 million, plus cash surrender value. There was a no-cost health package upon retirement. And there were the other frills: parties, fun outings to Branson, Missouri, and who knows where else. Perhaps taking its cue from Dick Cheney, MOHELA seemed addicted to noncompetitive contracts.

"There was a Bush administration-style lack of oversight," I said. "According to the auditor's report, after MOHELA moved into new headquarters, it paid over $1.25 million in lease payments for space it didn't need. Incompetence. I guess we'd better get used to it."

I read from the report: MOHELA had "no formal procurement policy prior to March 31, 2007." The outfit had another Bush era trait: It passed out noncompetitive contracts totaling millions of dollars. "The trustee bank received fees of $750,000 a year. A tidy little arrangement for all concerned, except investors," I said.

"So where's our money?" Sandy asked. There was genuine heat behind her words. Some of the more galling information was new to her. This was the first time she'd gotten the details of how MOHELA spent student loan dollars.

"I feel like a jerk for having believed my broker," I told Heyman, stating the obvious. "I feel even dumber for putting a penny in this rat hole operation, and—"

Heyman held up his hand, cutting me off in mid-sentence. "Okay, I get it," he said. Yes, he continued, MOHELA appeared to be a troubled operation. Questions of lack of due diligence were clear enough. There could be no doubt my broker had no idea what he was selling. Yet the overriding problem remained the ARS market itself and the manner in which it was manipulated and dumped on the investing public. I showed Heyman a copy of an e-mail I had received from my growing list of Internet correspondents:

> I have a Nuveen Real Estate Fund. It was sold by Wachovia as an extremely safe thing, no risk, seven day money, available any time. The broker didn't describe the risk factors to me whatsoever. It's my life savings for my kids for college. I'm totally lost without it. It's extremely scary to me.

"Do you have a lot of this kind of correspondence?" Heyman asked.

"Yes, lots."

He nodded and made a worried face.

"I realize you've got serious money at stake," Heyman went on. "If it's any consolation, I have a client with much, much more tied up, and it's killing his business."

He was trying to make me feel better. But the remark rolled off with a dull thud. Everything about the situation was surreal. The market existed in the twilight zone. In this uncertain, spooky vacuum, economies of scale were meaningless.

"You said you wrote letters of complaint to your brokers and to the corporate side," Heyman said. "May I see them?"

Heyman skimmed my collection of correspondence. Those early letters in March to my brokers and their manager were remarkably polite. Seeing the letters now, I was surprised by my initial sense of optimism, of hopefulness, thinking we were facing little more than a hiccup in the market. The correspondence, however, grew progressively more hostile.

A reply from Wachovia/A.G. Edwards corporate headquarters, dated March 12, 2008, was a tip-off that my correspondence (and optimism) was most likely futile. It was an ordinary form letter, a kind of go-away-and-don't-bother-us response. It read, in part:

Dr. Mr. Trupp:

Re: Information for Municipal Securities Investors

Our firm has received your letter concerning transactions in municipal securities. In connection therewith, please find enclosed a copy of "Information for Municipal Securities Investors," a publication of the Municipal Securities Rulemaking Board. At such time as we have completed an investigation of your letter, we will be in further communication with you . . .

The enclosed throwaway piece from the Municipal Securities Rulemaking Board was useless, a brush-off. I read through it and tossed it across the room.

Our next account statement showed that the interest rate on the MOHELA bond had dropped from nearly 4 percent to .09 percent. And the call date—the date when the issuer had to pay up—was 2044.

I showed Heyman another letter in which I again insisted that our money be returned. I received a virtual duplicate of the earlier response from Wachovia offices in St. Louis. I had sent to my brokers and their corporate mouthpieces a story from the *New York Times* detailing the hardships faced by ARS investors and the killer penalty rates being paid by the bond issuers. This was followed by a report via Reuters stating that a group of Wachovia employees had been named in a probe into laundering of Latin American drug money. I had sent an e-mail to Jim: What are we to make of this? I wrote. When I didn't hear back, I called his office.

Wachovia was headquartered in North Carolina. A lot of banks in the South get caught in that sort of mess, he explained.

Oh, well, now I'm supposed to feel a lot safer, my nagging internal voice taunted.

I told Heyman that Wachovia recently had been prosecuted for allegedly selling client names to Internet scammers, and that I had used this piece of news in a subsequent letter to the company.

The letters became more heated. Wachovia officers insisted that my concerns about risk disclosure had been fully explained on the company's web site: "Our web site features all the appropriate disclosures required," I was told. Yes, after the market imploded! The careful use of the words *appropriate disclosures* amounted to a farce. And there was more:

> In regard to the liquidity, at the time the security was sold to you, and until recently, our firm was able to offer daily liquidity to our clients. However, our firm had to discontinue offering this privilege . . . because of the illiquidity in the securities marketplace. This was an unprecedented event which our firm could not have foreseen or anticipated, and over which we have no control.

We would later discover that the last sentence of the letter was a bad joke. The ARS market troubles were not unprecedented and they surely could have been foreseen or anticipated. As for the claim of having "no control," this would prove to be the biggest stretch of all. We didn't have all the pieces of the puzzle as yet, although it was later revealed that the banks not only were controlling the market, they were manipulating it to make hundreds of millions of dollars in fees. *No control?* How gullible is a sophisticated investor supposed to be?

It wasn't until June and July that letters acknowledging my complaints arrived from FINRA and the SEC. It was just more formula stuff. More meaningless paper. The SEC said it was working with issuers of ARS "to find solutions to the current liquidity crisis." (Unknown to most of us at the time, the commission was also telling Madoff whistle-blowers to take a hike. Hardly a confidence builder.)

Heyman wondered if I had discussed my complaint with other attorneys. I told him of my conversations with Sam Edwards and Peter Panerites.

We had discussed fiduciary duties, deceptive sales pitches, lack of due diligence.

"So how did it end with Wachovia/Edwards?" Heyman asked.

"Badly," I said. I slid another letter across the table. It was from corporate headquarters and read in part:

> Mr. [broker's real name withheld by author] continues to claim that he did mention investing in auction-rate securities and explained all the features, including potential risks as he does with all clients. He categorically denies he ever used the term "free money." . . . While I understand your unhappiness and frustration . . . our firm respectfully disagrees with your assertions.

Heyman reached into his briefcase and pulled out a thick document. "Have a look," he said.

It was a class-action suit filed March 9, 2008, by Judy M. Waldman as trustee for the Clair Waldman Trust, individually, and on behalf of many others caught in the ARS trap. The defendants were Wachovia Corporation and Wachovia Securities. The complaint read like a lawyerly treatise on my letters to the bank. It was a nasty set of allegations against a firm whose reputation had taken a pounding on other matters. I told Heyman I'd read the details later.

"Do you think you can win this?" Sandy asked.

Heyman hesitated, leaned forward, and said, "I think I can. I definitely do. It's a matter of who knew what, and when did they know it." He sat back and waited for a response.

I looked over at Sandy. For some reason I checked out the platter of sweets she had purchased from the deli. The pastries looked unloved and lonely. Sandy grinned.

"Let's go for it," she said. "I'm psyched."

I agreed. It was a big step. Arbitration would not be inexpensive, and Heyman's fees were not exactly bargain basement. It no longer mattered. We were on our way to a resolution, one way or another.

Heyman was suddenly grave. "You realize, of course, that Wachovia is entitled to discover the information on your computer. It can also get access to your computer if an arbitrator orders it."

I was stunned. "What are you talking about?"

"You've been writing commentary on all kinds of financial web sites. You're gathering information. I get that. But securities lawyers are always looking for loopholes. They'll see you're deep into the financial community, you write *sophisticated* comments—and that's key. *Sophisticated*. And you've done a great deal of trading in the past. They'll argue this point in arbitration. They'll claim you should have known better, and they'll hang you with your own words." He gave me a stern look. "Stop it right now! And don't discuss this with any-one! You'll only be making witnesses against yourself."

"But—"

Now the softness was gone out of Heyman's voice. He was almost glaring at me. "No! Stop it! And quit sending letters to Wachovia. You're creating a big paper trail. They'll hang you if you keep it up."

"Do you really believe I'd let those guys take my computer? I'd sooner drop it in the Potomac. Nobody's going to get their hands on it."

"You have my advice," Heyman replied. His tone was no-nonsense and hard-edged. "If we're going to beat this thing, you have to trust me. Don't underestimate these boys."

We walked him to the door. He would send a retainer contract in a few days. In the interim, I was to shut my big mouth and lay off writing incriminating commentary on the Web. Message received. Smart asses get kicked. Dummies just might win.

Chapter 6

Power to the Blogosphere

All economic movements, by their very nature, are motivated by crowd psychology.

—*Charles Mackay,* Extraordinary Popular Delusions and the Madness of Crowds

By the end of July 2008, Heyman had drawn up our complaint against Wachovia. A check had been forwarded as a retainer, plus $1,800 to be held in escrow to cover the FINRA arbitration filing. It was a terse, well-documented complaint. I called Heyman at his office and complimented him. It felt good having taken another step forward.

"It's a strong case," he said. We chatted for a while. "Still writing for blogs?"

I knew it was coming. "No comment."

"You're sticking your neck out."

"I am not going quietly into the dark night. Why should I?"

Heyman's retainer was a necessary bite. You pay for what you need and just suck it up. It was strange having to pay a five-figure retainer in order to get back money that belonged free and clear to us. We had no choice. Wachovia showed no hint of ever giving up the money unless forced to do so.

The FINRA filing fee was especially galling. It was on the order of paying a gang of thugs whose mission was to break my kneecaps. FINRA arbitration was like a bad joke at the expense of tens of thousands of consumers. The bank-financed organization is often mistaken for a government watchdog; it is anything but. The organization is a front, a so-called self-regulator, run by and for the well-being of its corporate sponsors.

Ordinary investors watched from the sidelines as the big corporations with ARS investments took a shellacking on the same battlefield. Bristol-Myers Squibb, 3M, Texas Instruments, US Airways, among dozens of other big firms, had reported billions of dollars in losses and were suing the banks that had suckered them into buying auction-rate paper. FINRA was doing next to nothing to settle their complaints. It might be argued that corporate America was paying a price for its own bad karma; its pain, however, surely would be passed on to consumers. The major grief, along with the moral and intellectual insult of being mugged first by the banks and later by FINRA, fell more on ordinary investors, the least powerful 50 percent of the fraud victims. We would later learn that FINRA was playing its own ARS cat-and-mouse game; it would be a discovery that would unmask the organization's role in running interference for the wider financial-services industry.

Despite Heyman's warnings, I was in too deep to turn off the blogging. On the contrary, I had become so prolific that Google was following my comments on the *New York Times*' online DealBook and Seeking Alpha. Another outlet, Investment News, a web site for professional financial advisers but open to civilians, also provided a good online site to blow off steam and enlist the help of other investors.

There were many blog sites on my list and the pace of writing was obsessive. Within a few months, a strange transformation occurred. My financial commentary had overwhelmed virtually everything else listed under my name on Google. It was as if I was rewriting my life history.

In the meanwhile, I was making notes for this book about the scandal. It wouldn't be a technical book. Instead, I envisioned a kind of group diary detailing my own experiences and the hardships suffered by other victims of the scandal.

Momentum was building. I was coming at the subject from different angles and scattered Internet locations. What was desperately needed was a kind of ARS central—a web site devoted entirely to the subject and its permutations. I knew if I kept searching I'd find it. And when I did, I could go all out on the attack.

Feedback flowed in from victims around the country. Below is a sampling of howls from those initial correspondents (names withheld for privacy concerns):

> My broker kept assuring me it would soon resolve. I got an infuriating letter, one of those "Dear Client, We feel your pain" kinds of things. I wrote back telling him I'd personally beat him over the head . . . I'm 70 years old!
>
> I filed a complaint with FINRA on First Trust Four Corners and Hewitt Financial Services. I sent e-mails to Representative Bart Stupak and Senator Debbie Stabenow. I am filing a complaint with Michigan Attorney General Mike Cox. I'm retired, 65 years old, and receiving Social Security. . . . This is not pleasant in the current financial crisis.
>
> Our little group has exchanged a lot of information and supported people in their efforts to reach the SEC, Andrew Cuomo (New York Attorney General) and William Galvin (Massachusetts Secretary), FINRA, reporters—but we are . . . still stonewalled. It's hard to know what you've accomplished when so much is undone.

Correspondents sent their telephone numbers. I followed up and called them for interviews. Many victims were elderly and struggling with a variety of illnesses. Because their money was frozen, they could no longer afford medical treatments. In more than a few cases, their insurance companies had dropped them or refused to pay for certain services. Other victims had lost their homes. Others were now broke or close to it, and forced to sell off other savings in order to pay living expenses. More than a few were unable to pay their taxes, and the Internal Revenue Service was taking action against them.

A great many horror stories came from ARS victims who were at or near retirement. Every one of them had fallen prey to the "good as cash," "same thing as cash," "better than Treasuries," "completely liquid" set of sales ploys. They were confused and angry. Many said they were fed a phony pitch that went something like this: We're sorry we didn't give you all the details, but then we didn't expect anything like this to ever happen to the market. Be patient and you'll get your money back one of these days. Oh, and by the way, we can lend you money at 8 percent interest. It was the same line I was getting from my brokerage.

Here's a sample of an interview with an ordinary investor from Georgia. What follows is taken from notes made during our telephone conversation:

> My whole family's stuck with this shit. You see, the guy who sold us this stuff, he's a family member. Not to say which side or anything, just family. We trusted him. We listened to him. . . . No reason not to, right? Yeah, so he sells us these student loan securities, the ARS, he called them SLARS [Student Loan Auction Rate Securities], and a lot of different-ent auction-rate stuff. Sells it to me, my wife—to his own wife. Imagine that. And to his parents! They're not young or rich or anything. He's their boy—to be 100 percent trusted. He's looking after us, the go-to guy. Then, it's like one day he calls—I think I got the first call—with the news. Hell of a thing. Me, I'm number one on his list. Asks me to sit down, you know, like it's some crazy-ass TV show: "Are you sitting down 'cause I got some kinda hard news. . . ." Hell, I thought it was a joke. He's a joker, this guy. He's got maybe 90 percent of the whole damned family's net worth in auction bonds, safe as can be, he said. Then, well, he hits me with it. "Market's frozen," he says. I'll never forget how he put it, like it was temporary; it's going to be fine. "What do you mean, *frozen*?" And he says, "Illiquid," but it's going to

work itself out. He knows because he's on the inside, a broker, we trust him. Always did, because he's like us . . . doesn't like sticking his neck out. I was mad as hell. "How do you know it's going to be okay?" He says don't worry, he wouldn't screw the family, and I know he's got plenty in those bonds himself. They're in his kids' college fund. Jesus! How do I know? Well, he's my brother. Would you believe—my own brother?

* * *

"It's a gold mine," Heyman told me as we waited to be seated for lunch at a faux alpine ski and hunting lodge tucked away in the leafy suburbs between Washington, D.C., and Baltimore. "It's a web site," he explained as we waited for a table to clear in a quiet corner away from the noisy bar.

I had called Heyman and requested an interview with him, matters aside from our case ("Off the clock," I said politely) explaining the preliminary work I was doing for the book. There was something about Heyman, a certain subtle tough-mindedness that surfaced during our initial meeting in Washington. To check my instincts, I contacted a friend in Baltimore who knew him socially.

"Bill is a very principled man," she insisted. "Sometimes, honestly, I think he takes wrongdoing personally, even when it's someone else's problem."

Somewhere beneath that mild-mannered, lawyerly exterior, an idealist was waiting to spring forth.

"Are you still writing for the blogs?" he prodded.

"What do you think?"

"You're incorrigible."

"I'm a writer, for chrissake! It's what I do."

No way was I going to pace the floor waiting haplessly for the banks to come clean. I am not equipped with endless patience and good manners when it comes to dealing with financial types. The idea was to test public outrage, use it against the banks, and meanwhile do all I could to help expose the underpinnings of the meltdown and the role of those who enabled it in Washington—FINRA, the SEC, and the big talkers in Congress who engaged in the back-scratching nexus with Wall Street.

"Okay, okay," Heyman relented. "A book's a good idea. So this is good, because I have something very interesting for you."

"Great! We're off to a fine start."

"It's a web site," he said. "Someone in the office told me about it. It's got everything. Copies of all the ARS stories from day one." Heyman was animated, a little mischievous, as if handing over a secret code scrawled in invisible ink. There was a conspiratorial glint behind those rimless glasses.

"Aren't you afraid I'll start writing for it?" I asked. "I mean, you were pretty emphatic the other day."

"You're going to do whatever it is you're set on doing," he said. "I think this scandal is awful. I do. If you're going to fight on the outside, apart from your case, well, maybe this will be a little extra something."

We were shown to a table next to a window looking out on a stand of weathered oaks. Branches filtered the fierce July sun into a checkered pattern of light and shade across the wide lawn. Our table was equally woodsy: burnished walnut with lots of little darkened knots. I half expected to see a clutch of hunters hauling a slain buck over the floor.

"You're saying this site, it's like an archive of published ARS information?" I asked.

"Practically encyclopedic. Check it out."

I was stirred by his enthusiasm. He had just handed me a super lead. It might be exactly the kind of site I had been searching for. It would turn out, however, to be a lot more than either of us anticipated. Heyman probably knew I'd find a way to use it as weapon, or at least a tool that would allow the undermining of the stone wall behind which the Wall Street "banksters" were clinging to other peoples' money.

He wrote the web address on a slip of paper: AuctionRatePreferreds .org. I looked up at Heyman. Was this his sly way of joining my little crusade or was he merely being helpful, no ethical lapses visible to the naked eye? "Young man with a big conscience," someone said of him. Indeed, he had the makings of an activist, but one with sufficient experience to know that activism can be a one-way ticket to heartbreak.

An attractive young waitress in a kind of Hippie-style leather vest came smiling up to the table—obviously a college student working a summer job. She had a quickness about her, a kind of surgical way in which she handled her pencil, as if making incisions on the sheets of her order pad. She took us in with the quizzical curiosity of someone peering into a microscope. She made me feel a little older. There she was, at the beginning her life, seemingly carefree. And me—I was pushing the stone uphill and feeling it.

"Welcome to Tower Oaks," she said. "Can I bring you anything from the bar?"

I had a powerful urge to inspect the wine list. But I was on business to interview Heyman for the book outline that was taking shape. Wine at midday has a way of undoing good intentions. Heyman ordered a Coke. I went for the bottomless pot of black coffee.

"Okey-dokey," the waitress said, tucking her order pad into the waistband of her miniskirt. She brought the beverages to the table and asked if we were ready to order lunch.

We ordered and settled in for the interview.

I asked Heyman to tell me what he knew of this newfound goldmine: AuctionRatePreferreds.org. Preferred? Heyman explained that certain auction-rate paper held a higher ranking than ordinary ARS, the same way preferred stockholders had first dibs at getting their money back, while common stockholders needed to stand in line behind them. Billions of dollars of preferred ARS shares were in the mix, but they had been frozen along with the not-so-preferred shares. In the circumstances, the word had lost its meaning.

As we waited for the food, Heyman urged me to study the Sarbanes-Oxley Act of 2002 (SOX). He said certain portions of the act might be used to force banks and other issuers to face criminal penalties if they refused to redeem ARS.

"How so?" I asked. SOX didn't seem to fit. The law arose out of the scandals surrounding Enron, Tyco International, Adelphia, and WorldCom, whose creative accounting shenanigans caused those companies to implode.

SOX mandated enhanced financial transparency, Heyman explained. It also required disclosure of analyst conflicts of interest. ARS sellers were clearly violating these mandates. He tossed in the fact that violations of SOX and other white-collar crimes cost the taxpayers $200 billion a year, a figure later confirmed by the National White Collar Crime Center, a Virginia-based nonprofit sponsored by the Department of Justice.

The drinks and food arrived and were hurriedly polished off. Formalities out of the way, I began my interview of Bill Heyman.

"Wall Street lawyers are always looking for loopholes, technicalities," he began. "That's how they think. And that's how the ARS problem is viewed. It's like, 'What can we get away with?' Clearly the banks that sold these instruments violated their fiduciary duties. And, to tell the truth, in my handling of these cases it seemed the financial advisors, the FAs—most of them were told to sell ARS like a money market investment."

"Do you think most of the FAs understood what they were selling?"

He shook his head. "No, I don't. Now, Bank of America, unlike most of them, told their customers what an ARS really is—or was. They were unusually candid. Let's give them credit for trying to be honest."

I paused, gazed out at the oaks and the sun-dappled lawn. *Trying to be honest*! It seemed an odd way to explain what ordinary investors so often take for granted. Is honesty something unnatural in the financial-service industry? Is it inherently deceptive? I realized these were rhetorical questions. Anyone with a brokerage account knows the answer. Heyman said most FAs didn't know the details of most of the products they sold. Did this mean they were stupid or indifferent?

"It's hard to generalize," Heyman said. "They're sales clerks, most of them anyway. They do what they're told."

But they also are naturally curious. A broker with Jim's depth of experience had to be aware of some degree of risk. The way I saw it, he had been around way too long to be an unwitting conduit of misleading information. He and other brokers knew, of course, that the industry's lawyers would back them up if the market folded. Still, Heyman made a reasonable point. Jim, for all his experience, was likely following the company line, believing he was dealing in virtually risk-free debt. Maybe.

"Securities attorneys are paid top dollar to save their clients money," Heyman went on. "So, ultimately, bottom line, they'll hang their hat on anything, any technicality. In the case of the ARS thing, they assumed, out of nowhere, with no evidence, that their retail investors were savvy. And being savvy meant you knew what you were getting into. The attorneys gave the banks the nod. On the weight of legal advice, the banks told their brokers to push the product. But the banks knew the truth. A lot of brokers didn't. The way this was done—well, in my opinion, there's really no excuse.

"When it blew up in their faces, the state regulators got involved. The state attorneys general I'm talking about here. When the fraud allegations were flying, the industry circled the wagons. The advisors, the brokers, were told to shut down. Don't talk about it or discuss what was happening in the market." Heyman let out a weary sigh. "But, you know, that's just normal procedure. It's done in almost all fraud cases."

So, in Heyman's opinion, the brokers and financial advisers were dupes. Flunkies. This was the hard reality he had to deal with. If the financial advisors were dupes, what about their superiors? Where was their accountability? Brokers are, of course, salespersons. They make a pretty fair living pushing products that "make markets." They are paid commissions on whatever products they sell. I could accept Heyman's view of brokers as an incurious lot who, mule-like, pull their load without knowing or caring about the risk. I knew more than a few who fit this description. But to the best of my knowledge, Jim and Victor weren't mules. They knew how the business works and how risk can be measured.

Heyman wasn't the kind of person to be sarcastic or bitter. Still, it was hard to envision running a business—especially a business heavily dependent upon sales—without knowing the details of the products being sold. Would you excuse a dentist who filled your cavities with a toxic substance? Could there be an excuse for a physician who injected poison into your veins and later shrugged it off by claiming ignorance? No, it doesn't work that way in the real world. There's a cogent reason for malpractice suits; and more broadly, the basic principle of responsibility applies to anyone who provides a public service. Ignorance has never been an excuse—except in the murky realm of financial services.

I placed my skepticism on the table. Heyman stuck to his opinions.

"I personally believe most brokers, the financial advisors, were innocent, I mean for the most part," he said. "Not all, but most of them. They didn't know."

The waitress arrived back at the table with a big smile. "Got room for dessert?" She had her order pad at the ready. I asked for a coffee refill. "Oh, come on," she countered. "Live a little. Check out the sweets."

"Just coffee," I said. Heyman ordered another Coke.

"Okey-dokey."

"Do you think this waitress doesn't know exactly what's on the dessert tray?" I asked.

"Oh, sure. Of course she does. But she can't know the ingredients, what the stuff is made of. It just looks pretty. That's really all she needs to know."

"But suppose a customer keels over after eating the prune tart. Wouldn't management automatically get rid of that product?"

Heyman knew what I was trying to say, even though I wasn't making my point in the most precise manner.

"I'm saying only what I believe. I personally believe the advisors were mostly innocent. I don't have a high opinion of most of them. They're not the brightest of people. But they do have an obligation to be honest. They work under FINRA rules and New York Stock Exchange rules. There's the National Association of Securities Dealers Rule 2110, which calls for—" He stopped in mid-sentence to make sure I was keeping up. "Basically the rule calls for high principles of honesty," he continued. "It says that a broker, in the conduct of business, is bound to live up to, and here I quote: 'high standards of commercial honor and just and equitable principles of trade.'"

"Isn't that a contradiction? Really, what kind of high standards do you have if you don't have a clue, or even any curiosity, about what you're stuffing into your clients' portfolios?"

"Sure, it's contradictory. It's not right. I'm not justifying what happened. But those people rely on what they get from their firms and their bosses. They rely on management. They do what they're told. Lots of brokers are furious with their companies. Billions of dollars worth of business is trotting out the door in the wake of this mess. All I'm saying is that most of these guys are okay. Yes, the ARS thing is bad. Still, overall, I think the industry is doing better than it used to in policing itself."

It is ironic, to say the least, that more than two years after the ARS crash, FINRA got around to warning the industry that it had better get its act together when it comes to bonds. In an April 11, 2010, article in *Investment News* by Jessica Toonkel Marquez titled, "FINRA Cracks Down on Credit Disclosure," broker–dealer funds are warned to pay closer attention to the safety of the bonds they sell to investors. FINRA says it's taking a "tougher stance." What is meant by "tougher stance" remains to be seen.

Heyman, in defending brokers, could not have guessed what was coming. Our interview took place well before Wall Street kicked off what is now grimly referred to as "The Great Recession." On that quiet afternoon at Tower Oaks no one had yet dreamed that the banks would pull off the con job of the century and refuse to lend money, hoard taxpayer bailout funds, and threaten to shut down virtually all lines of credit. Who would have guessed that former Treasury Secretary Henry Paulson, a Goldman Sachs alumnus, would fall to his knees and literally beg Democratic House Speaker Nancy Pelosi to go along with a massive bailout, injecting billions of taxpayer dollars to rescue Wall Street? We were unknowingly on the cusp of creating the most destructive financial crisis since the Great Depression. More than $700 billion would be handed out in the form of federal welfare to the banks, based on little more than Paulson's two-and-a-half-page plan to save the financial system. Out of whole cloth Paulson would create the worst kind of moral hazard. Former President George W. Bush admitted he was confused by what was taking place. Yet the swaggering, presidential market guy went along with Paulson's essential looting of the Treasury. Neglected in all this was a little detail called *accountability*. The banks could spend the money any way they saw fit. All bets were off. Like the banditos in the classic Humphrey Bogart film, *The Treasure of the Sierra Madre*, neither Mr. Bush nor Mr. Paulson were forced to show "no stinkin' badges." And the same held true for the banks.

"Wall Street is two-faced. Never forget that," Heyman said, reaching for the check, although I beat him to it. It was only fair that I should pay. It was a future business expense. Heyman was off the clock and meeting out of the goodness of his heart and genuine concern for the soundness of the economy.

"The industry serves its own interests, and the ARS thing is a prime example," Heyman said. "They say they serve their clients and stockholders. But the brokerages will always come first. Is it moral? I don't know. Morals are broadly interpreted. There are ethics involved, and money. Between the two they will always choose the money."

✳ ✳ ✳

AuctionRatePreferreds.org—the wording of the web site struck me as being awkward, a little too insular and MBA-ish. Heyman had promised to send the link the afternoon we met at Tower Oaks.

With much impatience I negotiated my way back to Washington, playing involuntary dodge 'em cars on the impossibly congested Rockville Turnpike, zipping (with jolting stops) past garish strip malls that offered everything from Korean dining to mattresses so deeply discounted that I was tempted to buy a few as backups to our over-priced pillow top.

Somewhere on the drive back to Washington, I was struck by a gut feeling: The web site Heyman had raved about would be a turning point in the struggle. And sure enough, it was. It would be my *in* to a powerful and connected audience.

I arrived back at my office a little past four o'clock eager to turn on the computer. Then the phone rang.

"Phil, uh, it's me, Jim." I was stunned. We hadn't spoken for months.

"What's on your mind?"

"It's about your account."

I was planning to switch brokerages, removing all liquid assets from our Wachovia accounts and leaving the ARS in place, although I wasn't going to inform Jim of this move. I had become one of the squeakiest wheels in Wachovia's e-mail files. Unfortunately the ARS had to remain with Wachovia. If I moved them to another brokerage, neither the old nor the new brokerage would redeem them.

"What about the account?" I asked, trying to keep the pique out of my voice.

"I want to talk, you know, about the ARS thing. Okay by you? Can we meet near the office?"

Fifteen minutes later, I arrived at a deli on Wisconsin Avenue. Jim was crammed into a booth that seemed too small for him. He was a bulky fellow, barrel-chested with the arms and shoulders of a linebacker.

"I didn't expect this," I said, slipping into the booth. We shook hands. It was a bit eerie. He gave me what I can only describe as doleful stare.

"Where's you-know-who?" I asked, referring to his protégé and partner, Victor, my putative backup broker.

"Well, you know, he couldn't make it," Jim said. What he really meant to say was that his protégé *wouldn't* engage the subject of ARS with a client. He was a scrupulous company man who consistently refused to discuss the subject, except to say in the face of an ever-darkening fiscal reality that liquidity was flowing back into the markets, a notion that must have transported him to a state of runner's high. When he threatened to hang up if I ever mentioned the subject of ARS again, I stopped calling him.

Jim ordered ice tea. I ordered more coffee to pour into my already over-caffeinated system.

"What's on your mind?" I asked with a mildness that surprised me.

He wasted no time. Though he didn't say so directly, I got the idea that ARS had never been properly explained to him. Yes, he made a tail on purchases for his clients. He knew the bonds were unusual instruments, not so different, however, as to arouse his suspicion over the health of the auction market. Wachovia hadn't supplied a prospectus, and the brokers were told they didn't need one. He reminded me that at one time, when the equity markets were beginning to show cracks, I had parked a sizeable chunk of ARS in the cash portion of our combined portfolios. "I wouldn't have okayed it if I thought the market was going to crack," he said. He reminded me that once upon a time I felt good about ARS investments. "You liked supporting municipal projects. Liked helping student loans, hospital wings, all the social stuff. I should have gotten you out of the big one first," Jim said, referring to the MOHELA bond. "I did get you out of all the ones I sold. And I'm sorry I didn't get to sell all of them. I should have, but it was too late. I know it's caused you a lot of grief."

"It sure has!"

"I'm sorry," he repeated.

"So am I."

Jim explained that the auction market had stood for 20 years. He trusted it. His best clients were in it. Who could have guessed it would have come to this?

"It's a damned shame," he said. "I didn't see it coming, and that's the truth."

He was remorseful. He was embarrassed. And, to his great credit, he had risked stepping outside the corporate cone of silence. This could not have been easy. I asked questions for which he had no real answers. Jim wasn't stonewalling. He just didn't know what to say. He had trusted the market as I had so foolishly trusted it, and now it was costing both of us in personal ways. I imagined that fat client book of his and the other squeaky wheels grinding over his office phone. Maybe Jim was losing clients. Maybe lots of them. Possibly he'd been threatened with lawsuits. I felt bad for him. I genuinely liked the guy.

I reached down deep trying to find it in my soul to excuse him, to cast out my suspicions and say, "It's all right, Jim." But there was no clear road to empathy. If he knew the market was in trouble when he sold ARS, then he was guilty of deception. If he didn't know the market was set to implode, then he was guilty of a lack of due diligence. There were many maybes and what-ifs. In the end, the trust was gone. Still, I had to give him credit. At least he had taken a chance and reached out to me, and for that I think of him as a mensch.

When we parted that afternoon, I wanted more than anything to understand, to forgive. But as I drove back to my office, Heyman's words echoed: "Wall Street is two-faced. Never forget that."

Chapter 7

Radioactive Man

Today's free-market economists . . . aren't merely not philosophers. They're not even worldly. Has any group of professionals ever been so spectacularly wrong?

—*Harold Meyerson,* Washington Post

I was eager to explore AuctionRatePreferreds.org, but before I could get started, Sandy reminded me that we were invited to attend a gathering of Hoover Institution members and supporters at the historic Willard Hotel in downtown Washington, D.C. The new web site—the promising collection of all ARS news—would have to wait a day.

The Hoover bash was a glitzy meet-and-greet held in the vaulted, chandeliered hotel ballroom, replete with open bars and a galaxy of political and media stars. Sandy's client, Dr. Kiron Skinner, a Hoover Institution fellow, had invited us to attend. Members and supporters from around the country had gathered to survey the conservative political optics. And despite the GOP's dismal prospects at the polls, the mood remained festive, the food offerings opulent, and the buzz intriguing. For purposes of full disclosure, I'm an Independent; Sandy is a Democrat. But in Washington's political mixing bowl, labels are often stashed for the purposes of information-gathering. The Hoover Institution event offered the potential for news in every corner of the room.

I had only an academic interest in the fortunes of the GOP. The party's long-term strategy is legend: huff and puff along year after year running the world's most persistent political marathon, the prize being Karl Rove's wet dream of a permanent Republican majority. My focus was not on the strategy of permanent domination, coincidentally shared by Wall Street, but rather on the display of high-profile journalists and politicians orbiting with varying degrees of gravity around the gilded ballroom.

It's fun to be in this element. The plan: meet and speak with every big name player I could find. "Press the flesh," former President Lyndon B. Johnson's clever descriptive phrase of his own powers of personal persuasion, just happens to be my modus operandi. Show me a famous face and I will find a way to engage it. If nothing else, I figured this slightly giddy exercise would take my mind off my ARS woes. I had no idea that in the course of the evening I would encounter one of the Bush administration's most controversial cabinet officials, a man who might provide priceless insight into the administration's love affair with deregulation, and the long-standing political mania to transfer the nation's wealth to the top 1 percent of its citizens.

The late Robert Novak, the conservative political columnist, made his way through the crowd shaking hands, flashing his miracle of a smile, but inwardly brooding. I had occasionally bantered with the so-called Prince of Darkness when we were habitués of the National Press Club. We were never on the same page politically. He was smart and quick and possessed one of the most enviable Rolodexes in Washington. I knew him as tough, witty, and more middle-of-the-road than one might suspect for a guy who, in print, leaned hard right.

I hadn't seen Novak in quite some time. We exchanged brief greetings, but little else. Bob was ill and distracted; he has since died of brain cancer.

I spied Christopher Hitchens, the prolific author and *Vanity Fair* columnist hanging out at one of the many bars set up around the floor. He was in a jolly mood, laughing with a group of admirers. At a distance he appeared elfin—a compact Brit with an unusually deep tan, open collar, quick eyes, and a hefty drink in hand.

I introduced myself. Hitchens was very polite, very quick on the uptake. As a true intellectual he revealed the killer instincts and timing of a stand-up comedian. I was hoping to trade a few barbs, when out of the corner of my eye I saw the imposing former Republican senator from Tennessee, presidential candidate, and Hollywood icon, Fred Thompson. He entered the ballroom as if he owned the place.

Accompanied by his youthful bride, Jeri, whose stylish appearance that evening was the very antithesis of dowdy Hooverian fashion, Thompson commanded attention like a magnet attracts iron. Jeri was a vision straight off Rodeo Drive. Clad in a shiny red pants suit (the material looked like fluorescent polypropylene), expensive black boots, and a drop-dead pricey purse, everyone in the room turned to stare at her. Perhaps some whispered catty slurs about the 25-year age difference between the couple. Many snidely called her a trophy wife. But Jeri's glamour was deceptive. A wonky political pro, she had managed her husband's presidential bid and was rumored to play hardball with the best of the political strategists.

I disengaged from Hitchens and made a beeline over to Thompson. It was an opportunity not to be missed. I wanted to meet Jeri, too, but she was quickly engulfed by a bevy of Hoover Institution women and whisked away.

By the time I arrived, a small, elderly gentleman was busy speaking with Thompson. I stood to one side and listened. The presidential hopeful towered above his humble supplicant, who heaped praise on Thompson's perceived genius.

"You're going to make it!" the little man declared. "All my friends are voting for you."

With a red-carpet-worthy air of noblesse oblige, Thompson absorbed his admirer's breathless, if not embarrassing, compliments. He stood there and took it in with a forced grin and that characteristic hound dog look of enduring patience—his official worldly countenance on the hit NBC TV hit series, *Law & Order*, in which he played New York City District Attorney Arthur Branch. One could almost hear the show's theme music playing its dissonant chords in the background as the star-struck admirer gushed with praise.

"Do you have a business card?" the supplicant wanted to know, craning his neck to meet the eyes of his six-foot-four hero.

"Didn't bring 'em tonight," Thompson apologized. A real pro. Thompson didn't even crack a smile at this absurd request or let on that he was fibbing.

The man reached into his pocket. "Well now, here's mine," he said, offering his business card. "You'd make a great president," he enthused. "Just the greatest since——"

"Thank you so much," Thompson grinned. "Appreciate your support."

Then it was my turn.

"I really don't think you need a business card," I said, introducing myself to Thompson.

"Well, you know, some people," came the vague shrug of a reply.

Thompson's candidacy puzzled me. Why would a man who had served years in the House and Senate, who later became a multimillion-aire Hollywood icon, and was currently raking in big bucks as a lobbyist, set himself up for what Harry Truman called the "splendid misery" of the presidency? It was a question I just had to ask.

Thompson blinked nervously, composed himself, and replied, "Always had this feeling for public service. And a lot of people were urging me to go for it. The presidency, I mean."

"The backing is there, obviously," I said. "Still, it's an amazing personal leap."

He nodded. "Well, surely . . . of course . . . yes." Thompson is an imposing man, and as he spoke, his gaze wandered around the room like a periscope. Politician to the bone: He wasn't about to miss an opportunity to connect with any stray big-name Republicans who might help his campaign.

We chatted easily for several minutes. Suddenly Thompson did a strange thing. He glanced around like a wary safecracker, as if he wanted to be sure no one was listening. When he was satisfied he was out of earshot, he leaned in close and whispered, "And, to tell you the truth, I had that one ambition left over. Just that *one*, mind you. Had to, you know . . . you know, wanted to get it out of my system."

Yes, I said. Sure, I understand—not that I really did. If true, it was quite a confession.

"But suppose you win? There you'll be—the whole messy world on your shoulders. What then?"

Thompson stiffened, fired a .45 caliber expression straight at me, gunslinger style. His stare had real stopping power. I felt heat coming off him. It was the pique, or perhaps the exasperation, of a man who wasn't used to being provoked by a nosy journalist in search of a quotable quote.

"That will have to be a long discussion for another time," he huffed, brushing me off as he walked away with the haute indignation of a four-star general who'd been confronted by a buck private. Clever. He read between the lines. Thompson knew the implication: that, truth be told, he really didn't *want* the burden of presidency. It was later revealed in the *New York Post*'s "Page Six" that all along it was Jeri who had convinced him to make the presidential bid. He wouldn't need to worry about the small stuff. She would handle the details.

And then . . . was I imagining it? Yes! There he was, standing alone in a corner: Radioactive Man! I could hardly believe it. One of the most famous (some might say infamous) political personalities in all of Washington; a figure constantly in the news, controversy swirling around him like coils of razor wire—oddly alone, fading into the shadows. *No, this is impossible . . . just totally bizarre.*

"Is that who I think it is?" Sandy whispered, casually glancing over at the enigmatic figure in the corner vaguely grinning at no one in particular.

"It sure is."

"Nobody's talking to him. Can you believe it?"

"Maybe he doesn't want to talk."

"So why is he here?" Sandy gave me the knowing look of a PR pro. "If he didn't want to talk with people he wouldn't be here." She urged me to engage him. "Go on," she said, poking me in the side. "Do your thing. I'll catch up with you later."

I put down my drink and strolled over to him, introduced myself, and struck up a conversation as casually as I might with a next-door neighbor.

"This is a real surprise, a pleasure," I said extending my hand. (Editor's note: The author cannot disclose the name or title of Radioactive Man, who spoke on strict condition of anonymity.)

"Yes, it's a pleasure to meet you," he replied. There was relief in his voice, as if the simple greeting allowed him to exhale.

To my amazement he was totally unself-conscious. As we conversed, I half-expected to be shunted aside by a swarm of Hoover Institution guests. But none approached. It was well-known that Radioactive Man was more dangerous, perhaps more controversial, than Vice President Dick Cheney. Darth Vader certainly would have attracted more eager admirers. In Washington, as on Wall Street, you're up or you're out. Radioactive Man was definitely out. His days had become like a bitter November night, cold and uncertain. As an ARS investor, I knew what that felt like.

Not that this man's defrocked political career mattered to me. He possessed an amazing and controversial store of information in his official portfolio, insider facts that had much of the Western world buzzing, pro and con. And though his official position in the administration had little to do with Wall Street, he nevertheless knew which policy bodies had been slain and where they were buried. He knew the president's darkest secrets.

I jumped at the chance to make him my new best friend. If nothing else, he might provide insight into Bush's appointment of Christopher Cox as chairman of the SEC. Cox was another Radioactive Man, though hardly as controversial. He was a key figure not only in the ARS debacle, but a regulator whose central ideology and passive-aggressive political actions played into the broader economic tsunami that was to come.

After a bit of empty chatter, I told my new best friend I was writing a book about the auction-rate securities fraud. I wondered if he might be helpful in providing certain insights. Might he be willing to meet outside the Beltway?

"I'll e-mail you," I said. "We'll do lunch somewhere out of the way, if it's okay with you."

He wanted to know what manner of information I was looking for. I told him I wanted to talk financial deregulation. And I wanted to know more about how Cox wound up as the nation's presumed securities cop.

"I'm not an economist," he said. "Sounds like a matter for the SEC."

"It is," I replied. But perhaps Radioactive Man might be in a position to add unique insight about the commission and its chairman.

He thought it over for what seemed a very long time. An uneasy silence hung between us. I waited, still hardly believing I was speaking with this man on such a casual basis. Then, with a glimmer of cheer, he said, "Sure. Send an e-mail." He agreed to meet. I was delighted. "But this is strictly background," he emphasized with quiet urgency. "*No names.*" I gave him my word. He was not someone to be taken lightly.

✳ ✳ ✳

The restaurant was jammed with bureaucrats from the nearby CIA headquarters in Langley, Virginia. I was shown to a red leather booth by an attractive young maitre d' in her twenties. She was cheerful and just slightly familiar—the familiarity I took to be out of respect for Radioactive Man, whose wife had made the reservations and was well-known among the waitstaff.

"You're very perky today," I joked.

"Perky counts for a lot," she replied. She told me Radioactive Man had a special table. "It's discreet," she said. "Nice and comfy."

I slipped into the leather-covered booth near the rear wall of the restaurant. The perky maitre d' asked if I'd like a drink. Radioactive Man would be along shortly, she said. I ordered black coffee, sat back, and waited.

Time passed slowly. I kept looking at my watch. Finally, Radioactive Man appeared, the maitre d' at his side, guiding him toward the booth. He was a small, boxy man with a major crop of coal-colored hair. His movements appeared weightless, as if he were a spaceman beyond the hold of gravity. He floated without effort through the restaurant. Not one person at the crowded tables looked up. All eyes remained on lockdown. Was he invisible? Why didn't anyone notice him? And then I remembered: This is Radioactive Man, the boiling center of gossip and heated controversy. People are afraid to know him. Though he carried himself in a nonthreatening manner, the space around him was electrified and more than a little perilous.

"Sorry I'm a little late," he said, slipping into the booth. "Been waiting long?"

"Not really."

Was I interrupting any of his important business? He shook his head. "I have an hour or so," he replied mildly, with an air of unconcern.

"Thanks for taking time to meet."

"No, no, not at all." His words flowed easily, as if he was speaking with a neighbor. He looked the part of everyman in a suburban tweed blazer, open collar, and mossy Dockers. This was part of his political toolbox—an ability to charm, disarm, and to be a man possessed of the great good fortune of having been born professionally friendly. No obvious shadow of suspicion darkened his round, almost innocent face. It was the face I had viewed countless times on TV, on the front pages of the most prestigious newspapers. I had studied him for years, fascinated, as he ran the gauntlet of testimony before congressional committees. He had friends on some of those committees as well as lethal enemies who were gunning for him. Radioactive Man was bloodied but not entirely beaten. That would come later in an especially humiliating move by the White House.

"I know you're busy," I began, reminding him that I wished to discuss deregulation of the financial markets and that I had no political agenda to push. He was a Bushie to the bone; political debate would have been foolish, if not impolitic. I was interested only in matters of regulatory policy.

After a smattering of polite chatting, I laid out my point of view: The administration had gone off the regulatory rails. It had turned its back on economic policy, allowing the boundaries of financial prudence to lapse into a bloody free-for-all. The stock market was swooning. Banks were churning out absurd Rube Goldberg derivatives and leveraging debt to the sky. Thanks to the investigative digging of Wall Street-veteran-now-blogger Larry Doyle, we had learned that FINRA had been covering up toxic assets in its own portfolio, including hundreds of millions of dollars in ARS, which it sold relying on apparently inside information and without warning to the public. (In the months following the meeting with Radioactive Man, there was talk of FINRA having invested with Ponzi artist Bernard Madoff. Other disclosures would follow.) The SEC, under the serenely indifferent hand of Chairman Cox, had slipped into the zombie zone. The markets were being denuded of value by collusive short sellers. The DOW Index had shed nearly 6,000 points from its 2007 highs. The social fallout was calamitous, with states facing massive debt and unemployment climbing at a relentless pace.

As I laid out the scenario, Radioactive Man nodded, apparently making mental notes. Did he possess a photographic memory? I wouldn't bet against it.

Then there was the ARS problem, I explained, about which the administration had done nothing. I reminded Radioactive Man that tens of thousands of investors had been defrauded, that Chairman Cox, whose 17 years of congressional service had produced a record of mindless free market speak, appeared indifferent to the ongoing scam.

Radioactive Man listened without visible emotion as I took shots at the administration's economic record. He leaned forward as I spoke, occasionally tapping the tabletop with his fingers, as if keeping count of my indictments.

"Doesn't the president see what's happening?" I pressed. "He seems bewildered."

Radioactive Man smiled broadly. Another six-figure smile. He leaned back against the leather seat. He assured me President Bush was "acutely aware" of all these problems.

"He believes in markets, and he's right," he said calmly. "This is a free-market economy—an efficient and great economy. Government jumping in—well, it can only make matters worse."

Really? Was Chairman Cox right to ignore the ARS and other scandals? How could the SEC be so passive? How could Cox stand by as institutional fraud rolled over taxpaying citizens? Was the commission flying the American flag or a banner proclaiming caveat emptor?

"I can't speak for the chairman," Radioactive Man replied. "I can tell you the president has every confidence in him."

Confidence? I had to keep from laughing. "So the president thinks he's doing a bang-up job?"

The round face darkened. "Mr. Cox isn't Superman. And Congress— you can't discount them, now can you?" He had scored a point. Congress was also in the zombie zone. Toothless pronouncements came regularly from members of Barney Frank's House Financial Services Committee. Tough talk. No tangible action.

A waiter took our orders. He was a young man, the congenitally preppy type. He was a little too old to be a college student. I wondered if he was, in fact, a waiter. The CIA was just up the road. Were they keeping an eye on Radioactive Man? Was the waiter taking our orders or logging clandestine notes?

Radioactive Man scanned the menu, selected a meat dish, rare, with fries and ice tea. I ordered a small salad. It's interesting what people eat at lunch; it gives a hint of their personality. Radioactive Man possessed a characteristic he-man appetite, which I suppose gave him energy to fight the political firestorm that had overtaken him. The nature of the controversy stretched all the way into the Oval Office, and it had added injury to the wounds suffered because of the administration's adventurous decision to sue for regime change in Iraq. I couldn't—and wouldn't—debate Iraq with Radioactive Man. He had placed the subject off limits. Fair enough. To bring up the details of his involvement in that bloody arena, in a public setting, would be tantamount to identifying him, and I had promised to keep his role in the Iraq debate off our agenda and his name out of print. There are certain people you just don't cross.

"We didn't know what to do exactly, you know, with Chairman Cox," my source said, sticking to the subject of our meeting. He said Cox was "a good Republican stalwart." He had arrived at a point in his career, however, where the grind of congressional service and the extraordinary demands of campaigning for office no longer held appeal for him. Some in Washington speculated that Cox, in addition to facing career burnout, was apparently feeling the affects of an old motorcycle accident and other physical ailments. He had concluded he no longer was in shape to run for office, that he had had enough of what Radioactive Man called the "debating society."

Radioactive Man said he had discussed Cox's future with the president and the other cabinet members. The president, in turn, wanted to appoint him to a judgeship in his native Orange County, California.

"Barbara Boxer wasn't having it," Radioactive Man explained. Apparently Senator Boxer was no fan of Mr. Cox, and she allegedly had run a quiet campaign against his ever being seated on the California bench.

"The SEC job was open," Radioactive Man continued. "Cox and the president were close—eye-to-eye politically. So, the situation being what it was, we asked if he'd handle the vacancy at the commission."

"Was he happy with the offer?"

"It was a pretty good fit. He didn't jump at it. He's a brilliant man. He understood the potential."

I was tempted to say, *the potential to do next to nothing.* Cox was an ideologue watching the firestorm in the economy spread from Wall Street to every continent on the planet. There's nothing to be gained, however, by sarcasm, especially when it's thrown at someone as politically powerful as Radioactive Man. Still, it wasn't easy to keep smiling, to remain objective. The little voice in my head warned: *Who are you kidding? You have an axe to grind! But not here, not now. You've just been handed the key to a great blog. Save the hard political stuff for the right space and time.*

Radioactive Man wasn't familiar with the ARS affair. I did my best to explain the details, emphasizing the human casualties—emphasizing the charities that had suffered great losses. His administration was, after all, big on faith-based initiatives, and many of these had taken major hits as a result of the scandal. He fidgeted in his seat, as if the coils beneath him had begun to send out mild electric shocks. It was perhaps the first time that I realized, with discouraging clarity, how difficult it is to explain the mechanics of a complicated economic situation, let alone appeal to the human side and hope for empathy. Radioactive Man held one of the highest and most sensitive positions in government. It was amazing that a man in his position was clueless about a multibillion-dollar scandal perpetuated by the most ardent supporters of his administration. Was it too much to presume that he would have knowledge of this matter? Perhaps he'd heard of it, though only faintly, amid the cacophony surrounding him on a daily basis. He had little apparent interest in Wall Street rip-offs. He had his own battles to worry over.

I showed him a copy of a class-action complaint against Wachovia Securities. It was dated March 9, 2008.

"What's your take on this?" I asked, hoping to get a response—anything—from this super-seasoned attorney who had held several high political offices. I read to him straight from the complaint:

Defendants knew, but failed to disclose to investors, material facts about auction-rate securities. In particular, defendants knew, but failed to disclose that these auction-rate securities were not cash alternatives, but were instead, complex long-term financial instruments with 30-year maturity dates, or longer. Defendants knew, but failed to disclose that auction-rate securities were only liquid at the time of sale because defendants were artificially supporting and manipulating the auction market to maintain the appearance of liquidity and stability. Defendants knew, but failed to disclose that auction-rate securities would become illiquid as soon as defendants stopped maintaining the auction market. On February 13, 2008, 87 percent of all auctions . . . failed when defendants and all other major broker-dealers refused to continue to support the auctions.

"I can't comment," Radioactive Man said.

Was I boring him?

He sliced his meat into tiny portions. It was a matter for state regulators and the courts, he insisted, tasting a small chunk of meat. It wouldn't be fair or ethical for him to make a judgment.

He was covering himself. Anything he might say could well affect the complaint I had shown him, and he knew it. Little lines appeared at the corners of his mouth. His lips pursed. He was miffed at being confronted, although he did a masterful job of covering his irritation.

"Excuse me, sir," I said. "I know I'm asking a lot. Still, you're high up in the administration. Hard to imagine you'd have nothing to say, no comment at all—and you know I won't use your name. I promised."

He faked a hollow laugh. It sounded vacuous and sentimental. "Sounds like a Black Swan to me," he replied. Well, maybe. After all, what could be more improbable than this meeting!

Suddenly the conversation took an unexpected turn. Radioactive Man leaned in close. His gaze narrowed. It was the focused stare of someone who is about to make a very intimate disclosure. It was puzzling, and little unnerving.

"Who do you think killed JFK?" he asked. His words stabbed at the air between us.

I felt a sudden jolt. *Who killed JFK? What kind of question is that?* Like just about everyone else in the United States who was around at the time of the president's assassination in Dallas, I had opinions gleaned from countless conspiracy theories. I told him my theory, which involved the Mexican Mafia. I was uneasy. What was this leading to?

"Did you believe the *Warren Commission Report*?" he continued. I shook my head. "You're right. It was a complete whitewash," he insisted. "A lot of crap."

What about Bobby Kennedy? Did I have a theory about his assassination in the kitchen of the Ambassador Hotel in Los Angeles? Yes, I had my theories, my raw speculation. Radioactive Man gave me another long, curious stare, the kind of hard-edged look cops give suspects under questioning. He kept his eyes alert, holding me fast. The room was starting to feel chilly.

"I *know* who was in on the King assassination," he said it with an air of certainty. He looked at his wristwatch.

This turn of subject made no sense to me. It would have been foolish to ask questions about the King murder. It was creepy. Was this his way of turning the tables, throwing me off my line of questioning? I didn't know, and I didn't like it.

"Jimmy Hoffa. You know anything about him?" asked Radioactive Man.

Well, in fact, I had heard quite a lot about Mr. Hoffa and his battles with former Teamsters President Frank Fitzsimmons. I knew more than I wanted to know, even if it was only anecdotal. In the 1970s, I won an award for a series of investigative articles on crime in the trucking industry. It was one of the scariest times in my life, especially when the Teamsters marched on Washington demanding to know why the Interstate Commerce Commission hadn't quashed the "purely speculative" series being written by a punk reporter—me! But I wasn't about to bring up the subject with Radioactive Man. I was content to believe that his odd switching of subjects was a way of telling me to get off his back concerning bank fraud, especially at a complicated time in his professional life.

I called for the check. Radioactive Man pretended to a friendly squabble over who should pay. I held fast. My treat. That was the deal. I also gave him one of my books.

"I'll read it with interest," he said.

Sure you will. It was like handing him a lump of coal.

A group of diners walked past. You could tell they were CIA employees. They huddled together, uneasy, silent as muted birds with downcast eyes. Not one of them looked at the famous man seated across from me.

We departed the restaurant. I was glad to be out of there.

Later, I e-mailed Radioactive Man thanking him for taking time to meet. And then again, some months later, I sent an e-mail when things appeared to be going a little better for him. The last communication I received came in the form of an e-mail response: "Was I supposed to do something for you?" was all he said.

Chapter 8

Armies of the Unseen

These guys are doing more to destroy capitalism than Marx.
—*Nell Minow, co-founder, The Corporate Library*

With the coming hints of spring, I could sense a kind of groundswell. Not the big hammer I was looking for. My avenue to big clout had yet to be captured. The avenue would involve Harry Newton's web site. But something was holding me back from making the connection. This puzzled me. The stakes were high. Maybe I feared rejection. I had never before been afraid to approach someone with an idea, no matter how far out the idea might be. But each time I picked up the phone to call Mr. Newton, something stalled in my head. Until I overcame this block, I would be forced to continue on my own, writing commentary in a scattershot fashion on a variety of web sites. I was enlisting the identities and active co-operation of more ARS victims. Sooner or later my "Harry hesitancy" would end, and my efforts would come into sharper focus. I desperately needed to make that connection. But I just wasn't ready.

Still, something positive, something energetic, was starting to happen. Pissed-off investors were at last looking for ways to make noise. Except for the banks, who were still raking in fees on nonexistent auctions, no one could be happy about the ARS situation. Yet there was a growing restlessness that was beginning to push back. It was exactly what I was hoping for.

I was receiving ever-increasing volumes of e-mail. Some messages were from investors seeking advice; others from people who wanted to vent. Both were valuable resources. If I could plant myself on a single, well-known web site, that unseen army would grow and coalesce. I knew Harry Newton's site would act as a lobbying force, an integrated base of operations. *Pick up the phone and call him*, the inner narrative nagged. And a countervoice, a little softer and more cautious, replied: *Give me more time . . . I'll get there.*

Interaction. My online mailbox was beginning to fill daily with communications from strangers caught up in the ARS vice. I had placed an appeal on the popular web site, Seeking Alpha, explaining my plans for a book. I requested firsthand, personal accounts. I wanted to find out what others were doing about their problem, aside from joining class-action law suits. It was my early attempt to form the hammer, the blunt instrument bankers might respect.

There also was a need to find other blog sites, alternative avenues to amplify the energy. I didn't for a moment believe it would be easy for strangers to spill their guts to yet another stranger, someone with an odd-sounding e-mail address who might be a con artist. Trust had been widely shattered by the scandal; communications and disclosures carried a risk. But if I became an advocate with a byline, trust would flow. This was my plan for approaching Harry Newton. When I was ready and sufficiently confident, I'd take the plunge and suggest that I become the web site's official investigative journalist.

All had become risky territory. Sacred economic beliefs had fallen. Rating agencies had proven to be as greedy as the banks, essentially selling Triple-A ratings on junk. Alan Greenspan's efficient-market hypothesis (deregulation) had been debunked. George Soros pointed to the obvious: "The salient feature of the current financial crisis is that it was not caused by some external shock like OPEC raising the price of oil. . . . The crisis was generated by the system itself." Even the near-religious faith conjured by mathematical financial modeling had turned out to be a phony god.

None of this debunking of sacred myths was sufficient to silence ARS victims. It was amazing how ready they were for an all-out fight. The initial pace of incoming e-mails was inconsistent at first, although there was seldom a lack of outrage: *Rotten bastards. I'm not a youngster, I was born at night, but not last night. This is shit! This cannot stand!*

Those faceless legions of correspondents needed to find to someone who understood what they were going through, someone who would stand with them. An attorney could apprise investors of their legal rights and temporarily boost their spirits (while lightening their purses). Helpful as legal advice often is, it isn't a substitute for basic human empathy. Liberal billionaires such as Soros might side with them, but at a very great distance. Bill Heyman provided a calming influence, but my instinct, like those of others, was to fight. The close, human touch was effective and much in demand. Bill Clinton proved it with his famous "I feel your pain" remark. This was my appeal: You're hurting, I'm hurting; together we can generate a world of hurt for the banks and get our money back!

E-mailers couldn't know for sure who I was or if I possessed a deeper understanding of the situation than anyone else. I was still working through the puzzle of the credit crisis excuse. I viewed it as a smoke screen created by the bonfire of securitization. ARS victims didn't start the fire. The banks and brokerages had plenty of money, and they would get much more from Henry Paulson's Keynesian bailout scheme—the simple fill-in-the-blank document he had created at Treasury that demanded no accountability. The banking chiefs subsequently launched a stock and bond buying binge and handed out hundreds of millions of dollars in bonuses, this without a hint of embarrassment and without push back from Paulson.

But I was confident. And emphatic. I had to be. There was good reason to suppose the offended voices would grow louder and more insistent. It was daring, a long shot; yet I could begin to imagine the digital torches and pitchforks glowing in the distance. One correspondent fumed: "Where is [New York Attorney General] Andrew Cuomo? Where are the regulators?" Indeed, where were the cops?

One of the earlier indications that I was getting somewhere was the following e-mail that showed up in my in-box:

I saw your comment in DealBook. Do you think this mess is going to resolve? What is it going to take? What is SEC doing?

I'm feeling sick—I am sick! I am not a kid. Am retired but maybe not much longer. What's happening? Are we screwed?

We need to get into this together.

* * *

I was unconsciously making a sharp transition from my real life, the one I enjoyed: the life without blinders and a sinking feeling about our future. I found myself glued to the computer most waking hours. New people were entering my life via the Internet. They wanted answers. There was considerable research to be done before I could get up to speed and help myself, let alone make a stab at a collective effort against the banks. I know, I know, shrinks call it obsessive. I call it survival. Everything was at stake.

"You've got to get out of the house!" Sandy implored.

"Later," I most often responded when she attempted to unglue me from the computer screen, although *later* never seemed to come. I was losing track of time, working into the night and barely sleeping.

Although I knew I wasn't alone in the struggle, this knowledge didn't soften the fact that the ARS fraud wasn't the only game being played on investors, and that millions of people were losing everything—jobs, homes, trillions of dollars in savings. Obsession is the least you can expect when the busy, impersonal corporate hand has picked your pocket. It happens every day, constantly, and when that greed has violated your life and your sense of self-worth, you are liable to do anything to strike back.

Each day I woke up to the dismal fact that I now had a new full-time job I never wanted—getting our money and our life back. Overcoming the sting of having been deceived by those you trust is next to impossible. Truth to tell, it takes someone with the hide of a rhinoceros, or a brain the size of a walnut, to go on as if nothing has happened. In the process of trying to put one's life back together, there is the risk of sinking beneath despair. Anxious nights sap energy and shorten one's fuse. But in the end you have no choice: You keep up the fight despite the unseen psychic damage that builds layer upon layer.

A few years earlier, exploring a volcanic island off the coast of New Zealand, I had stumbled into a quicksand pit. The memory of that close call on White Island, the ever-steaming volcano in the Bay of Plenty, hovered over my thoughts. Helplessness in the grip of the quicksand, not knowing the depth of the pit, boulders the size of Volkswagens spitting out of the caldera and whizzing through the air like cannon shot—this experience was made fresh again by the helpless sensation of having been caught in a scam. I had barely struggled out of that soupy quicksand trap, thanks to the strenuous efforts of my companions, and now I was going to spring myself out of the sinkhole created by our equally life-threatening financial situation.

"The quicksand incident," I suggested to Sandy. "Maybe I should use the analogy."

"Oh, God!" she replied. "*Please* don't. You'll just give these poor people more of a sinking feeling."

A laugh. The first one I'd had in what seemed like forever. An actual laugh. "That's pretty good," I said. "A sinking feeling. Very funny."

It was imperative to grab more attention. Out of 146,500 debunked ARS investors, how many would stick their necks out and actually put up a fight? There was a steep learning curve to be engaged. The situation had hit us without warning. The plot was dense and surreal, the cover-up criminally effective. Investors were being kept entirely in the dark. The silent treatment was just the latest cheap trick. Did Jim and all those other brokers know what they were doing? Did they understand their behavior was unethical—perhaps illegal? Jim had been contrite. I was cheered when e-mailers reported that their brokers had apologized, although this was a rare event. Unfortunately, apologies didn't get their money returned. We needed more direct action. And the only place I knew to get it was through the great sprawling blogosphere.

Who was this audience of unseen warriors? They were made up of those who worked harder and longer, saved, invested, and reached a certain maturity: a time of life when all the work and saving might allow a little comfort, even a few small luxuries. I was searching for people who were lied to and exploited, whose money had been stolen. I wanted citizens who understood the cruelty of life in the United States when you're broke or near broke; people who knew how the laissez-faire meat-grinder works when you're net worth goes negative. Individuals who know what it feels like when the Grim Reaper of Money comes knocking, demanding not only your destruction but also a perverse fealty toward those who have cleverly cheated you out of meaningful segments of your life.

✻ ✻ ✻

The following found its way to me over the Internet from a 2008 news brief from the Texas law firm of Shepherd Smith Edwards & Kantas:

> Just how rigged was the market for auction-rate securities?
>
> A recent Bloomberg report shows just how actively UBS submitted bids in ARS auctions in order to sustain the market. . . . From January 1, 2006, to February 28, 2008, UBS submitted support bids on 27,069 auctions for preferred shares, and its bids were drawn upon to prevent auctions from failing 13,782 times. During the same period, the firm submitted bids in 30,367 auctions for municipal and student loan securities, and its bids were drawn upon 26,023 times. These figures demonstrate the extent to which brokerage firms like UBS sustained the ARS market. . . . It is no wonder, then, that the ARS market collapsed when UBS decided to stop supporting it.

Was UBS saying, "Hey, there, investors. The joke's on you!" The revelation provoked an image of Wall Street stalking the boundaries in full predation mode, setting up for the kill. The auction freeze was a fait accompli. Now it appeared the banks and Treasury Secretary Henry Paulson were setting the stage for what later turned into the multibillion-dollar Troubled Asset Relief Program (TARP).

Politics obscured much of these preliminaries. It was, after all, perfect Machiavellian sport. There was historical precedent. At an especially troublesome time in the history of Italy, a wave of populism overtook the countryside. When Machiavelli's Prince was informed that the people were restless, that wealthy aristocrats feared a populist uprising, the Prince found a cynical solution. "Give them festivals," he told his nervous advisors. In a way, the 2008 presidential primaries were the twenty-first-century equivalent of those festivals. People were stressed between being nervously hopeful ("Yes, we can!") and fearful of losing everything to yet another anticonsumer Republican administration. This time, unlike the Machiavellian model, festivals were passé. Jesters and trained elephants wouldn't do. We needed a makeover for the financial industry, regulations to protect against the nonstop predations of Wall Street.

Again the inner narrative was sharp: *Come on, call Harry Newton and get it over with. It's your best shot. Maybe the only one that makes sense.*

✳ ✳ ✳

During the weeks immediately following the ARS crisis, I attended an art exhibition of works by my good and talented friend, Ann Purcell. The gallery was alive with art lovers stroking their chins in that curious way of collectors contemplating the *right* purchase. There was plenty of talk of promising new artists and somber reflections about the old ones we missed.

Ann's show was a much-needed break. My computer screen had begun to fill almost hourly with cryptic messages from ARS victims who had seen my invitation to exchange information. Many of these correspondents believed I knew more about the situation than I actually did. I chalked it up to the usual outside the Beltway assumption that living and working in Washington gives one special access. It's mostly a myth. Washington is so insular that even the insiders walk around scratching their heads wondering who can move legislation forward.

The unsavory mix of politics and the ARS mess required scaling a steep learning curve. If investors were going to make waves and show a collective outrage we needed inside knowledge and strong political allies. When a question was asked of me, I wanted to have an answer. Vague opinions wouldn't do. Given the broad scope of the situation, added to the growing numbers of e-mails that had begun to consume hours of attention each day, it was important to dig in and examine a range of scenarios. But on the night of Ann's opening, I returned briefly to something resembling normal life. For a few hours, I was no longer the "Dear Abby" of the auction rate scandal.

Being a mostly Washington-New York crowd, there was lively political talk and occasional bloviating. Could this then-obscure guy with the funny name, Obama, come out of nowhere and win the presidency? What would happen after the Bushies got their talons off the public purse? Would we ever get rid of Cheney and Rove? Or would they become, like so many before them, creatures that would take root here and spawn? Would they stalk us as opinionated political has-beens after their cowboy president packed his six-guns and returned to Texas where, he said, he would "stuff the ol' coffers" giving speeches. (At this writing, Cheney and Rove have taken root. Outside of Washington they are virtual nobodies, a condition few politicians can tolerate.)

I roamed the gallery taking lots of time to mull over the paintings. It was great to see Ann. It had been a long time between visits. She cheerfully reported that other exhibitions of her work were in the planning stages.

"It's only talk for now," she explained, her modesty coming with a hint of anticipation.

Though Ann had long ago become a creature of Manhattan, she had a deep political background, having once worked on Capitol Hill with the late Senator William Proxmire. She had the perfect gimlet eye. Ann had forgotten more about political in-games than most of the yammering heads who appear on 24/7 cable news shows would ever learn—the exception being Chris Mathews of MSNBC *Hardball* fame. I asked her about Obama. Could he win? Could he manage to govern? Could he protect the public from the financial terrorists?

"Well," she said with sly knowing, "he's got to be nominated first. And, you know, you may have heard there's somebody out there named Hillary. She's not one to be fluffed off."

"Understand. But *could* he win?"

Ann laughed. "After what this gang has done to the country," she said, referring to the Bushies, "you could get Elmer Fudd in the Oval Office."

I wandered to the bar, sipped an acidic red wine, and did my best to be absorbed in the colorful surroundings. I floated, a bit heady, into Ann's paintings. Her brilliantly constructed collages, the slashing strokes of color that had arrived straight from her heart to her brush and onto the canvas, gave me a needed boost.

There it is, I thought. The real deal. This art is honest, creative work. It is not the unsettling act of making money appear out of thin air and then pretending it has the quality or integrity of real innovation. The financial shell game is played with oddball numbers and formulae designed by would-be swamis. I was reminded of JPMorgan Chase's Jamie Dimon who, as reported by *Vanity Fair*, liked to say before a deal, "Let's make friends with these guys before I eat them." Cannibals can be so witty prior to dumping your body into boiling water.

Ann introduced me to a bond trader at a major New York bank. He was a pleasant young man, one of those commuters to Manhattan from Connecticut (funny how pockets of that otherwise pleasant state have become Wall Street's garish bedroom community and strip mall). I sized up the bond trader as a decent enough guy, one of those comfort-food-eating people who probably never missed a meal, and who had taken the trouble to come from New York to Washington out of respect for our mutual friend Ann. I couldn't help liking him, although I knew his presence would pull me back into the ARS scene and all those e-mails on my computer screen that needed to be answered.

"You're the writer. Gotta be a hell of a job," the bond trader said shaking my hand.

I couldn't help smiling. "Like construction," I said. "But more frustrating and probably less useful."

He wanted to know if I was working on anything new. I told him my idea for the ARS book, and we drifted into a slightly dicey financial conversation.

He said the banks were busy "hoarding" money and that Washington wasn't going to stop them from doing so. What came next was more of a jolt. He started explaining the makeup of various securitization models for mortgage-backed securities. He drew a verbal picture of something resembling an old-fashioned Dagwood sandwich. The best stuff—the Triple-A paper that was virtually assured to pay off—was the top 20 percent layer of the sandwich, followed by the riskier mortgages in descending order to the "sour mayonnaise" loans, those tricky adjustable rate sucker traps sold to clueless home buyers on the basis of *no job, no assets, no down payment, no problem*. These so-called Alt-A mortgages were at the bottom of the Dagwood sandwich. These lowly subprimes fueled the Great Recession of 2009, but at the time of Ann's show, the secret was that many of the banks selling these securitized time bombs were betting against them with the intention of making fortunes on the ultimate collapse of the market.

"It's a reasonable model," the bond trader explained. Sure, there was some real crapola in the mix. The sour mayonnaise blend of mortgages at the bottom of the sandwich were loaded with toxicity and bound to fail. But the pitch made to investors in these derivatives went something like this: When measuring risk in the composition of the mortgage sandwich, there were plenty of good loans you could count on. If the bad ones went belly up, the good mortgages would more than offset the losses. It was a clever though deceitful pitch, and it worked because investors didn't know about the downside bets the banks were making.

A year after my conversation with the bond executive, the outcome of this securitization model stands as unscrupulous homage to the recklessness of Wall Street's client trap. It resulted in record foreclosures, joblessness, commercial real estate on the verge of collapse, and a multibillion-dollar bailout by taxpayers to the geniuses who paid themselves handsome bonuses for having brought the financial system to its knees. Many banks and hedge funds profited greatly from the collapse, especially Goldman Sachs. As for the investors, maybe they should have seen it coming. Or perhaps they should have realized that if you have a broker, you may have a problem.

"Financial algorithms are flimsy things," I said. "Intervening variables are endless and unpredictable. All those models assume that tomorrow will be like today, and when has that ever been true?"

"Well, those models are close enough to bet on—or bet against," said the bond swami.

"Speaking as a reporter who once covered NASA, I think it's easier to put a man on the moon than it is to predict human variables—market swings, war, irrational exuberance, panic. Rockets don't have pockets and they're not greedy."

"We hire guys from NASA," he said with obvious pride.

I listened as this executive explained the presumed flawless thinking behind modern mortgage securitization. I was shifting nervously, drinking my wine a little faster. When your money's been expropriated without so much as an explanation, even a phony one, you are in no mood to hear about tranches and pie-in-the-sky mathematical constructs. Unfortunately, my attitude was a little too obvious.

"Your industry's artwork is on display at the Museum of Constant Confusion," I snipped. "No disrespect. It's like bankers gone wild, but without any of the fun. Please don't get me started."

The bond trader's face darkened.

"You can't condemn all of us," he insisted. "Some of us do hard, honest work."

Some . . . the word sounded defensive. A nod was all the satisfaction he was going to get out of me, although there was a sense of humanity conveyed to him by this acknowledgment, this gesture that recognized the sincerity of his words. I'm sure he worked hard. Sure, he was a good and honest guy, someone to count on. Still—

"Good enough," I told the bond trader, who was sipping the off-brand Champagne typically served at art openings. With great care he selected an offering from a tray of pigs in a blanket.

He was adamant. One couldn't deny that Wall Street provides jobs, enviable salaries, a nice tax base for New York; and there's always the opportunity to underwrite growth around the world. The man was a true believer.

"Working a bond desk—I'm not knocking it, or you," I said. "And I agree Wall Street can do good things. It's just that the way it gets done these days is disturbing. There's a lot of outrage these days."

"All this hating of us," he sighed. "It isn't right. Nobody gives us a break. They forget. Financial institutions are inherently unstable. It's too bad. But it's always been, you know . . ." he made a gesture with his free hand, a sort of wavering motion. "Well, I'm sure you get my meaning."

He informed me that his bank and the other too-big-to-fail zombie banks were slashing lending to near zero. The bank needed its massive reserves, and if the rest of the economy contracted like a punctured balloon, well, we'd just have to find a way to reinflate it.

Perhaps he didn't know the 2008 bailout was being discussed behind closed doors at the Fed and the Treasury, that SEC Chairman Cox was being pressured to rein in the short sellers who were killing bank stocks. A less competitive Wall Street was in the works. Only the biggest players would be left to duke it out under the banner of "Moral Hazard Are Us!"

On October 16, 2009, the *New York Times* would declare, "Bailout Helps Fuel a New Era of Wall Street Wealth." The story, by Graham Bowley, stated, "It may come as a surprise that one of the most powerful forces driving the resurgence . . . is not the banks but Washington."

But all this was future tense. That evening of Ann's show had her bond trader friend citing economic history—the cycle of recession, crisis, boom, bust, and recovery. He compared the ARS collapse to the Savings and Loan rip-off of the 1980s. Americans are used to uncertainty, he claimed. "We're our own worst enemies."

"But that's not what the economy wants or needs," I said. "You can't justify it. Ordinary people wind up paying for recklessness and arrogance. And the banks—they go AWOL while the rest of us sink out of sight. They act as if they don't need rules or a country. They have their own country—the State of Oligarchy."

"I never said it was pretty." It was the culture of the Street. It wasn't perfect; it was reality. He repeated the word "culture" several times, making a distinction between the world most of us live in and the one occupied by the big investment institutions.

The bond trader had tried his best to explain what he believed to be a reasonable position. He seemed honest, diligent. But his core principles, his integrity, were outflanked by his industry's culture, and I was too far gone that evening to be of a moderate disposition. Besides, an art opening is hardly a proper venue for debating the unpleasant truisms of financial gaming.

I was tempted to say something nasty, something inappropriate. Being at the tipping point, I was relieved to see that syndicated columnist Mark Shields had entered the gallery. He and Ann were old friends from the political jungle of Capitol Hill. Shields had worked in a former life with Ann Purcell's mentor, Senator William Proxmire. They met on Capitol Hill in the turbulent 1960s, when Proxmire was a liberal firebrand.

"Great-looking show," Shields was saying to Ann when I approached the two of them.

"Mark, you know Phil," Ann said.

"Oh, yeah, sure," he replied, extending his hand. We had discussed politics during brief encounters at various Washington events, and I followed his regular Saturday night appearances on the political panel show *Inside Washington*. We aren't pals, although we were most of the time on the same side of the political fence.

Built like a small armored fighting vehicle and decked out in his on-air uniform—blue blazer, gray slacks, striped necktie—the presence of Mark Shields brightened my spirits. No matter how serious the topic, he always had a playful take on it.

"Think Obama can pull it off?" I asked.

Mark shrugged. "He's got a lot going for him." It wouldn't be a snap outrunning the Clinton machine, he added. "It's an exciting prospect though." He paused, shook someone else's hand, ever the gracious political celebrity, and then turned back to the subject of the upcoming election. "Whoever gets in is going to have quite a time getting anything done," he admitted. "Government's more dysfunctional than ever. The caucuses are swinging more and more to the extremes. It's going to be gridlock."

He was prophetic. Soon after Barrack Obama took the oath of office, both political parties headed hard left and hard right. It was what political guru Norm Ornstein called "bipolarization."

Mark asked if I was writing anything new. When I told him the subject, the mischievous glimmer vanished.

"Oh, gawd," he replied with his characteristic New England drawl. "You've sure got a messy job on your hands."

I told him my proposed book would be about ordinary investors whose lives had been thrown out of joint by the ARS collapse. When I mentioned Wall Street culture, Mark sighed.

"Gawd," he repeated. "Those people are impossible. I sure don't envy you." The look he gave me implied a little more: Keep your head down and watch your back!

More than a year later, in October 2009, U.S. District Judge Jack Weinstein, overseeing the first headline grabbing criminal charges in the ARS scandal, would say what most people knew—or should have known—about the dangers of Wall Street culture and the ARS problem in particular. Weinstein told defense and prosecution attorneys handling the cases against Credit Suisse AG fraudsters Eric Butler and Julian

Tzolov, brokers found guilty of defrauding clients to the tune of more than $1 billion, that when considering sentencing, "the culture of corruption" in the securities industry had to be factored in. Judge Weinstein described that particular culture as "pernicious and pervasive." The *New York Times* called it "a classic case of greed and glory on Wall Street."

Everyone, it seemed, had discovered new ways to vilify the money savants. The Masters of the Universe had outsourced their greed to MIT graduates and math majors who were paid to predict the future. It was mission impossible that had been sold to the public during the stock market boom between 2002 and 2007. Now, on the downward slope, the algorithms were being shredded. Yet even as the efficient market theory was unmasked as a myth and the new science of mathematical prediction was stripped bare, Wall Street was planning its comeback at enormous taxpayer expense.

"What a world these guys live in," said Mark Shields.

What a world, indeed.

✳ ✳ ✳

I was going to write the book. Yes, it was certain. It was the socially responsible thing to do. At least it might keep me sane as the ARS situation continued to unfold. Perhaps the writing would break whatever it was that kept me from calling Harry Newton with my investigative journalism idea. In the meantime, I was determined to help crack the code of the presumed illiquidity that was causing havoc with peoples' lives.

It was imperative that any writing I might undertake be geared to break that code. *Never forget, Wall Street is two-faced*, Bill Heyman had warned. I couldn't get the phrase out of my head. Wall Street was built on trust, the most precious and fragile of commodities. Yet it was this trust that the Street violated day in and day out. Already banks that had sold ARS were screaming foul at state regulators who were gearing up to investigate the fraud. Any intrusion or demand of repayment amounted to something like extortion in the eyes of Tom James, CEO of the Raymond James brokerage. James wasn't alone in this attitude. Almost a year after the market collapsed, James wrote a January 5, 2009, apology for having sold ARS to his clients. It was an apology with caveats. He said he and many Raymond James employees held these bonds in their own accounts. Clients would be redeemed ahead of the brokerage's executives, he promised. The caveat was that the Raymond James and other "downstream" brokerages didn't underwrite the securities but merely sold them to clients. The issuers, he implied, should be forced to redeem the bonds.

What was going on was pure ruthlessness. The victims who were communicating with me were entitled to fight back with as much venom as the engineers of the ARS fraud. A letter writing campaign was under way to state attorneys general. Tough political threats were being made. They were, indeed, ruthless in their demand for justice. Rage by investors who felt used; fury at having been taken for fools— it was spilling out like bile. Furious investors used words like thief, criminal, liar, and this heated rhetoric would be used with increasing intensity. There was a growing sense that, yes, being conned was at the root of the anger, and, yes, a mood of revenge was being created.

An e-mail arrived from an aggrieved Wells Fargo client. It contained a copy of a note written by a broker to the client concerning his ARS situation: You know that if I had the power to write you a check I would. . . . Let's talk tomorrow and feel free to vent.

"Feel free to vent," the correspondent wrote. "Vent? What horseshit. I want my money! Somebody needs to *pay*!" Curious about what the correspondent meant, exactly, by "somebody needs to pay," I replied with a question.

"Are you suggesting what I think you are?" I asked. "Isn't it dangerous to suggest violence?"

A few days later the answer appeared on my computer screen. "I want to put my fist through a wall. You can guess what that means."

Ruthless: It was the only way to describe the attitude on both sides.

Take someone's love, job, or money and the result is that civility disappears and a fist comes crashing through a wall or on the side of someone's head. It was best, I figured, to steer clear of violent exclamations. People suffering severe distress or life-altering trauma have a way of finding a target—any target of convenience. Build up enough stress and anything can happen.

It didn't take long to see that a trend was becoming obvious among certain of the ARS victims—those fist-through-the-wall people. These were mature, educated, mostly elderly investors whose fury and unceasing anxiety, when viewed objectively, might be considered troubling.

They were ranting—and scared as hell. They were apparently willing to ramp up their fury to *The Godfather* level.

I certainly didn't envision a nascent movement of vigilantes. "Torches and pitchforks" was a somewhat humorous metaphor. An actual uprising to the level of extremism was not to be dismissed. There were rumors of underground cells whose inflamed leaders wanted bloody, violent payback for having been conned. It was impossible to confirm the vigilante movement, and yet it couldn't be discounted. There were plots to descend upon Greenwich and literally take back the spoils of the ARS players—their homes, cars, art collections, anything that wasn't nailed down.

This group of irate investors most likely later became the supporters of Sarah Palin and the know-nothing extremists who thrived on unrequited outrage. These morally offended individuals wanted to see Wall Street in flames. Even my gentle and even-tempered friend, Janell Cannon, the much-acclaimed children's author and illustrator, sent me a paper banner: RAHR!! it shouted in bold red type. It was her witty contribution to the angry roar of an author (me) who was determined to bring down the ARS fraudsters, and Janell was cheering me on with an appropriate bumper sticker of a roar. I taped the banner to the bottom of my computer screen and glanced at it whenever I paused between sentences. RAHR!! succinctly captured my determination to punch holes in the scandal and discover who and what was behind it.

There was, however, a line not to be crossed. While it was easy to empathize with the vigilantes, I wanted nothing to do with violence or the incitement of violence. Most of us just wanted our money. Simple justice.

I made a policy of deleting inflammatory e-mails. Faced with the prospect of FINRA arbitration, it seemed risky to have such crazy material on hand. There was always a chance that Wachovia's attorneys might find these messages and argue that I was a head case, a dangerous character who well might be part of a violent conspiracy. The politics of personal destruction, after all, isn't confined to the political killing fields of Washington.

* * *

It was in spring 2008 when online correspondents reported that Robin Carnahan, the Missouri Secretary of State, was on Wachovia's

ARS case. The news, though unofficial, was encouraging. It certainly brightened my outlook. The e-mail that popped up on my computer screen was a ray of hope:

> It's backdoor talk, but we're told it's from a good source. Carnahan is under pressure from investors. Wachovia not making it a cinch for sure. They're big players in St. Louis.

Robin Carnahan has a reputation as a racket buster. You'd never guess how really tough she is by her appearance. She has the look of a polite mid-Western equestrian who hosts outdoor parties and chatty book clubs. Unlike some other state securities enforcers, however, she has no tolerance for fraud. I was delighted to learn that in her two terms in office she beat Wall Street on numerous occasions, returning $9.5 billion to investors. The rather bland slogan she uses to describe her political persona, "A straight shooter who gets things done," is something of an understatement. Her father, the late former Missouri governor Mel Carnahan, beat former Attorney General John Ashcroft in a run for the Senate, but he was killed in a plane crash while on the campaign trail. Her mother, Jean, was appointed to take his seat in Washington. Thus Robin Carnahan's political roots go straight to the Wall Street-Washington nexus. She knows the darkest regions of the game and almost always comes down on the side of ordinary citizens.

Soon after getting the news, I made an appeal for more information. Through various blogs correspondents I learned that Carnahan's office had received more than 100 complaints within weeks after the ARS market collapse. One correspondent said those initial complaints amounted to nearly $120 million. Of that total, $80 million came directly out of the pockets of Missouri investors.

I telephoned Carnahan's office. It was an early stage investigation, I was told. And, yes, it was true that the office had received an unspecified number of complaints. I was pleased to learn that most of those complaints arrived via e-mails. Since the matter was in its preliminary stages, no official comment would be forthcoming.

After taking a few deep breaths, I called Jim. Was this for real? Was Carnahan chasing Wachovia?

"Can't talk about it," he mumbled. "You know I can't." Besides, he added, he wasn't privy to such information.

A day later, I tried speaking with his partner, Victor, my backup broker.

I got an angry response. He said if I called again he would hang up on me. He had made it clear that he was toeing the corporate line. His cone of silence was proudly unbroken. Though his response didn't surprise me, his threat to hang up if I mentioned ARS gave me a queasy feeling.

"You have a hell of a lot of nerve talking to me like that," I shot back. "How do you sleep at night?" I slammed down the receiver, walked into the bathroom behind my office, and splashed water on my face. The voice in my head was raging: *You're not going to let them get away with it. No way. You made a lot of money for these guys and they treat you like shit. But it's going to turn on them; you're going to kick their corporate asses. Expose them for what they really are.*

I later learned, again from Internet correspondents, that Carnahan's office was also bringing the Missouri State Higher Education Loan Authority into the probe—the MOHELA monster, where much of my now-illiquid cash was invested. The incriminating state audit of the student loan authority proved that MOHELA, like much else in the realm of finance, deserved to go down. Hard.

Each day brought me a little closer to making that call to Harry Newton.

Chapter 9

Day of Deliverance

We as an industry cannot avoid the simple fact that we caused a
lot of damage, and we have to make sure it doesn't happen again.
—*Brian Moynihan, CEO, Bank of America*

August 15, 2008.

It was one of my mad-as-hell mornings. The moment I opened
my eyes, I was prepared to turn on the computer and wade through the
usual stream of e-mails from ARS victims. Despite the ever-increasing
volume of mail, their stories still resonated, still had the power to inflame
the senses. Scattered among these stories, also per usual, would be the
glut of financial web sites. Their challenged syntax, dubious analysis and
prognostications, mixed with the never-ending police blotter of white-
collar crimes, made for a potent cocktail of emotions, especially first
thing in the morning.

"Lighten up," said Sandy. The collective energy has to go somewhere. Energetic matter, the physicists claim, is indestructible. "Keep pushing but keep your cool. Drink your coffee!"

I had an enemies list of ARS fraudsters. It was taped to the wall beside my desk. Anyone looking at it might remark that it was a list of the very best financial institutions in the United States. Super blue-chip outfits. Each played a key role in the ARS crash and the broader economic meltdown. Each had engaged in an arrogant game of Leveraged Monopoly with shareholder and client money, and they had moved their individual game pieces closer than ever to that square on the board that proclaimed: "Go to Jail." There was fine print inscribed on this unfortunate penalty box. Written with invisible ink was the good news for the banks: Go to jail and give yourself a huge bonus. It will make yourself feel better about yourself!

Again, I glanced at my hit list.

I couldn't read it any longer. Too upsetting. The list was emblazoned in my brain like a series of wanted posters. It was just too infuriating. Suddenly, a strange thought popped into my mind: It would be easier to reverse the orbits of celestial bodies than to impose civilized culture on Wall Street. Not even the belated confessions of deregulation advocate and former Federal Reserve Chairman Alan Greenspan would alter the mind-set of the Ayn Randian true believers. Walk into almost any investment bank and ask, "Who is John Galt?" In a flash you will be surrounded by the faithful. They will admit that even superheroes will make occasional missteps. But not to worry: Those stumbles will be borne on the backs of shareholders and taxpayers, Rand's loser class.

The flow of printed e-mails piled up like an unrelenting storm of paper. They cluttered just about every spare corner of the office. These e-mails had become more than ordinary printed words; each was a life—each a sad, infuriating story.

The good news was that Attorney General Andrew Cuomo earlier in the month reached settlements with JPMorgan Chase, Morgan Stanley, Citigroup, and UBS. The buyback of ARS by those firms amounted to $26.3 billion. The multimillion-dollar fines were, of course, passed on to the stockholders, and the banks walked away without denying guilt or claiming innocence.

By now, Wachovia also was in Cuomo's crosshairs, although his office was in the official no-comment zone regarding the open investigation. Our online gang was inundating the attorney general with e-mails. We had sources in touch with investigators who were inclined to leak. The leaks piled up and formed the basis for online stories I planned to write for Harry Newton's site, presuming Harry would cooperate. We knew Cuomo was contemplating a run for the governorship. New York ARS victims were threatening to make their dissatisfaction known at the polls if he didn't beef up his investigations and bring home more results.

Sandy and I were anticipating a break. With Cuomo and Carnahan targeting Wachovia, waiting for them to act was a little like waiting for our first child to be born—a time when anticipation and hair trigger anxiety made time slow down to the point of exasperation.

We had opted for arbitration by FINRA and sent our filing fee to Bill Heyman. He was a few days away from forwarding the money to FINRA to cover the hearing, about which we had very mixed feelings. Heyman was confident. I was dreading what I feared would be a farcical kangaroo court.

To keep our minds focused on other realities, Sandy and I had attended a foreign policy dinner and seminar at the National Press Club in early August. The speakers focused on Iraq and the unsettling pressures building around the United States' involvement in Afghanistan. During the dinner, Sandy chatted with a 50-something policy analyst who had taken a beating in the equity markets. I conversed with a gentleman, now retired, who had worked as a CFO on Wall Street. I told him about my experience in the auction-rate market.

"You should have read the prospectus," the former CFO declared. It was the standard line. But there was no prospectus, I replied. "Well, you could have gone online and found a disclosure statement." A disclosure statement? "Yes," he said. "It has to be there." Has to be there? I'm afraid not. "Well, then," he grumbled, "it's those damned brokers. Christ! What they do to people. It's a crime."

I was ruminating over the CFO's comment the next morning when the phone interrupted my thoughts. I ripped the receiver out of its cradle so hard I nearly dropped it.

A familiar voice greeted me on the other end.

"Good news." It was Jim, my now-former broker. He spoke in a quiet, even voice. "You're liquid, good to go," he said.

The shock was immediate. I did not expect to hear from him, and in the moment my voice failed me. When I regained it, I wanted to make sure I understood him correctly.

"You're telling me the MOHELA bond is being redeemed?"

"That's right."

"It's *real* cash now?"

"It was always real cash."

"Yeah, sure. Real until it wasn't."

In the tremulous space that hung between us, I realized I had missed Jim; missed his familiar voice and the enthusiasm he brought to the task of trading. It was a perplexing irony. Much of my resentment had been directed at my initial broker who had left the company soon after sticking me with the MOHELA bond.

"I should have gotten rid of MOHELA first," Jim said. It was the same confession I heard at our recent meeting. When the ARS market began to slip, Jim was quick to redeem the ARS he had purchased for our accounts. He ran out of time to dump the MOHELA bond in mid-February.

"Yeah," I said. "It should have been the first to go."

"Couldn't sell it," he told me. "Nobody wanted student loan paper."

"Would've been nice to know that before I bought it."

"I didn't buy it," he said. "That was your last broker. Remember?"

He sounded genuinely apologetic. Still, I resented the way I had been treated, although the resentment was softening. Listening to him now, on this day of deliverance, I imagined him at his desk wearing his ubiquitous Yankees shirt, the energetic "stock guy" with whom I had broken bread and exchanged personal information; the guy I once trusted and who was proud of his market smarts. Later, I would learn that Jim had only cursory knowledge of the auction market. Like many brokers, he had been kept in the dark and away from the ugly details by upper management. This information would seep out later. But now it was time to revel in the news Jim was proudly delivering.

"Fill me in," I said, incredulously. "I want to make sure I under-stand what you're telling me."

Jim said, "You're going to be made whole."

I was still skittish. "Are you sure?"

"Cuomo settled with Wachovia. Game over." The official news had flashed across the Dow Jones News wire only a few minutes earlier.

"So I get the money back in my lifetime?" I must have sounded pretty bitter, although my heart was pounding with mixed joy and resentment.

"Yep."

He explained the money would be returned, in full, no later than November 28, 2008. It couldn't be wired to my new account, the one I'd ripped away in anger from Wachovia and placed with another brokerage. Jim explained the full sum would come in the form of a check.

"Your nightmare is over," he said. "I'm happy for you."

For the first time in recent memory I was speechless; the last time had been when I learned our money had been frozen. I took a long breath, glanced at my watch, amazed by the split-second changing of reality.

"We should get together for lunch," I said. It was a sentimental notion.

"Okay," Jim responded. "We can do that." Pause. "Maybe you should have stayed with us."

"Impossible—especially after the silent treatment."

He was instantly defensive. He said all brokers, nationwide, had been instructed to clam up when the auctions failed. I don't know why he said it. It wasn't true. Any number of correspondents had written about long, painful conversations with their brokers. Some had gone so far as to resign because, like their clients, they, too, had been suckered into believing the ARS pitch concerning safety, liquidity, and so forth. They had been made to look like fools and worse. Some were stuck with ARS in their personal accounts.

Thankfully, this was no longer my problem. I knew on some level that I had another decision to make, a decision I needed to discuss with Sandy. It could wait.

For the first time in months, I breathed normally. Even the sunlight appeared brighter, more energizing. Why spoil it? Taking on Jim's claim of universal silence was a zero sum game. It no longer mattered.

"I'll call you," I told him.

"Anytime," he replied. "I'm not going anywhere."

Deep down I knew it wasn't to be. I might have enjoyed seeing Jim again; I would have liked to pretend none of this had ever happened, but nothing would rub out the stain of disgust. You can do your best to repair a broken bond of trust. You can make an uneasy peace with it. Still, like one's tongue relentlessly probing a sore tooth, fractured trust sends a persistent and palpable warning that your survival instinct keeps flashing to your brain.

* * *

I Googled the latest news release from the New York Attorney General's office. The headline appeared on the computer screen like a declaration from the gods of crime and punishment:

> Attorney General Announces Settlement with Wachovia to Recover Billions for Investors in Auction Rate Securities; Wachovia to Pay $50 Million Penalty
>
> New York, August 15, 2008—Attorney General Andrew Cuomo today announced another agreement to provide liquidity to consumers who purchased auction-rate securities. Under the latest agreement, Wachovia Securities, LLC, and Wachovia Capital Markets LLC . . . will return over $8.5 billion to investors across New York State and the nation. The agreement settles allegations that Wachovia made misrepresentations in its marketing and sales of [ARS]. Wachovia marketed and sold [ARS] as safe, cash-equivalent products, when in fact they faced increasing liquidity risk.

The press release explained that within the past eight days, Cuomo had signed agreements restoring nearly $35 billion in liquidity to thousands of investors. In addition to Wachovia, other settlements had come from Citigroup, UBS, Morgan Stanley, and JPMorgan Chase. It was a bright win for all those investors who had inundated the attorney general's office with flaming e-mails demanding to be made whole.

Lesson number one in the battle of digital torches and pitchforks: Complain Loud and Often. It had paid off. Not that the fight was over. Hundreds of billions of dollars remained frozen.

Wachovia had agreed to buy back auction-rate paper from all its retail clients, charities, and small businesses. The company would pay damages to investors who sold their securities for a loss in the secondary markets. Big corporate interests would have to wait in line until June 2009 for their payoff.

The victory, Cuomo said, "injects confidence into the entire market." He added, "The industry is now taking responsibility for correcting a problem they helped create, and we'll continue to make all investors whole."

He went on to thank the North American Securities Administrators Association's multistate task force and Missouri State Secretary Robin Carnahan, whose office had also been besieged by letters, e-mails, and phone calls from investors, for her "personal involvement." It felt good to have been among those voices.

Sandy was ecstatic when I gave her the news.

"I *knew* it, I *knew* it!" she exclaimed with the confidence of one whose prophecy has come to pass. All along she had nurtured a kind of dualistic point of view. In the beginning, she believed the situation would unwind on its own. Later, she transformed into fighting mode. "Who's got our money?" was her persistent cry. It was her rhetorical call to battle.

"So, we win," she said. "We win and they lose. What a relief." She was laughing now, and this time it was without a hint of cynicism. "I'm so, so happy. We can get back to our real lives."

We talked, excited, the long-held tension pouring out. The release of that tension was one of the greatest physical and emotional experiences of my life. The bitter gall evaporated in warm, pure truth. We were *free*—free to resume living with hope, free and unfettered to plan for the future. I felt like a kid starting over again, wiser now and more nimble. The entire world seemed to stretch out its warm inviting arms.

Sandy treated us to a fine dinner that evening. It was a delight. By the time coffee was poured to soften the effects of the bottle of wine we had consumed, she had a question I knew was coming my way.

"You could just walk away from all this mess," she began. "But will you? You've built up quite a following. A lot of people depend on you for information—and a little inspiration. Would it be right if you walked away now?"

I didn't need to reply. She knew in advance what my answer would be.

✳ ✳ ✳

It was an extraordinary victory, and it burnished Cuomo's political credentials to run for governor. Major banks and brokerages had been forced to give up their ARS game and repay investors. A great victory, indeed, though hardly a final one. Some $300 billion or more remained in the hands of various "downstream" brokers such as Charles Schwab, Raymond James, TD Ameritrade, and Oppenheimer, among others. These smaller firms would turn out to be ruthless defenders of their actions.

In the weeks ahead, I would find myself debating officials at the Securities Industry and Financial Markets Association (SIFMA). There had been talk at FINRA of "dinging" the records of brokers who sold ARS that were later redeemed in global (nationwide) settlements such as those engineered by Cuomo and Carnahan. The FINRA proposal would inscribe a permanent black mark on a broker's reputation, provided that a client had made a formal complaint against the broker or the firm that employed him. I thought it was pure political theater, a hollow show of accountability. But SIFMA was livid.

"They [FINRA] are making it a sin to have sold ARS," Andrew DeSouza, SIFMA's manager of global communications told me in a telephone interview. "The brokers weren't involved in settlements," he said. "Their companies handled it."

DeSouza became agitated when pushed on the details of what brokers *should* have known. Auction-rate bonds were a financial product like any other, he insisted. Investors should have done their homework. Brokers acted in good faith. "They didn't break the rules," he insisted.

DeSouza was paid to defend his base. I couldn't fault him for loyalty. But how did he know for sure that brokers didn't break any rules? Future developments—and the e-mails stacked in my office—would reveal a far more complicated set of facts: evidence of deception that might give pause to the staunch Mr. DeSouza.

For now, however, it was all hail Cuomo! A major tactical battle had been won. And furthermore, justice had reared its head in an unfamiliar setting: the swamp of Wall Street culture. Cuomo's victory represented a powerful assault against the ongoing fraud, and the broker-dealers knew it. Cuomo and Carnahan had fired the first volley. Their actions marked the end of the beginning.

* * *

A few days after the Cuomo announcement, I told Sandy I had decided to stay in the fight.

"That's wonderful," she cheered. "Wowie!"

I was speaking rapid-fire, like one of the speeded-up disclaimers you hear at the end of broadcast commercials. "I—I, uh, I'm racing," I jabbered. "I can't back out now."

I was psyched. No arbitration nightmare. I was free and soon we'd get our money back. Over the anxious months of waiting, I had kept the ARS matter secret from our two grown children. I didn't wish to complicate their lives. As the elder of the family, the one who is assumed to be wise, I wasn't about to hand our kids needless worry; they had their own challenges to deal with. In addition, I was reluctant to present an image of their father as a sucker who had fallen for a Wall Street con. Now, with redemption money soon to be in-hand (ironic word under the circumstances: redemption, implying forgiveness, or rebirth) it was possible to let them in on our dark little secret. They'd be surprised, but they'd learn from my mistake.

"Go on, tell them," Sandy urged. There was approval in her voice, the bright green eyes alive with the happy news and also a quiet pride. Sandy never really doubted we'd come out on top. "Let's celebrate," she said. "How about dinner at Tosca? On me."

"How about instead we just hang out at the house with a bottle of Perrier-Jouet," I countered. "Put on that Diana Krall album of yours."

"Sounds like a plan. Oh, and yeah, you're doing a good thing."

* * *

It would be an understatement to say I was feeling expansive. Not only did I buy the Perrier-Jouet Champagne, I also ordered in the best pizza in the city. Pizza and Champagne: the perfect oddball victory fare.

We danced. We sang. We finished the entire bottle. This is how it must feel to win the Pulitzer Prize. I wanted everyone to know how good I felt.

Bill Heyman phoned his congratulations. We had a long conversation, not a word of which I could recall the next day. It no longer mattered. The sleepless nights were over. I was free. Sandy and I would not go broke. Life would go on. And so would the fight.

Who knows, I said to Sandy, we might consider retiring. We'd buy a little boat and furnish good wine and gourmet finger food to the yachting crowd sailing through the Sir Francis Drake Channel in the U.S. Virgin Islands. The Caribbean would be our swimming hole. We'd get as far away as possible from the corruption of Washington and the greed of Wall Street. Start a new life or return to my former life as a journalist traveling the world and writing adventure stories.

The old daily oppression had vanished. Yet beneath the roar of our great good fortune, which the online warriors had worked to bring about, something less innocent was stirring. A sense of strangeness, a whisper of stubborn indignity; it nagged at the euphoria. It was almost imperceptible in the rush of victory, yet it was undeniably there, urging in a persistent voice. Was it the old anger—the passionate desire to win?

"This is so great," Sandy said, cutting into my inner narrative. "See? I knew it would work out."

"It didn't just work out. People made it happen. Cuomo's no saint. He wouldn't have acted without a radical push. You know, it's the old bit about the tree falling in the forest. If no one's there, does it make a sound? Well, we chopped down a hell of a lot of trees, and Cuomo was there to hear 'em fall."

Sandy gave me a high-five. We put on another CD and refilled our glasses. The unmistakable sounds of Miles Davis and John Coltrane filled the room.

"So it's over," Sandy said, speaking above the warm sound of the music. "What's next?" She was happy that I had decided to keep up the fight.

Next? Good question. I was at last free to write anything I wanted. How would I operate, and when would I get over the hump and call Harry Newton? His web site had the juice I needed to keep up the fight.

I don't recall what time it was when I finally crept upstairs to my office computer. Sandy was in bed. The house was silent. Flopping into the swivel chair, I reached over the desk and turned on the computer.

The Perrier-Jouet still had me floating on its gentle, disorienting cloud. I clicked on the e-mail icon. The screen filled with entries. Some were familiar, although the majority were from unknown sources.

There were congratulatory notes from many auction-rate warriors praising the attorney general. I answered every one of these e-mails with what I hoped was quiet satisfaction, all the while trying to keep from jumping up and shouting thanks to the heavens. I resisted the temptation to quote from the Old Testament book of Ecclesiastes regarding there being seasons for all things, good and evil. No. That would be too pompous. It's not a good idea to sermonize in the face of good fortune, even if you believe you've helped bring it about.

Not all the e-mails were congratulatory. There were other messages: messages telling me the battle was only beginning. The e-mail that really got my attention was a story written by Daisy Maxey and Jaime Levy Pessin of Dow Jones Newswires. The headline announced: "Advisor Alleges UBS Forced Resignation." The lead read as follows:

> New York (Dow Jones)—A financial advisor who sold millions in auction-rate securities to municipalities while working for UBS Investment Services Inc. has filed a federal whistle-blower complaint against the firm, alleging that he faced retaliation after cooperating with a Massachusetts investigation into the sales.

This was not a story to be ignored. It came from Daisy, in whom I had complete trust, and the rest of the tale reached in and touched my inner narrative, the RAHR that stirred below the surface. The story continued:

> In a complaint filed with the U.S. Department of Labor in mid-June, Timothy Flynn, a former senior vice president at UBS Financial Services, alleges that he had not been informed of the liquidity issues in the auction-rate marketplace, the UBS AG (UBS) unit locked him out of his office, preventing its staff from talking to him and ultimately suspended and prevented him from doing his job. Flynn, who, along with his team, has sold more than $30 million in auction-rate securities to Massachusetts towns and public clients since 2006, according to the complaint, resigned from UBS last week.

I printed the story and flicked open another e-mail. It read, in part:

I have seen some of your writing on the Internet about the
auction-rate problems. You published your e-mail address and
said you want to write a book about the problem, and so I am
writing to you in the hope you can use my story to break this
awful situation to the public. . . . I am 82 years old. I live alone
in Florida. . . . I am blind in one eye and have other illnesses. . . .
I cannot get by without my savings, which are frozen in auction-
rate preferred securities. . . . I have Social Security, thank God,
but not much else. . . . I sold most of my stock holdings last
year. I kept a few utilities for dividends. . . . The proceeds of
my stocks sales were supposed to go into my money market
but my broker said I'd be safe and get better returns from
the auction-rate preferreds. . . . I never heard of auction-rate
preferreds and asked him to explain. He said they were "floaters"
because the rates changed every week or so, and the yields were
better than money market funds. . . . I have known this broker for many years and trusted him when he told me the funds
were safe as cash and that I would be happy with more income
and nothing to worry about with regards to safety. . . . He said
the auction market was guaranteed by the government, like a
Treasury bond. . . . They were AAA, so I'd be fine. Now I can't
get my money. My broker refuses to talk with me so I am in
the dark. . . . I am wondering if there is any way you can help.
I cannot eat or sleep and I am fearful of my future. Do you
have any advice to help me out?

✳ ✳ ✳

I was still feeling the Perrier-Jouet. But when I reread the e-mail from
the Florida correspondent, a spike of anger pierced the Champagne
high. For the first time since February 14, I was free of the fear of loss.
Life had returned to normal. But anger was still alive. *What's wrong with
you? Take the win and walk* away, the inner voice urged, sensibly. In a few
short months, I'd have my money back, along with its piddling interest.
During the freeze, MOHELA had cut the interest rate on the bond to
near zero. I recalled worrying that the value of the bond would be

written down. This whittling away of value had occurred with other ARS bonds. I'd been lucky. The value of the MOHELA bond didn't decline. So why was I still raging?

When did we become captives of this parasitic force known as Wall Street? My business professor friend Bruce Freeman traced it to 1987, the beginning of the Savings and Loan scandal. It was at this point, he said, that Wall Street began to overwhelm the real, tangible economy.

Until and unless Wall Street was brought down to size, jobs would be lost, homes would be foreclosed upon, investors would be cheated, a dangerous oligarchy would take shape, and the country would suffer wounds that might require many generations to heal.

Again I read the e-mail from Florida. I shut down the computer. It was getting late. It occurred to me that I would need plenty of rest.

I slipped into bed beside Sandy. She was sleeping, her breathing barely audible. I touched her shoulder.

"Mmmm . . ." she mumbled.

"Are you awake?"

"Sort of . . . now."

I bit my lip. "I'm definitely going to keep at it," I whispered.

"It's late. Aren't you tired?"

I told her about the Florida correspondent. "I'm not going to stop. I'm going to put it in a book," I said. "I mean it."

"You're sure?" She was wide now wide awake.

"Yes."

"David and Goliath?"

"Hardly," I laughed. "You know the deal. The most honest thing a writer can do is write. And this is a story people need to know."

"I knew you'd say that. Now go to sleep. *Please.*"

Chapter 10

The Newton Factor

As I write, highly civilized human beings are flying overhead
trying to kill me.

—George Orwell, writing in 1944 for the BBC

Harry Newton's web site, the one Bill Heyman had called a
"gold mine," captured me at first sight. In a fraction of
a New York heartbeat, I was hooked.

"Auction Rate Preferreds.org" was emblazoned in thick black letters the size of a bullet against a blood-red background. And below
the banner, against a yellow stripe, was Harry Newton's declaration
of war:

"Auction Rate Preferred Securities is the largest fraud ever perpetuated by Wall Street on investors. It dwarfs all frauds in history, including
Madoff."

I read the sentence several times. It is impressive that someone involved in finance had written a clear, declarative sentence. I continued reading from the site:

"There are three takeaways from this fraud," Newton continued. "First, you can't believe anything—absolutely anything—that anyone on Wall Street tells you. Second, Wall Street is only interested in the fees it can extract from you. Third, Wall Street (i.e., its representative) has absolutely no interest in whether the item(s) it sells you has any long-term (or short-term) value whatsoever."

My instinct was that this declaration, this stick in the eye of the financiers, was written by a unique and savvy individual—a realist without fear.

I sensed that I had found an alter ego. Harry's web site was the perfect vehicle for my slog through ARS land. Everything and anything of importance, every news story and commentary concerning ARS, was memorialized on Harry's site. In effect, it was the complete editorial history of the scheming and scamming of 2 percent of national GDP. It was pure journalism. Taken as a whole, the stories read like Dashiell Hammett's *The Big Knockover*, although Hammett probably never envisioned a knockover of such magnitude.

Among the links attached to the site was Harry's daily column, which had nothing to do with the auction market. The column, "In Search of the Perfect Investment," (ISPI) was written from Harry's New York office in his Central Park West apartment. That he could easily afford to live on the East Side of the city, but didn't, also impressed me. (I confess I never delighted in the East Side's pretensions.)

ISPI focused on the broader markets and market trends. The column was written in clear, stand-up prose. In the financial world, where clear English narrative is virtually nonexistent, ISPI was an anomaly. I later learned that Harry, in an earlier life, was a fellow jour-nalist, an award-winning investigative reporter for his native *Australian Financial Review*, that nation's version of the *Wall Street Journal*.

His column steered clear of the hyperbole of the typical online financial pap. With a few exceptions, most financial web sites are sales gimmicks designed to lure the uninitiated into investment schemes promising quick, triple-digit returns—for a hefty fee. Harry's col-umn was devoid of hucksterism. It was concise, honest, spiked with

Chinese Candlestick charts, and nicely finished off with good jokes and cartoons from *The New Yorker*. Civilized. Honest. Amusing. Three attributes I much admired.

At the bottom of the column was a headshot of the author. Harry Newton appeared to be slender with a huge shock of silver hair and an expensive smile. (I would later learn that Harry and I shared a mutual attachment to dentists.) I have seen middle-aged actors on movie lots trying their best to imitate the same look of worldliness and healthy charm, but they were not quite up to the persona due to an overarching ego and insecurity that clouded their nip-tuck charisma.

Below the ISPI column was another link: "About Harry Newton." I clicked on it. There was the headshot again, along with a bio:

> Harry Newton, CEO
> Technology Investor.com
>
> Harry Newton is a leading figure in the development of the telecom industry and an early-stage investor and advisor in all areas of technology. Newton and his partner, Gerry Friesen, founded the key publications that shaped this industry: *Call Center*, *Telephony* (now *Communications Convergence*), *Imaging*, *LAN* (now *Network Magazine*), *Teleconnect*, and *Telecom Gear*. They also co-founded the immensely successful shows Call Center Demo and Computer Telephony Conference and Exposition, which attracted up to 26,000 people to the Los Angeles Convention Center. They also published over 40 books focusing on networking, imaging, telecom and computer telephony.
>
> Newton writes the best-selling *Newton's Telecom Dictionary: The Official Dictionary of Telecommunications, Networking and the Internet*, now in its 25th edition—1,273 pages and published most recently in June 2009. The dictionary now contains definitions for over 24,950 terms. It has sold over 770,000 copies.
>
> In September 1997 he sold his publishing empire to Miller Freeman (now CMP) for $130 million.

"One hundred and thirty million," I laughed, nervously. "Why, that's walking around money for a guy like me."

Sandy failed to see the humor in my self-deprecating remark.

"Oh, stop it," she said when she finished reading the bio. "Big deal. Approach him personally. He's your kind of guy." She moved closer to the computer screen, gave Harry a hard, quizzical look. "Yeah, call him," she said. Sandy is one of the best public relations and media professionals in the country. She is constantly in demand by politicians, movie stars, and author/big-dealers like Donald Trump. She leaned in again for a closer look at Harry's photo. "Perfect," she said. "It's a good match."

"Me? Doing business with a $130 million hell-raiser?"

"Jesus!" she snapped. "You've worked with billionaires. What's this 'aw shucks, little me' crap?"

This was not false modesty on my part. Yes, I had worked with billionaires like the great entrepreneur/land baron/inventor John Perry, of Perry Oceanographics, and Dr. Harold "Papa Flash" Edgerton of MIT, the inventor of stroboscopic photography and the 1973 recipient of the National Medal of Science. "Papa" had once shown me his pictures of milk splatters that looked like white crowns, bullets passing through apples, and stunning photos of the first atom bomb tests at the instant of detonation. The man was a genial, certified genius. One day, as Papa and I were tooling about Cambridge, Massachusetts, he stopped on a side street and opened the titanium briefcase he always carried around. Inside was $3 million in stock certificates. I stared, baffled by the sight of all that negotiable paper. When I looked up, I saw the strobe light atop the Prudential Tower flashing on the surface of the river. The strobe was placed there to honor Papa. I wondered if he had invested in Prudential. I later learned it was a clean, unencumbered tribute. No strings attached.

"Why are you carrying that stuff around, Papa?" I asked.

"Oh, heck," he chuckled. "Can't say for sure. I guess it just makes me feel better."

"Is that why you decided to show it to me?"

He looked toward the river, this elderly genius who had shown the world the bottom of the sea with his strobe lights, who had seen things most of us never imagine, had revealed a side of himself few people had ever experienced. "You got a kick out of seeing it, right? It's fun," he said. "It's just a bunch of paper anyway."

Over the years, I had done business with varieties of the rich and famous, thus my hesitancy regarding Harry had little to do with his relative wealth or power. Maybe on some level I associated him with Wall Street. But this couldn't be the reason. He was antiestablishment when it came the money-manipulating crowd. Maybe it was Harry's Australian background. An air of mystery clung to him like an other-worldly shroud. What kind of enigma was this? Maybe it was all in my head. Totally irrational.

There was good precedent for my hesitancy. For starters, I was no stranger to Aussie ways. I had toured the country and had sailed and crewed with Australians along the Great Barrier Reef and in the Coral Sea. Once, as a gag, the crew put me ashore on Flinders Reef, 200 miles off the nearest coast. To my amazement and utter horror, the zany Aussie crew then sailed away over the horizon. I had become an instant castaway.

Flinders is a tiny spit of sand in the middle of a shark-infested sea, a gleaming barren strip visited by the occasional booby and not much else. Many an explorer has perished there. At high tide the islet is awash. I had faith, of course, that my mates would return. I waited. And I waited. The tide had risen and was lapping against my ankles. I could see the sharks: dark shadows visible below the transparent waves washing ashore only a few yards away. I have experienced other adventures with Aussies in Indonesia, but being made a castaway on Flinders was an experience I will take with me to the grave.

Given these intense native high jinks, I knew in my gut that Harry Newton, aside from his wealth and power, was possessed of a particular brand of personal drive and a wicked sense of humor. Not a man to be taken lightly.

"Harry is exactly what you've been looking for," Sandy per-sisted. "He isn't going to strand you on Flinders." I stared at her. The light formed a halo around her hair and lit her face. Irresistibly, I was being coaxed in the right direction. Sandy knew exactly what she was doing.

She was right. I didn't know it yet, but Harry and I had much in common. Besides, his web site was *the* premier ARS news center and perfect for what I had in mind. He had launched the site March 27, 2008. He had not constructed it from a sense of pure altruism. He was, at the time, stuck with his own auction-rate problems. But now he was safe, liquid. Like me, he could have taken his money and walked. But for reasons unknown he continued to support the cause. It was important to find out why.

✻ ✻ ✻

The first story on the site gave me a clue to Harry's continued interest in ARS. The headline read: "My Personal Nightmare Is Over, but Yours May Not Be."

Harry Newton's nightmare amounted to $4.5 million in frozen auction-rate preferred paper.

"Nuveen got me out of some," he wrote. "Deutsche Bank got me out of the rest. Thank you, Andrew Cuomo, New York Attorney General."

So—Cuomo was our mutual hero. The New York AG was going after the big ARS sellers.

Another positive was that Harry and I shared a profession in common. He had made a fortune turning his journalism into a successful magazine business. You have to be a writer to understand what this means. My career consisted of more ink than cash, but I had lived a big life and did pretty well in the magazine and newspaper business. And like Harry, I had been in on the creation of several successful magazines. All I had to do now was pick up the phone and call. Still, some enigmatic counterforce held me back.

✻ ✻ ✻

Later that evening, I returned to Harry's web site and slowly scrolled through more of the entries. An almost endless procession of news articles and commentary scrolled down the screen. It was past midnight, and my eyes were starting to rebel. All the while, the headshot of Harry lingered in memory. *This guy is serious, serious business*, my inner voice reminded me. I hated to admit it, but Harry was slightly intimidating. It was most unusual for me to feel this way. I knew I had to connect with him. It was the sensible, positive next step. Just pick up the phone. . . .

And as I was about to do it, the thought of confronting Harry gave me a case of sweaty palms. It was driving me crazy.

What was behind the hesitancy? In the past I've suffered the sweaty palm syndrome, but only in the face of physical challenges, like heading up a team of journalists living under the Caribbean Sea for a week in Hydrolab, the United States' only underwater scientific outpost. Living in an 8-foot by 16-foot tube on the sea floor and being responsible for other lives is enough to make anyone sweat. Hurricanes also made me nervous, having lived through the 1979 killer blow named David as it tore through my billet on St. Croix. There were a few moments of sweaty anxiety when high winds threatened to fling me off a 4,000-foot-high volcano in Guadeloupe. And I still have vivid dreams of the time I was caught in a shark feeding frenzy in the waters off Moorea. One of my crew was attacked, her blood turning the water emerald green, and I thought for sure I was next. But meeting new people never caused sweaty palm syndrome. Not presidents, not Hollywood stars nor famous artists, and certainly not business types. People filled me with enthusiasm. Like an adolescent autograph hound, I always was eager to meet the most famous, controversial, or (sometimes) detestable characters. I felt at home with all of them.

Harry might have been intimidating, although everything else about him clicked. I reached for the phone. My hand froze. I needed to gain my composure. I gazed out of my window. The trees stood out, ancient, stately, and indestructible as the earth. There was a sense of the familiar mixed with an inexplicable strangeness in Harry's image—the crisp, Harvard-educated publishing whiz whose web site was a link to thousands of investors whose stories, whose trials and fears and hatreds, I would soon come to know in great detail. But first I needed to pick up the phone.

Damn it! It would have to wait. The nagging hesitation wouldn't let go. I couldn't afford to make one false or self-serving move. I had to convince him that I wanted to help others.

Finally I came to the end of the web site. There was another Harry headshot. The man in this photo wore a gray t-shirt that bore the words "Good Guy." This was not the official Harry of techno fame. The man in the Good Guy t-shirt was totally relaxed. An array of computer screens like mini-billboards lit up on a wide desk behind him, and beyond the screens, through a big picture window of his office, were the blurry outlines of apartments and condos along Central Park West.

Later, Sandy returned to my office and looked over my shoulder at the "good guy" image on the computer screen.

"Imagine that," said Sandy, smiling at Harry's headshot. "The t-shirt—'Good Guy.' It's the most obvious thing about him."

I wanted to believe she was right. *Good Guy*, I voiced silently. *Yeah, Harry Newton looks to be a mighty fine mate, good as gold.* I could not have imagined how much supercharged power he would bring to the fight.

✳ ✳ ✳

While contemplating when and how to approach Harry, I busied myself with figuring out—back-of-the-envelope fashion—how much the ARS situation, the withholding of 2 percent of GDP—was costing the country by way of jobs and productivity. This was hardly a rigorous academic exercise. There are scams that hurt a few hundred or a few thousand people. But 2 percent of GDP sitting frozen in bank vaults had to be punching a significant hole in the economy.

A reporter at *Bloomberg News*, Dunstan McNichol, calculated that the U.S. economy would enjoy a $63.5 billion boost if businesses were able to free up funds trapped in the ARS student loan segment of the moribund ARS market. McNichol wrote:

> Businesses haven't had access to about $25 billion in the auction-rate bonds since February 2008, when investment banks that managed the sales quit serving as buyers of last resort. Including student loan securities held by banks . . . [McNichol quoted Mark Murphy, a spokesman for SecondMarket Inc., a New York-based clearinghouse.]

If the federal government were to restructure the ARS market for these so-called SLARS (student loan auction rate securities), businesses holding the illiquid bonds might create as many as 441,000 jobs and begin expansion projects delayed for lack of credit, according to a report by University of Delaware economics professors James Butkiewicz and William Latham. The report was commissioned by 25 nonbank holders of SLARS pressing for federal intervention—essentially a federal bailout. Members of the coalition included retailers Abercrombie & Fitch; Family Dollar Stores Inc.; Digital River Inc.; Texas Instruments Inc.; Duke Energy Corp.; Standard Microsystems Inc.; Ash Grove Cement Co.; and Heartland Express Inc.

Further impact was seen when 205 publicly traded companies holding SLARS reported that 96 percent of them had marked down their value by an average of 12 percent, according to a study of regulatory filings by Pluris Valuation Advisors LLC.

These were serious financial numbers. I wondered how many jobs we could buy if the entire ARS market were to be made liquid.

* * *

On a street level, meanwhile, unfortunate events were occurring. Scams built on scams. ARS scams were breeding related scams. I thought of them as "compound injuries." Everyone on Wall Street knows how this inside game works. On a "sophisticated" level, one way of creating compound injuries is through the creation of financial bubbles that are designed to burst, often at predetermined levels. This model, or a variation, appeared to be at work in the auction-rate heist. This model was applied repeatedly in the 1990s during the infamous tech bubble. Firms with insanely high price-to-earnings ratios were sold to investors by those with inside knowledge that failure would soon follow the initial public offerings. The tech bubble, like the 2008–2009 real estate disaster, was a scheme made to take down what Wall Street insiders call "sucker money"—retail investors.

In 2008, the ARS scheme was giving rise to blatant "phishing" scams. Fake FINRA e-mails had begun to appear on computer screens across the country. Fraudsters promised compensation from phony settlements in exchange for personal information. These e-mails informed recipients of purported regulatory actions, including fines imposed by FINRA related to ARS. The phishing parties promised that the recipients were due $1.5 million, regardless of the amount of their ARS loss. Desperate people were taking the bait, handing out their personal information, which the scammers then used for all manner of illegal activity, including identity theft.

It wasn't until October 15, 2009, that FINRA acted to warn investors that phishing parties were cropping up everywhere. By that time, FINRA itself was under the microscope for its dumping of more than $647 million worth of ARS out of its portfolio in 2007, a clear indication that market insiders were aware the auction market was about to crash. Apparently this heads-up came from the very banks that supported

FINRA's operations. Unfortunately, the investing public was kept out of the loop.

FINRA in 2006 was headed by Mary Schapiro, now chairwoman of the SEC. Her salary was reported to be $3 million. The *Washington Post*, among other news outlets, reported that she was handed $7 million when she left to join the SEC in the Obama administration. It was also reported that the number of fraud cases handled by the Schapiro-led FINRA, and the subsequent collection of fines, had diminished by 30 percent, and 36 percent, respectively. Apparently FINRA was part of the problem.

The hero of this FINRA-ARS dumping scandal was an online warrior, Larry Doyle, a Wall Street veteran of 23 years who culminated his career as national sales manager for securitized products at JPMorgan Chase in 2006. He currently heads a web site called Sense on Cents. He had come on the blogging scene two years after Harry. Doyle's daily columns and his online show, *No Quarters Radio*, were gaining an authoritative presence.

Doyle and reporters at the *Wall Street Journal* had raised a host of issues regarding Schapiro's stewardship. In January 2009, Doyle wrote: "The main regulator of the financial industry [FINRA under Ms. Schapiro] happens to be an investor in securities which virtually every attorney general in the country is going after every Wall Street institution for improper marketing and distribution! Are we looking at gross negligence, ignorance, incompetence or all of the above?"

At this writing, Doyle's pointed questions remain unanswered. He continues to push. Along with Harry Newton he would prove to be a rough-and-tumble warrior against the dogs of Wall Street.

✼ ✼ ✼

In late August 2008, more than a week after reviewing Harry's web site, I was still a bit sweaty-palmed about picking up the phone and calling him. It was time for some serious soul searching.

I was setting myself up to become something of a partner in Harry's crusade. I was prepared to make a bold proposition. He was digitizing virtually every article and commentary written about the ARS situation and placing them online. He also had added a few of his own remarks, essentially informing those stuck in illiquid bonds what steps they needed to take in order to get their money back.

It wasn't terribly complex language. Harry dealt in simple, straightforward prose. He was the Prince of Declarative Sentences. His was a practical to-do list designed to help form a coalition of angry voices. It was Harry's intention to make these voices loud enough and sufficiently hot to scald the most elite of Wall Street's CEOs and foot-dragging state attorneys general. Harry did not gladly suffer whiners. His approach, which made perfect sense, was to stir up populist anger—energizing those burning digital pitchforks and torches.

This was—and remains—Harry's online call to arms:

1. You need to find each other and band together. Contact FINRA.
2. You need to do massive attorney general lobbying to get them involved.
3. You need to threaten to individually sue the broker/financial advisor who sold you your ARPS or ARS.
4. If you haven't the stomach for all this, you can try selling your ARPS or ARS on the secondary market. You won't get 100 percent of your money back. But it may be preferable to the ongoing aggravation and sleepless nights.

He added to this what he called "some general investing lessons I have learned." These were brutally frank truisms: Never trust brokers or financial advisors. Do your own due diligence. Remember the old adage, "When in doubt, stay out!" Don't chase yield. "Most people got into [ARS] because they were chasing yield, and their brokers were chasing a small commission." Wall Street's advertising says it cares about its clients long-term. The advertising and the sales pitches are "unmitigated horseshit," Harry insisted. What Wall Street cares about is making commissions. "Wall Street is a product machine—pure and simple. It makes things to sell to you. They don't care. End of story."

The Aussie was being an Aussie: blunt, smart, no sparing of the rod:

As I wrote this site, I met people who put their entire life savings into [ARS], thus violating the rule of diversification. Today the world is moving so fast . . . that you can't predict.

So to put all or most of your money into one thing—no matter how persuasive the arguments—is not the wisest deal. In fact, it's plain stupid. There is no free lunch.

*　*　*

My plan to write original investigative stories for Harry's web site had taken shape. By now I had dozens of sources. I spent hours each day, seven days a week, corresponding and responding, and working out what amounted to a digital lobbying force. I knew upfront this was a big commitment; once begun, there would be no backing out. As long as people were being robbed by bonus babies, I would be in the fight—and the fight would not be refereed by gentlemen and gentle ladies. No, this would be a throwback to the old days of the bare knuckle boxer-brawlers, when a knockdown counted as one round, and fights continued until one of the fighters was beaten and bloodied and unable to continue. I would be ruled by the Law of Jungle Journalism.

My opponents would be people for whom I had little respect, people whose sense of honor and self-worth was spelled out in the crudest form: *net worth*. There was plenty of anger and talent willing to pitch in. These were forceful, no-nonsense investors. You can't debate the worshippers of Ayn Rand. They are the Alan Greenspans, the Lloyd Blankfeins, the misogynistic Larry Summers, the T. Boone Pickens, and practically anyone who ever passed through the bloody tombs of Goldman Sachs, aptly described in the July 2009 edition of *Rolling Stone* by writer Matt Taibbi. In a wonderful article titled, "The Great American Bubble Machine," Taibbi took on the company with a rapier. "The world's most powerful investment bank is a giant squid wrapped around the face of humanity, relentlessly jamming its blood funnel into anything that smells like money," he wrote with merciless humor.

As if this weren't damning enough, Taibbi added: "In fact, the history of the recent financial crisis, which doubles as a history of the rapid decline and fall of the suddenly swindled-dry American empire, reads like a Who's Who of Goldman Sachs graduates."

This is hardly the kind of language one might find in the puffy, self-congratulatory columns of *Forbes*. Taibbi used the same language and attitude that popped out at me when I first read Harry Newton's web site. It was HarrySpeak. And I liked it.

I wanted to ask my friend Harwood Nichols if he thought I might be temperamentally up to approaching the ARS disaster as a *reasonably* objective journalist.

"You were burned," Harwood said. "Don't tell me you aren't pissed."

We were dining together in an upper northwest D.C. Italian café called Arucola. Harwood looked a bit incredulous as his picked through his pasta dish with knitted brow. I respected him as a disciplined thinker and debater and one of the few money men I could trust. He was an honest friend, and the first person I called on to explore a financial quandary.

"Sure," I said. "I'm pissed. I admit it."

"And still you think you're going to be objective? Gimme a break."

"I can try. Besides, facts have loud voices."

Harwood put down his fork and gave me one of his looks. It was the uncompromising stare of the seasoned Vietnam combat veteran, a man who had sat in foxholes as bullets whizzed past his head. He had seen his buddies fall in battle. It was the unique Harwood look that says more than words, an expression you can feel piercing the thickest armor of self-delusion.

I once told him that I reserved the right to debate markets with him. But when it came to combat, he could say anything and I'd accept it. He was suggesting that Harry's web site was a form of combat and I might have to play duck and cover.

"Yeah," he said quietly. "You know what you're doing. But I wonder, I just have to ask, are you sure you want to get into the weeds?"

At that moment a group of smiling women passed our table with a big, aromatic whoosh. One of them glanced at us and grimaced. Ouch! She obviously sensed right off that it would be no fun to be seated close to us. We must have looked like a solemn pair of political hacks. As the aroma of perfume swept over the table, I slid down in my seat. I felt like a Grinch, a Dickensian character. The perfume smelled nothing like money.

"Maybe this isn't a time to be cool," I said. "Maybe it's time for pushback."

"So you're back to being yourself," he said. "Are you going to call yourself Junk Hunter again?"

Junk Hunter was the name I used before Cuomo saved the day for me and brought my ARS nightmare to an end. I naively believed Wachovia would never figure out who this Junk Hunter character was, cropping up every day as a furious commentator on different blogs. When considering writing this book, I toyed with the idea of continuing on as the mysterious Junk Hunter. I had grown fond of the name. It had a certain revolutionary appeal.

"This book, or whatever," Harwood said. "You know, it may make you famous in ways you'd rather not be."

Though I didn't know it, Harwood had uttered prophecy.

In the end, I received Harwood's blessing. I left the café a few centimeters closer to making that sweaty palm telephone call to Sir Harry Newton.

Chapter 11

Harry the Hit Man

I'm doing God's work.
> —*Lloyd C. Blankfein, chairman, CEO Goldman Sachs,*
> *TimesofLondon.com, November 9, 2009*

I picked up the phone and dialed Harry Newton's office.

"Harry Newton," he answered in a gruff Australian accent. It was close to noon. He sounded busy. Impatient.

I introduced myself. It was an abbreviated version of who I was and why I had called him. Within seconds, my initial hesitation vanished. *This is it. You had better sell yourself in a big hurry and sound convincing*, the inner voice pressed.

"You want to contribute original stories to the web site?" Harry asked, incredulously. "We have very few of those, you know."

Yes, that was the point, I told him. I'm a journalist; a persistent type, I wanted to write investigative articles under my own byline.

There was a long pause. I heard a cell phone cheeping in the background. "I can add a lot to the site," I pressed.

"Are you stuck?" Harry wanted to know.

"Stuck? What do you mean?"

"In auction paper. Are you trying to write your way to liquidity?"

I laughed. Harry didn't expect laughter. "No, no," I said. "I'm out, 100 percent. Free and clear."

"Well then, you're taking on angel's work?"

"Do angels have fangs?"

By now, only minutes into the conversation, I realized I had no reason to be timid. No sweaty palms. I was at ease. I pictured Harry as I had seen him in his online headshot: The neatly trimmed mop of white hair, rimless glasses, eyes alert, keen, the expensive, worked-on smile. He sounded awfully busy. I wondered why, but this was a time to stick to the point. So much was at stake. This was my superhighway with all the off-ramps to other investors willing to join in the fight.

"Well, so," Harry went on. "How old are you?" I told him my age. "Oh, I see. We're both a few steps from the grave."

He meant it as a joke. Not a very appropriate joke. I recalled Flinders Reef. The Australian mates sailing out of sight. Harry was engaging in a bit of Australian elbow-poking. His remark pulled a hint of temper out of me. I don't find age jokes to be funny.

But snapping back would have been silly and self-defeating.

"Speak for yourself," I said. "I will dig up stories. Raise a lot of hell. Trust me, I have plenty of experience in that department."

I wondered if Harry was checking me out on Google as we spoke. I hoped so. If he did, he'd see dozens of my comments from the *New York Times* DealBook, Investment News, Seeking Alpha, and other web sites. He'd also find my publishing resume—40 years as a reporter, columnist, magazine feature writer and creator, and so forth. He'd know for sure he wasn't dealing with a disgruntled freak but rather someone like himself who had earned his living in the word trade.

"Look," he said. "Let's understand each other. You want to contribute to the web site. Fine. But I'll be the judge in the end." Pause. Perhaps Harry was waiting for a snappy comeback, some self-serving version of nobody-judges-me!—the sure sign of the amateur. Harry was the $130-million dollar man, not a dime of which had come easy.

And yet, like other ARS victims, he'd been caught up in the same freeze. Beneath the gruff exterior I could sense the man in the Good Guy t-shirt.

"What do you expect to accomplish?" Harry asked.

"*Force majeure*," I said. Fresh stories might gather a following, a determined group, carefully selected and vetted, willing to push the SEC, the state attorneys general, FINRA, the banks, the brokers— all the reptiles in the swamp. I had been there before, in different swamps, I went on. I loved investigative journalism that produced not just sensational insights; it was getting the action going that mattered most, the building of a coalition of dissenters willing to take the fight to the banks and brokerages. I was in search of more pissed-off people who had been robbed by the brokers in whom they had placed their trust. The web site was an excellent central information and strategy center. "I'll dig up the dirt," I promised. "I think I can make plenty of noise."

"My God, you actually want to help those *poor people*," Harry said. The way he said *poor people*—it stopped me cold. It was as if he couldn't believe what he was hearing. "You do, don't you?" he went on, his voice incredulous. But I could tell he was leaning my way. "They are poor people," he continued. "Really they are, and they don't know what to do."

"Right now, I get dozens of e-mails," I said. "I—we—can put this together on a bigger scale." Fortunately my computer screen was filled with e-mails as we spoke. "Here's why I think it'll work," I told him as I read the following e-mail out loud:

> I expect individuals to go bad. But an entire segment of the economy? With the cooperation of the government? Whatever separated us from acting like a third world despotic regime, that difference has frayed. . . . The ARS mess has had a devastating impact on me personally—not from loss of money but from loss of trust. Naively I believed people in financial institutions could be relied upon to behave responsibly. . . . I thought we had laws that required them to do so.

"Incredible," Harry sighed. He'd received plenty of e-mails from the disenchanted and none of it surprised him.

It was clear enough that a majority of those caught in the ARS fraud were at or near retirement age. Harry agreed. "They failed to realize that the banks have great brokers," he said. "When you have obscene amounts of money in the float, you'll have criminal activity." No point debating the "great brokers" remark. This wasn't the time to start a disagreement. I wanted to get a sense of Harry and I wanted to come off as the real thing—a person with genuinely good motives.

I read another e-mail:

> My broker said if I go to arbitration it'll take about four years. I'm 70 years old! I'm really glad you're pursuing this. It has appalled me from the beginning to see everyone turn away from this crime. I wish I could testify to the power of group action.

Harry was warming to the subject. We agreed that Congress was equally to blame for the financial meltdown the nation was experiencing. Wall Street and Congress are, in the end, inextricably bound together. I had excellent sources in both places, I told him. We agreed, too, that despite the cliché of a "mess in Washington," no other segment of our society is more dysfunctional, delusional, and sick with greed than Wall Street. Its culture, lack of accountability, its disdain for what the old philosophers called the "general good" was unmatched since Roman times. It was also the problem of the Street's disconnecting from the "real" economy. Wall Street was like a moon that had pulled away from Earth and viewed the mother planet as a separate entity to be exploited from a distance.

"You may find your e-mailers a bit more sheepish than you imagine," Harry suggested.

"Maybe. It hasn't been easy to find people willing to stick their necks out. We'll just have to see what develops."

The context in which this conversation took place was one of mounting financial chaos. It was the beginning of the "great recession." ARS had been a tip-off. Still, the conservatives who fretted over the perils of "moral hazard" would soon be jumping into the hazard pit with both feet. Our most reliable creditors and allies were becoming increasingly disturbed. It was clear that the trouble was about more than money. What was going on at Wall and Broad revealed not only corruption, but also a lack of discipline compounded by incompetence that had the rest of the world wondering what was going on. In the following year, during the March 2009 G-20 summit in London, French leader Nicolas Sarkozy pleaded for a means by which the West might fashion what he perceived to be a "civilized capitalism," an ethic that might guide us into the future and rescue capitalism from the vices that had grown on its organs like tumors.

"I want to be honest with you," I told Harry. "I really am Junk Hunter. Every morning when I turn on the computer, the screen howls in my face. ARS people screaming their heads off." It was painful, I explained. But it energized me, kept me going. There's a certain virtue in being able to listen, to empathize. "My aim is to shake it up," I said. "I want to help beat this monster."

"All right," Harry said. "Look here, I'm very busy. Send me something. If it works, I'll put it on the site."

"Thank you," I replied. "I'll do my best."

* * *

Harry's willingness to take a chance wasn't the most enthusiastic of endorsements. His was a let's-see-what-you've-got invitation; it struck me as more of a challenge than anything else.

There was still a good deal of preparation to be made before contributing editorial reports. Top among them was the gathering together of reliable sources—sources I could count on who were working on the inside. Most important, these sources had to be romanced, cajoled, and made to feel they could trust me. It was a familiar task, but a tedious one.

There was no way of building a financial news-producing Rolodex without the willingness of others to offer up sources—names, phone numbers, titles. Much of this was a slow job of enlisting the confidence and assistance of those whose e-mails swamped my computer. It was necessary to let them know what I intended to do. The goal was to fill in the gaps not covered by the mainstream media.

These gaps were a source of frustration for many ARS victims. Most of my correspondents, while grateful for occasional news coverage by the *New York Times*, the *Wall Street Journal* and a select group of online blogs were of the opinion that, for the most part, the mainstream press had abandoned them. My clear intention was to lead, not follow, in news gathering. It would also mean trading tips on stories with those I knew in the mainstream press. Daisy Maxey was among those with an ambitious and open mind. She was willing to follow strong leads on strong stories and give them a proper venue.

Regardless of how many stories I wrote, or the exclusive nature of the articles written for Harry's web site, exposure in the mainstream press was far-reaching and ultimately influential. Despite the digital revolution, people still respect print. I wanted to find stories the mainstream media would follow. If I didn't have all the answers, someone else would.

While many of the ARS victims were fighting mad at their seemingly intractable situation, it would take time to win their complete trust. Victims of financial crime are understandably skittish and reluctant to trust others. They fear having their names appear in print. Confidentiality is key. I had to promise not to reveal sources to anyone. This was not easy. I was dealing with all kinds of correspondents— ordinary investors, corporate types, attorneys on the tort side, and those who specialized in securities litigation. I was a virtual stranger to them, merely a name on a web site. The selling job had to be sincere and to the point.

"You're Junk Hunter? It's a made-up name. So how do I know you're telling the truth?" was a question frequently asked.

It was necessary to explain why I had assumed this pseudonym, having been warned by Bill Heyman that disclosure of my real name, along with indications of my market experience, would paint me as a sophisticated investor and ruin any chance I might have in FINRA arbitration. I no longer had to worry about that.

But other investors were still facing the possibility of arbitration. They knew that identifying themselves in print would work against them. Dozens of times it was necessary to explain the dangers of the process. FINRA arbitration is a bad comedy where the joke's on the investor. The lack of balance and FINRA's consumer-unfriendliness was to give birth to a bill in the Congress sponsored by the House Financial Services Committee, chaired by Barney Frank: The Investor Protection Act of 2009, HR 3817. The bill contains a section that seeks to restrict predispute arbitration agreements written into most brokerage account contracts. This special section was to become a pet project of mine.

At this writing, the proposed Investor Protection Act has yet to be passed, but chances are better than even that it will succeed—unless Wall Street buys its way out or acts on its own to correct the situation, the latter being unlikely. Investors are fed up with stacked decks and the humiliation and expense forced upon them by cold-calling, account-churning, stock-tip-hawking brokers who are allowed to get away with murder. The ARS scandal helped bring the congressional proposal to the surface, and it was one of the prime goals of Junk Hunter.

On November 11, 2009, Daisy Maxey sent me a story that cheered Wall Street and inflamed backers of HR 3817. Her story was headlined, "Citigroup Unit Wins in Major Auction-Rate Case." The news was that Citigroup Global Markets, Inc., walked away with $118.7 million in cash invested by Banco Industrial de Venezuela in auction-rate paper. "We're pleased with the decision," a Citigroup spokesman declared. The Miami agency of the Banco Industrial filed its claim in September 2008, asserting fraudulent and negligent misrepresentation, breach of fiduciary duty, and civil theft, among other infractions.

"What did you expect FINRA would do?" a Capitol Hill source lamented. The source hinted a possible political motive: a stick in the eye of Hugo Chavez, Venezuela's president. With the finding in the Banco Industrial de Venezuela case, it was now becoming clear that FINRA served not only the well-being of its financial sponsors, it also had a possible weapon against perceived enemies of the U.S. Hugh Chavez was not amused by the outcome of the case.

"It sets a terrible precedent," I responded, "and I'm no fan of Chavez."

"Sure," my source said. "You sound surprised—you who have been following this ARS business. It's FINRA, stupid. It's mama bear defending her young."

I wrote detailed commentary on the way and means of arbitration on a number of web sites. Correspondents were surprised to learn that Wall Street attorneys could seize computers and all other records in what they liked to call "vigorous defense" against the poor schmucks who showed up before the industry-slanted three-judge panel.

What I discovered rather quickly was that many of my correspondents were unaware of the anticonsumer bias of FINRA. They assumed the organization was somehow connected to the federal government, when, in fact, it was a supplicant to the banks. It appeared the word "regulatory" threw investors off, causing them to imagine a government link. Many didn't want to hear the truth. It was just too painful. Warning investors that their odds of winning were thin, at best, made me into the messenger of bad news, and some of those correspondents dropped off the radar.

It remained for the official media to publish a FINRA scorecard. Gretchen Morgenson, reporting in the November 8, 2009, edition of the *New York Times* revealed how determined FINRA was in its battle against consumers. In an article titled "A Way Out of the Deep Freeze," Morgenson wrote that nearly 500 ARS claims had been filed since the market freeze almost two years earlier. A total of 253 cases were still pending; 242 had been closed. Only 17 went all the way through the process. Of those, Morgenson wrote, investors won in four cases.

She also reported that 146 of the 242 closed cases were settled by the parties in dispute. She added: "Although the settlement terms aren't public, lawyers who have handled these cases say that such deals typically involve refunding much, if not all, of investors' money." This paints an overly rosy picture. It is stunning that so few claims were filed by a universe of 146,500 victims. We may never know what happened to the silent majority.

"So you're out to beat up on FINRA," one correspondent complained. He said I was being unfair in my attacks. But he was one of those who refused to believe the organization was a creature of the industry.

"Maybe," I said. "And maybe if we all work together, we can get it done." The moment I said it, I realized I sounded like a flake, an airhead idealist. But what the hell! All I was asking for was a chance to join in the fray, to get people's money returned, and to have some impact on the slanted FINRA playing field.

* * *

Through the winter of 2008 I was busy proving my bona fides to complete strangers. And I was making progress. There were contacts in Congress, in big corporations such as American Express, and among dozens of individual investors.

It was becoming clear that most of these contacts and sources were prepared to hand over names and phone numbers of their brokers. One thing they didn't want was having their names in print. I had to promise absolute confidentiality. This promise earned me an "in" at the New York Attorney General's office, thanks to a handful of disgruntled ARS victims who were big players on the periphery of Wall Street.

Copies of broker e-mails were coming my way from infuriated investors who continued to get the runaround. How ironic. The brokers and the banks, in their arrogance, were helping me along. Investors came to realize that what I was touting as "advocacy journalism" was a tool, a voice to be trusted. Feeding information to me began to appear a lot better than trying to deal with the individuals and institutions that had taken investors' money and destroyed their trust.

If they, or I, could peek into the future, these investors would understand that their trust in what I hoped to do was well placed. The banks would pull out all the stops to keep from redeeming ARS holders, and FINRA would play along. For instance, a day after Gretchen Morgenson's November 8, 2009, article, the online site Investment News, an outlet for industry professionals, announced with great triumph: "Smith Barney, Raymond James Victorious in Auction Rate Cases." It was a glowing report on how these brokers, before a three-member FINRA panel, "won major arbitration claims involving institutional and individual clients seeking tens of millions in restitution for the purchase of auction rate securities."

In the same report, Investment News crowed that a month earlier, FINRA had knocked down a claim from an investor who bought $10.7 million in ARS from a Raymond James broker in 2006 and 2007—this at a time when FINRA was on notice that the auction market was about to implode and quickly cleaned out its own ARS stash.

By the time the Investment News article and similar reports surfaced, I had gathered a small, vocal group of squeaky wheels who were in touch with others whose battles against the ARS problem was a daily ritual. There was, however, a growing realization that the grunt work would be left to a few tough-minded types willing to go up against the concerted powers. Frankly, I had hoped to enlist hundreds of active players, although the truth was that many had no clue how the game was played. Others, like the blind physician in Florida, were intimidated into silence. She wanted to tell her story but was afraid to have her name in print. Her broker and the company attorney had warned her to keep her mouth shut if she hoped to stand a chance in arbitration.

I kept telling people: "Read *The Godfather*. It's the best business book ever written. An MBA from Harvard pales by comparison."

"Jesus! It's about killers, fucking crooks. How can you make such a stupid remark?" one correspondent fumed. (Some others were equally miffed, though not quite as blunt in their assessment of my suggestion.)

It was simple. *The Godfather* told people what they had to do to stay on the right side of events. If they complied, good things happened. If they didn't do what was asked, bad things happened. Very bad things. The TARP bailout—the looting of the Treasury—was played by Godfather rules. Either the taxpayer did what the banks wanted them to do, that is, shell out nearly $800 billion without questioning how the money would be spent, or the financial system would come to a screeching halt. You don't need to have an MBA to get the gist of the threat.

Chapter 12

The Raymond James Caper

An insidious modern spy must be a combination of broadband surfer and vintage gumshoe.

—Handbook of Practical Spying

I t all began with an anonymous phone call.

"Are you Phil Trupp?" The caller spoke in a hushed voice.

"Yes, who are you?

"Can't give you my name. Not yet. But wait—don't hang up. I'm with a group of brokers, and we want to thank you for all you're doing."

What I was doing was churning out headline stories for Harry's web site. Harry was posting them and urging me on. Thankfully, the stories were attracting attention. E-mails were coming in from all around the country, along with a great many phone calls from ARS victims.

I asked who the caller worked for and wondered why he was speaking like a man who had someone on his tail. I let him know, gently, that I wasn't fond of anonymous telephone calls.

"I work at Raymond James," said the caller, referring to Raymond James Financial, Inc., headquartered in St. Petersburg, Florida. "We're hoping you can help us. We've got big trouble with auction rates."

Nothing new there, I figured. Yet the urgency in the caller's voice was intriguing. Maybe this was a new angle, a new twist to the story.

"We feel we can trust you, which is why I'm taking this chance," the caller said. "We have some unpleasant truths you might be interested in."

I was skeptical. Was this no-name disembodied voice trying to pull a fast one? In 2009, Raymond James was named best full-service broker for the second year in a row by *Smart Money* magazine. I knew little about the inner workings of the brokerage. My focus had been on the big banks. Still, how bad or unusual could the caller's problem be? ARS was trouble wherever it happened to be.

"The problem—it's ugly," the caller said.

I pushed. Why wouldn't the caller tell me his name? It was off-putting to be presented with a plea on one hand and two-sided rules on the other. The caller knew me, but I had no idea who was on the line. "I shouldn't be talking to you at all," I told him. "If you're afraid to say who you are, why should I listen to anything you have to say?"

The caller's voice rose. "*Please.* I'm sorry, but this is important. *Please.*"

If it's so important, why all the secrecy? Again I pressed for a name.

"You don't know these people. A whole bunch of us could be fired just for making this call. We're taking a chance," he said. He explained he was calling on behalf of a half-dozen Raymond James colleagues, brokers. He took a breath. "We have *documents.*"

"What kind of documents?"

"The ARS pitch handed out to Raymond James brokers."

Now the caller had my attention. I wanted to know if he had the real thing.

"The pitch? That's not news," I said, growing a little impatient. I wanted to play this fish my way. The basic pitch had been recited to me countless times by other brokers. I had never seen it in writing, of course, let alone on any bank or brokerage letterhead. Maybe the caller had the hard copy I was searching for.

RJ is trying to distance itself from the problem, the caller explained. "But they were in the game, and now we're caught in the middle." He said many RJ advisors were stuck holding auction paper in their own portfolios. As for their clients, "They are not happy."

"You're a broker. You're implying you didn't know the deal?" I shot back, leading him on. "You were selling and buying this stuff in the dark? That's kind of far fetched."

"Not really," the broker said. He claimed the RJ group he represented didn't understand how the auctions worked. The complexities were never explained. Risk was played down. Not that it's an excuse, he pleaded. "Our clients don't want excuses. They're walking out the door and they want their money."

"Imagine that."

"I want to send the documents to you," he went on. He said they would reveal the company's strategy. "Read them, and then the head of our group will call—if it's okay with you."

"Who's the head of your group?"

"Sorry. I can't tell you that," he replied. "She'll call you next week."

She? Now he had my attention. A female ringleader. You can't ignore that.

I was curious and miffed all at once. But I was willing to play the game. I had received countless anonymous calls from disenchanted brokers. They were invariably stingy when it came to putting their names behind their allegations. This guy was pulling the same stunt. But he was the first to offer real documents from a real brokerage.

The annoying no-name crap was another iteration of the cone of silence. Or was it simply another form of cowardice? This caller was proving once again that brokers are a timorous lot. They'd tell you all manner of stories about how they were duped by management. Ask them to back it up in print and it's no dice. Until now. If it weren't for the female ringleader angle and a chance to get my hands on company documents I might have hung up.

"Okay, send what you've got—FedEx." I had nothing to lose. Plus there was the possibility of getting my hands on a smoking gun.

"But no promises on this end," I insisted, careful to maintain proper distance. Beware of strangers bearing gifts.

"You're very patient. We'll get back you," the caller said.

I looked at my watch. "Fine," I said, careful not to show enthusiasm.

The caller was pleased. "You'll be helping a lot of us."

Well, Mr. No Name, I thought, that remains to be seen.

I didn't waste time tracing the call. I dialed star 69. The phone number was located nowhere near St. Petersburg. It was more than 1,000 miles away in Ohio. When I dialed there was no answer. I suspected it was a public telephone.

The call had come on a Friday morning. By the time I knocked off work for the day, the idea of obtaining a smoking gun, under any circumstances, had taken on an exciting edge. The anonymous caller might be a fake or a real mole. Whoever he was, his motive seemed obvious. He knew my style. If indeed he handed me solid, incriminating evidence, I'd use it.

* * *

By the end of 2008, I had written a number of stories for Harry's site. The articles were less than casual indictments of the banks and brokerages. They carried grabby headlines: "TD Ameritrade Founder Buys Chicago Cubs; Online Firm's ARS Clients Still Striking Out." "Oppenheimer Strains to Reassure ARS Clients but June Statement Fuels Pointed Skepticism." "Advice and Encouragement to Oppenheimer Victims," and others aimed at the less-than-altruistic heart of the financial-services industry. There were other sharp headlines aimed at the usual suspects. Raymond James had not yet raised a blip on my radar.

A little research over the weekend turned up an apologia to RJ clients by Thomas James, chairman and CEO of the company. It appeared in a January 9, 2009, article by Margie Manning in the *Tampa Bay Business Journal*.

"I apologize for being involved in your purchase of these securities," James said. "We will redeem all customer holdings prior to redeeming the [ARS] holdings of our employees."

It had all the earmarks of a genuine mea culpa. If so, it was a big one. RJ's clients were holding about $1 billion in illiquid bonds. How deep into the market were the RJ employees? Mr. James didn't say. Nor had Mr. James redeemed a dime of auction-rate paper.

The story underlined the clear motive behind the anonymous call. The caller made a point of saying clients were heading out of the door because of the ARS headache. This could not have made the brokers happy. More likely their unhappiness involved being stuck with frozen money in their own portfolios.

"You're entirely cynical," a friend said when I told him the story.

Entirely cynical? What kind of an indictment is that? *Entirely cynical* is probably the title of some long forgotten book about Wall Street trading practices. Here are a group of people whose modest ambition is to hold the whole world hostage. They dream up plots and counterplots, cons and super cons, Ponzi schemes and poisonous derivatives, dark pools of money and shadow banks. They succeeded in their hostage-taking plans—the hostages having been the American taxpayers. Aside from self-interest, nothing in the financial world is what it appears to be—save for the cynicism.

I called a friend and asked her to tell me everything she knew about RJ. She had never worked for the company, but her time in the business had provided a wealth of juicy inside stories. She was one of the best sleuths in the city.

"An old family firm," she reported. "They're huge in the St. Pete area. Can't find any big scandals there. No indiscretions that might wake up the local sheriff. Company's into sports sponsorship. A pillar of the community. White bread. White guys. Disgustingly upstanding."

The less white shoe side was Raymond James Stadium, the "Ray Jay," home of the Tampa Bay Buccaneers and the NCAA's South Florida Bulls football team.

A colleague in Tampa didn't have much to add. "The James family? Well, they're not exactly the Flaglers, of course. But they're getting there," he laughed.

* * *

The FedEx package arrived first thing Monday morning. It had been sent from an obscure address in St. Pete. The sender's name was an indecipherable scrawl. No clues on the shipping label. It was naïve to have expected more.

A thick package of material was inside the package, along with the following letter:

Dear Mr. Trupp:

We know you've been instrumental in helping solve the auction-rate securities disaster. We recently forwarded this information to the SEC.

Nothing has happened.

We need your help! The Raymond James investors need your help, too.

I will telephone your office Friday at 2 P.M. to see if we can furnish more information.

Thank you in advance.

Jones

There was another note, this one quite detailed, on Raymond James letterhead. It was dated March 11, 2009. It was a general appeal to Raymond James clients and contained emphatic allegations of corporate misconduct:

"My colleagues and I believe our firm, Raymond James, has acted in an illegal and unethical manner. We hope you will pressure the firm to fix this problem," the letter began. Before reading the long list of allegations, I skipped to the end. The letter, signed by a Ms. Jones, an alleged Raymond James branch manager, turned up the heat. But first Ms. Jones (who did not sign her last name) explained her bona fides:

"I am a Series 7 and Series 24 registered representative with 14 years experience in financial services. My clients are my friends. Raymond James has now brought tremendous hardship to them and thousands of other people."

The list of allegations by Ms. Jones was, by now, a familiar series of financial clichés. I'd heard them from countless ARS investors. There was the push to offload auction paper onto clients, regardless of suitability; descriptions of ARS as Triple-A in e-mails, booklets, and conference calls; assurances of liquidity; management allegedly dictating which ARS issues were to be pushed into client accounts; lack of a prospectus; an allegation that Raymond James management on February 1, 2008, on the eve of the market collapse, promoted the idea that many ARS issues remained "strong buys."

The most serious allegation was that the company's board of directors and the Chairman's Council were advised to sell their own auction paper holdings on or about February 1, by which time it was clear the market was headed into the tank. There were more allegations:

> The firm has lied, manipulated the truth, and threatened its own employees if any disclosure was made. . . . The firm has brazenly and repeatedly said it has no intention of resolving complaints unless forced to do so.
>
> On the last earnings conference call for stock analysts, Mr. Tom James, the CEO, said: "When it comes to auction rates, I am not worried about class-action lawsuits or the government. The regulators are engaging in extortion, pure and simple." [The replay of this call and its transcript are still available via the Internet.]
>
> This attitude is infuriating given the firm pushed auction rates onto financial advisors and clients. There was no natural demand for ARS until Raymond James created it.
>
> We hope you will bring enough pressure to bear on Raymond James to fix the auction-rate securities problems for our clients. These clients are not rich people. Some have medical bills, some have kids in college, and some could lose their homes. The firm is causing real hardship for investors—and real hostility.
>
> Indeed, our own firm has become our adversary. You seem to be the only hope of resolving this issue. We financial advisors share some of the blame with our firm. But the clients are completely innocent in all this. Yet, they are being made to pay.
>
> My colleagues and I must remain anonymous for now; sales supervisors made it clear they will fire anyone speaking to the press or regulators concerning ARS. But we will furnish whatever additional information or assistance we can.
>
> Ms. Jones, branch manager

Along with the letter were reams of documents dating back to November 15, 2006. Most of them touted the advantages of ARS over money market funds; essentially, they were detailed sales tools for use by the brokers.

My eyes crossed reading through the package of materials. It took a long time to get past the verbiage, at the end of which I was left waiting for a phone call from the mysterious Ms. Jones.

* * *

The call came exactly on time: noon. Monday. "Did you receive our package?" It was a woman's voice. I tried to guess her age. She was in her early 40s perhaps, but with a wisp of a younger woman's eagerness.

I acknowledged receipt of the materials. "You, I assume, are Ms. Jones," I said.

She said she was a manager of one of RJ's Florida branches. She didn't identify which one. It didn't matter; all the evidence of her group's claims was in the FedEx package, she insisted. The sales policy, the pitch, applied to all of RJ's brokers. They had apparently been deserted by management and left on their own to deal with the blowback.

"You must be very angry," I said.

"Yes, I'm angry," she said. "And sad. Do you think you can help us?"

She spoke quickly. I imagined her glancing over her shoulder now and again to make sure no one was listening. Was she calling from a phone booth? Was she being watched? The sound of her voice— hurried, breathy—betrayed her paranoia.

Ms. Jones and her compatriots had taken a few pages out of a John Le Carré novel. Perhaps Ms. Jones was the spy who wants to come in from the cold, although she was going about it the wrong way.

"Can't make any promises," I told her. The material needed to be vetted. It would be best to have some legal eyes scan it.

"We thought you'd be open to our problem," she said. "You sound awfully cautious."

"Well, I'm not hiding anything. You know who I am."

The lack of direct attribution was a problem she hadn't considered. It apparently hadn't occurred to her that she might be tying my hands. How could I tell for sure if someone, or some group of disenchanted clients, might be trying to whack the brokerage and leave me holding the bag?

"I can assure you that isn't the case," she replied. "What I'm telling you, and the documents—it's all true."

My mind was racing. If she were merely a disaffected investor she wouldn't be talking to me and sending documents to make the case. More likely, she'd be calling on the state attorney general or taking advice from a securities attorney. Taking the official route of filing complaints with regulators would force her to come clean and use her name, sign various sworn statements, and then hope against the odds to find another job in the industry. Brokers don't sue their employers and walk away without a stain. Landing a job at another financial-services outfit would be a little like trying to find diamonds in a coal bin.

"Come on," I said. "Tell me your name. No one will ever get it out of me. That's a promise."

"I'd like to, but I just can't."

"Then I can't make any promises."

"Understood," she said. "I do hope you'll reconsider helping us."

I looked at the stack of documents. My hunch was Ms. Jones was telling the truth. The papers were too detailed to be forgeries. Still, I wasn't ready to commit to anything in print. The material would be vetted and I'd check in with Harry for his take.

Attorneys were shown the documents. No one doubted their authenticity. As for the problem of direct attribution, I was reminded that Richard Nixon's presidency was wrecked in large part by an anonymous source whose name appeared in print only decades later. "Deep Throat," the shadowy informant who steered reporters Bob Woodward and Carl Bernstein into the bowels of the Watergate scandal, remained a secret until May 31, 2005, when *Vanity Fair* revealed that former FBI agent William Mark Felt Sr. was the mysterious source behind the reporters' investigative tour de force for the *Washington Post*.

About a week later, and after review by others, I decided to go with the story. Harry agreed. It appeared on Harry's site in mid-March, 2009:

Insurgent FAs at Raymond James Stage Revolt; Reveal Company's Tactic to Push Auction Rate Securities

By Phil Trupp

Washington, D.C., March 17—A group of irate Raymond James financial advisors have turned to insurgency, charging the firm and its board of directors "lied, manipulated the truth, and threatened employees" if disclosure of the company's policy regarding the sale of auction-rate securities was made public.

The company's board first discussed the liquidity problems of auction-rate securities in October 2007, but failed to alert its clients or brokers, according to documents and e-mails made available exclusively to AuctionRatePreferreds .org. The Raymond James FAs said their firm "aggressively pushed ARS onto both financial advisors and clients without regard to client suitability," describing the securities as "AAA and totally safe" in company e-mails, booklets, and on conference calls.

Sources said the company, while using the typical sales pitch of ARS liquidity and safety, "just like mutual funds," dictated which ARS issues would be placed in client accounts, "without consulting FAs or clients." The company failed to provide a prospectus to its FAs or clients, these sources said. When the market collapsed in February 2008, the firm told its brokers and clients, "You should have read the prospectus," according to company sources.

As late as February 1, 2008, Raymond James warned its FAs to avoid purchases of Nicholas Applegate, but said "other ARS are still strong buys," according to an internal memo. The insurgent FAs, many of whom are left holding frozen ARS, said the February 1 message was followed by a notice to certain board members and the Chairman's Council to sell their ARS holdings.

Referring to the research analysts, the FAs said their effort was "minimal."

"The firm has brazenly and repeatedly said it has no intention of resolving complaints unless forced to do so," these sources said, adding: "On the last earnings conference call for stock analysts, Mr. Thomas James said, 'When it comes to auction rates, I am not worried about class-action lawsuits or the government. The regulators are engaging in extortion, pure and simple.'"

AuctionRatePreferreds.org received more than 150 e-mails from aggrieved FAs.

The purpose of the supporting materials, they said, was to demonstrate "how vigorously the firm sold ARS as liquid cash equivalents, both to financial advisors and to clients."

The FAs complained there was no "natural demand" for ARS "until Raymond James created it."

They said their clients are not wealthy people. "Some have medical bills, some have kids in college, and some could lose their homes," the FAs explained. "The firm is causing real hardship for investors—and real hostility."

✳ ✳ ✳

Several class-action attorneys were in touch after the story appeared online. They wanted to see the documents for possible use in ongoing complaints against Raymond James. By now, I was used to phone calls from curious lawyers seeking details of the various stories appearing on Harry's blog. Copies were made of the RJ documents and sent to those who wanted to peruse them. It was routine.

Not long afterward, in July 2009, I signed a contract to write this book. My role as a conduit took a backseat to full-time editorial duties. The RJ caper slipped out of sight for six months.

Attorney Aaron M. Sheanin, of Girard Gibbs LLP in San Francisco, was among the first to request copies of the RJ papers. His firm was pursuing a class-action case against the company and needed additional information to file an amended complaint. I phoned Sheanin in January 2010 to see how the case was going.

The amended complaint was still under consideration by the judge, he said.

"Raymond James is claiming they had no knowledge of any reckless conduct" in the sale of auction-rate paper, Sheanin explained. "They pose themselves as a small player and didn't know how the market functioned. This really defies logic," he added. "I think the court smells a fraud here."

What about the documents and the RJ people who contacted me?

The papers were helpful, Sheanin said. Then came something unexpected. "The people who contacted you contacted us. They're for real." So real, in fact, that they were providing additional documentation. Sheanin said the combination of the documents and what they told Girard Gibbs "makes a very strong case."

"Are they part of the class action?" I wondered.

"No. They're offering the information for the benefit of other investors. We see them as 'inside informants.' Officially, they're confidential witnesses—CWs."

There are four RJ confidential witnesses. "And yes, they're scared," Sheanin explained. One of them is a branch manager, as initially advertised in the anonymous call to me. Apparently she is the mystery woman, "Ms. Jones."

I asked Sheanin to forecast the outcome of the case.

"To just get in the door, the court wants you to present just about enough evidence to make the case. The bar is very high in securities cases," he said. "The court wants chapter and verse before they'll show a pulse."

Does this mean the court system is set up to favor the banks?

"Congress did it," Sheanin told me. He was referring to the Private Securities Litigation Reform Act of 1995 (PSLRA). This piece of tangled law was developed as part of Newt Gingrich's "Contract with America." On its surface the legislation was designed to reduce frivolous cases filed in federal courts. It was part of the never-ending war against legal representation. Hardly lawyer-friendly, it mandates that investors can't move ahead with a case "without having evidence in hand that strongly suggests deliberate fraud," Sheanin added. In financial cases attorneys need to present a set of facts that are proof-positive before their plaintiffs can get a fair hearing.

The act was passed over former President Bill Clinton's veto. Every Republican in the House of Representatives voted for PSLRA. Only four Republicans in the Senate voted against it. One of the major sponsors in the House was then-representative Christopher Cox, the very same burned-out legislator who wound up as head of the SEC in a deal described by Radioactive Man in Chapter 7.

"The RJ informants are very real. They're sort of acting as angels," Sheanin said.

"Okay," I said. "Will you tell the angels something for me?"

"Sure," Sheanin said.

"Tell them I think they're cowards. Tell them I believe their story, which we've both vetted and verified. But they need a lesson in honor. I don't give a damn if they are angels. They're clueless angels. They owe me a phone call, and they owe me a name."

"Okay," Sheanin said. "I'll tell them."

As any mystery writer knows, exciting beginnings sometimes wind up in long, drawn-out denouements. It may be a long time before the "Raymond James Caper" is buttoned up. In the meantime, I'll be waiting for that telephone call.

Chapter 13

What's It All About, Barney?

At issue is the human mind, which has to be shocked, seduced, or otherwise provoked out of its habitual stupor.
—*E.L. Doctorow,* Creationists: Selected Essays

I had to dig up a good story, one that would show that Harry's web site was expanding into the realm of political clout. The site reprinted virtually all ARS news articles, as well as opinion pieces. What it needed was something truly original, a story geared to the exact needs of our audience.

This was a turning point. If we were ever going to find a group of like-minded investors, this was our moment, and Harry's web site was our instrument of mass money recovery.

My first chance to find congressional insiders willing to talk came in the wake of the September 18, 2008, hearings on the ARS situation held by Rep. Barney Frank's Committee on Financial Services. But I would have to chase down this insider for all I was worth. Attendance at the hearing would guarantee little more than a news story. What I needed was someone willing to provide insight—not hype, not political convenience-speak, but a clear, objective voice. Fortunately the hearing provided an opening.

The auction-rate session was held at the Rayburn House Office Building on a brisk autumn day—sunny and cloudless in that mid-Atlantic way that makes all things seem possible. The gold- and red-tinged leaves stood out splendidly against the scrubbed autumn sky. On days such as this it's easy to forget Washington is built on a foundation of political sausage-making. The pleasant illusion swept clean doesn't carry a long shelf life, but it's pleasant while it lasts.

Hearing Room 2128 was practically devoid of spectators. *How can the freezing up of 2 percent of GDP be of so little public concern?* The apparent lack of public knowledge should not have been surprising. ARS wasn't exactly a household acronym. The middle American economy was shedding jobs, homes, futures. ARS represented 146,500 investors: not an inconsiderable number, but small compared to the nationwide financial dislocation caused by an administration and a Congress that hated any form of regulation. Americans sitting around the kitchen table were worried about losing their homes and jobs. They had little time to focus on the intricacies of Washington's tacit cabal with bankers more than willing to take advantage of Washington's indifference to arcane forms of robbery. Who has time to ponder the ARS problem when you're one paycheck away from homelessness?

I watched the proceedings on C-SPAN. I chose to do this because it gave me the option to stop the action or to go back, as needed, to make sure what I was hearing was correct. It also allowed me to make accurate notes and check out the visuals presented by the committee and the witnesses. It might be argued that real-time observation is a better way to go. But I have covered countless hearings in person, and all I can say is thank goodness for C-SPAN. The digital forum allows a reporter to keep the pace and often enough get ahead of the action.

Many of the witnesses who were prepared to testify before the committee appeared eager and ready; others, not so much. The SEC witnesses appeared antsy and sat at the front of the room fidgeting with papers.

The subject of the hearing was: "Auction-Rate Securities Market: A Review of Problems and Potential Resolutions." The witnesses shifted nervously, shuffling their prepared statements, muttering to one another as the committee members took their places on the raised platform. I recalled how these hearing rooms give off the mixed aroma of very old paper and fresh disinfectant. This was something else I didn't miss. What would a visitor from the heartland think of this place? Would the visitor feel welcome in this vast space with its cast of hardball players: slick, well-known politicians; lobbyists whose pricey outfits would make Sarah Palin blanch; administrative assistants scurrying about like ROTC students preparing four-square bedsheets for morning inspection. Would a visitor know where to sit? Or have any idea what the hearing was about? A newcomer from the heartland would be on his own, left to challenge a political jungle with the skills of rugged individualism. It was hardly a fair match.

Barney Frank walked in holding a sheaf of papers that looked like a collection of telephone directories. As usual, he was several minutes late. There is probably no busier elected official in Washington than Rep. Frank. Everyone, it seems, wants an audience with Barney. They should be careful what they wish for. The congressman from Massachusetts is notoriously impatient. His attention span is counted in seconds, not minutes, and he wields a quick, killer sarcasm.

He appeared rumpled and distracted, like a man who had just been awakened and handed a number of conflicting missions, all of which were of equal weight and needed instant attention. It was said of him that no matter how cluttered his agenda, he would find a way to get through the mountain of business in front of him, pit bull style. Barney Frank is known to snap at anyone he believes is wasting his time. "People ask a lot of dumb questions," he remarked famously during a CNBC interview. For a man who can be extremely witty ("That's right," he once told a reporter back in the 1980s when he came to Washington from Massachusetts, "I'm the only gay, Jewish, left-handed congressman in town!")

"I apologize for being a little late," he began, sliding into the chairman's seat. "Can we get the door closed back there?"

He went on to explain that the committee had a vast agenda of problems to confront, in addition to ARS. He and the members were facing an economic meltdown, and the committee's mission was to "diminish the likelihood of this happening again."

Frank allowed himself a few subtle swipes at the Bush administration (no one even smiled). These were serious times. Wall Street was clearly in control of Washington—Henry "Hank" Paulson, the Treasury chief, handling the economic joy stick. The money *machers* were in control of most everything. Pillaging the economy of the Western World was a job for financial savant control freaks with other people's money to gamble. There was a sense that the committee members knew who was calling the shots, and the members were doing their best to avoid even the smallest appearance of culpability. Many had received substantial campaign contributions from the banking sector, although to see them seated in their respective high-backed leather seats, looking brisk as the autumn morning, an uninitiated observer might believe these elected officials were twenty-first-century incarnations of Diogenes seeking honesty with no taint of unsightly political reality.

Rep. Spencer Bachus, the Alabama Republican, was the first to follow Frank's introduction. The first thing he did was praise Linda Thomsen, then-director of the SEC's Division of Enforcement. She had cracked down and issued tough language on the abusive short selling that was sucking the lifeblood out of the equity markets. Thomsen, a scholarly looking woman with a slightly hesitant voice, had harsh things to say about the shorts—never mind that her condemnation was years overdue. The damage had already inflicted a bloody setback for the equity markets. Bachus, giving her a thumbs-up, rambled on about the obvious:

"I think it [shorting] has weakened a lot of our financial institutions that probably would have survived had it not been for those abusive practices, because as short sellers often acting in concert with each other. . . ." The rest was a long-winded and discouraging recitation of what everyone already knew. I was thinking, *Mr. Bachus, what took you so long to see a problem that was so obvious that even Jim Cramer had to speak up about it?*

From the start of Bachus' homage to Thomsen, who later would resign her SEC post under what some in Washington alleged were twin clouds of industry favoritism mixed with a pinch of incompetence, it was clear that any real news might be difficult to extract from the bonfire of political posturing. I was wrong about that part. Much solid information would be placed before the committee, albeit occasionally hedged by a certain defensiveness on the part of the regulators.

"I have compared these packs of short sellers to jackals," Bachus said, possibly waiting for applause from the meager gathering of observers. I kept wondering when he'd get around to the subject of the meeting: ARS. When at last he did get around to it, he called the now-illiquid bond market a "roach motel" (laughter all around). Bachus continued: "As we deal with the stability of our financial markets, a large component of that is going to be the auction-rate securities market, and I do believe that is one area where we are making real progress, and it is beginning to resolve itself."

Within the first 15 minutes of the hearing, it was clear some of the committee members had no real grasp of the ARS situation. Bachus' remarks were the first clear indication of cluelessness. A few members estimated the total of frozen auction-rate cash was $160 billion; the actual figure was more than twice as much. Rep. Carolyn Mahoney, the New York Democrat, pointed out that four years earlier, former SEC Chairman Arthur Levitt had warned of problems in the auction markets. Why didn't anyone listen?

"What becomes clear," Rep. Mahoney continued, "is that too many issuers were left in the dark. Many had no independent advisors. And those that did not hire advisors often found themselves receiving advice from parties that were conflicted since these advisors also worked as bankers in the auction securities market.

"He [Mr. Levitt] also reminds us that problems in these markets have been known for at least four years as a result of an SEC investigation into the broader market in 2004 and 2008, and that a lawsuit by the Massachusetts Secretary of State revealed that going back to 2006, nearly 85 percent of the auction[s] would have failed."

Now we were getting somewhere. Massachusetts Secretary of State William Galvin was solemn, almost grave in a less-than-flashy gray suit, white shirt, and dark tie. He had the look of a man who knew the story from beginning to end and had adroitly placed the denouement beneath the pile of papers in front of him on the witness table. Now he waited with strained reserve to reveal the backstory.

The question that stood out was why the market froze all at once in February, this despite internal problems that had been known for years? This was the dark heart of the mystery. I wondered if anyone, congresspersons or witnesses, would come up with a clear and simple answer to this market failure. How and why the crash occurred: This was my central point of focus.

Rep. Randy Neugebauer, a Texas Republican, took off on a disjointed statement about student loans—a subject of particular interest to the situation I faced with Wachovia. While he touted the importance of creating a viable market for student loans, the gentleman from Texas wanted to place his economic views, his philosophy, on the public record: "I'm not a big-market interventionist from the federal government," he said with a kind of spirited Texas twang. "Maybe the best thing for us is to get out of the way and let the markets start functioning again."

Georgia Democrat David Scott jumped in with a counterattack:

"I hear a lot of discussion on the other side about getting out of the way and letting the markets take care of themselves," he began, leaning into the microphone. "We have learned that is absolutely the wrong thing for us to do. If anything, we need to get in the way, and we need to get in the way quickly, because this is not just a problem in the United States anymore. This is a worldwide problem. Our prestige as financial leader of the free world is at stake. . . . As we responded to the Savings and Loan crisis in 1984, I believe, so this is a very serious issue."

Scott was just getting heated up when his time began to run out. He was straining to get in his last words:

"Could more have been done to assess, to anticipate, and, further, to have prevented the auction-rate mess? Were investment firms and broker-dealers well aware that the ARS market bubble was about to burst? There's a lot of culpability here—the nature of the auction settlements—the role of the auction manager—"

His time ran out in midsentence.

Christopher Shays, the Connecticut Republican, pointed out that 19 of the top 100 student loan lenders had jumped ship and no longer were in the student loan business. (Others have since given up, making student loans hard to get and very expensive. The Obama administration has recently moved to eliminate student loan middlemen and has proposed loans be made directly by the federal government.)

I looked at my watch. Nearly an hour had passed. Barney Frank called an end to the series of statements by committee members. He was eager to hear from the witnesses. Meanwhile, I was still hoping to get a sense of how the market collapsed so quickly and with such a bang. *Who engineered this setup and made it appear to be simple coincidence?*

✳ ✳ ✳

Chairman Frank set the tone for the round of witness testimony:

"We have had debates . . . over whether or not there should be a preemption at the federal level of the role that the states play in securities law," he began. "And anyone who wanted some evidence that it would be a mistake to wipe out the state role or substantially diminish it can look at the history of this issue, because it has been at the state level that we have seen from my own state of Massachusetts, from New York, and elsewhere . . . that in a number of states it has been the state securities officials and law enforcement officials who have taken the lead."

Frank then called on Linda Thomsen to act as the lead-off witness. It was immediately apparent that this soft-spoken bureaucrat, charged with facing down some of the administration's most egregious con men (while letting Bernard Madoff off the hook after numerous warnings about his $65 billion Ponzi scheme) was not exactly comfortable in the charged environment of the hearing room.

Thomsen was aware that the SEC under Chairman Christopher Cox had become something of a joke. The agency was regularly accused of neglect of duty and philosophical posturing over the joys of deregulation, all in the name of a free market that attracted sizeable campaign contributions from right-wing ideologues. This is not to say the lefties were innocent. Like the right-wingers, the Democrats and the liberals were, by and large, well-acquainted with Wall Street largess. The well was poisoned top to bottom. But Thomsen, apparently fighting an uphill struggle against the passivity of Cox, was not to be deterred by the low esteem in which her commission was held. A year later, she would be asked to leave the SEC. But now she was fully prepared to make a case that the commission, led by a man whose hands-off philosophy was helping defeat capitalism itself, was up to the task of making the ARS players come clean.

In a small but clear voice she explained that the ARS debacle was the result of a "variety of reasons, including the subprime mortgage and credit crisis unfolding throughout the second half of 2007."

Her confidence rose. "The Division of Enforcement began investigating, and deployed tremendous resources to the effort," she went on. In March 2008, after receiving more than 1,000 investor complaints, the division interviewed 26 broker-dealer firms. Investors were likewise interviewed, "including employees and broker-dealers and issuers. We established a dedicated e-mail box to receive investor complaints," Thomsen told the committee. She spoke of these actions as if they were something special when, in reality, such oversight was part of the law that created the SEC. None of these actions added up to much.

The committee members listened politely, shuffled papers, and whispered to one another while Thomsen continued her testimony. Seeing this, Thomsen raised her voice. She was not going to be ignored.

She alleged that Citigroup and UBS "made misrepresentations and omissions" to their customers when pushing ARS. No news there. What she handed up as revelatory disclosure was by now yesterday's news. It was already known that these two huge ARS sellers were madly shoveling auction junk into the portfolios of trusting clients before the market imploded. The firms later settled the complaints filed against them, without admitting or denying guilt—another get-off-the-hook charade by which regulators allowed the banks to pay chump change fines with investor dollars and walk away with a clean record. Citigroup and UBS walked away with slaps on the wrist, while the down-and-out schmuck who might steal a box of doughnuts from a convenience store would be facing jail time.

"The agreements in principle with UBS and Citigroup established a general framework for other settlements," Thomsen said. "It was [Massachusetts] Secretary Galvin who filed the first suit with respect to auction-rate securities."

This was more old news. Every investor who followed the ARS situation knew these basics. Why was Thomsen taking up valuable time paraphrasing stale headlines? Her presentation would not go down well with certain of the committee members, and the subsequent Q&A would become heated.

It was discouraging to hear Thomsen assert that the settlements would provide a mechanism through FINRA for investors to participate in what she called "a special arbitration process" to seek "consequential damages," the latter being costs incurred after the initial investor fleecing on the secondary market and efforts to recover the par value of ARS in a subsequent expensive legal action.

Given FINRA's anticonsumer bias, Thomsen's final remark practically sucked the air out of the hearing room.

Next to testify was Susan Merrill, FINRA's executive vice president and chief of enforcement. One of the first things she emphasized was FINRA's determination to "hold industry participants accountable and provide investors with real and tangible relief."

Someone at the back of the room issued a hollow cough. Or was it a guffaw? The TV camera briefly swung around to reveal a small group of well-dressed, middle-aged men and women seated near the back wall. The sound came from someone in this group, who I presumed to be ARS victims. I wondered what they made of these high-sounding promises by Merrill and Thomsen. These people might have something real to say—something less politically correct than the clichés handed out by Merrill and Thomsen.

Merrill was prepared to dazzle the committee with numbers. FINRA, she said, had sent sweep letters to 2,000 firms asking about their involvement in the auction market. The letters were sent in April 2008. More letters were sent during the summer. Fifty-three staff members conducted on-site examinations at more than 32 firms in over a dozen states.

"On-site examinations are continuing as we sit here today," Merrill said with a shade of cops and robbers drama.

Can FINRA be tough? Oh, you betcha, Merrill assured the committee members:

"In August, FINRA announced special arbitration procedures," she said. "Under these procedures, individuals who have worked for a firm that sold auction-rate securities since January 2005 will not be eligible to serve as arbitrators."

Talk about tossing a bone to the starving! Once again the TV camera flashed on the group seated against the wall. They were as stone-faced as statues under assault by a flock of overstuffed pigeons.

✳ ✳ ✳

The star of the show, William Francis Galvin, Massachusetts state secretary and chief securities regulator, quickly punched the button that activated his microphone. He was introduced by Chairman Frank as "the real leader in efforts to provide protection here, and, incidentally, a former legislative colleague."

There was some banter between the two men and some laughter. It would be the last laughter heard in the hearing room for a long time. A slightly built man with an oversized sense of righteous outrage, Galvin has a long history of tangling with financial bandits. He has the surface calm of a clergyman, though below the surface he is quick and testy, and the bad guys he goes after are never the same again when he gets through with them.

"I am here today to discuss our findings and investigations into UBS and Merrill Lynch sales of auction-rate securities," Galvin began, softly. His understated demeanor didn't last long. He continued in a clipped, almost angry tone. "I feel compelled to say at the outset that there is a much larger issue here, and that is this: The auction-rate securities scandal is just one more variation on a reoccurring theme that we have seen before."

There was another pause. Galvin, who is considered to be too intelligent to allow Wall Street to lure him into its cult, was an expert at making effective points, and he was proving his talent once again. His lifted his gaze from his prepared remarks and let his eyes roam over the panel of legislators.

"And that theme is the documented belief of large segments of the financial services industry that they are above the law," he said forcefully. "They [believe] they are entitled to special privileges, entitled to engage in conflicts of interest, and have no duty or obligation to average investors."

A smattering of applause arose from the group of observers. Chairman Frank shot a hot glace at them. The room fell dead silent. Galvin continued:

"Without stricter regulation and sustained and diligent enforcement, this theme will again emerge. Specifically, five basic facts, I believe, arise from the auction-rate debacle. They are: Conflicts of interest need to be more aggressively monitored and disclosed to investors with real and tangible relief; financial advisor incentives need to be disclosed;

financial advisor training needs to be enhanced; supposedly objective research reports need to be more tightly regulated; self-regulation is not effective to prevent a scandal such as this one; and state regulators, in conjunction with their federal counterparts, need to continue to be actively involved in enforcement actions."

After another pause to allow his message to sink in, he offered what amounted to heresy to Wall Street's lobby, the American Bankers Association, and others who serve an industry that has ripped the guts out of the United States economy and brought misery to the global markets.

"Government intervention," said Galvin, "is more effective when it monitors aggregate risk-taking and prevents bubbles from building instead of having to bail out the parties after the bubble has burst."

It was a truth everyone knew. The difference was that Galvin was plain-spoken about it. The industry, enabled by deregulation flag wavers such as Larry Summers (who has shifted from deregulator to market overseer) and Robert Rubin (likewise, on both sides of the issue), had lost all semblance of efficiency. Those who wished to make a moral case spoke of the market's lack of decency. There is an old saying on Wall Street: Bulls struggle up the stairs. Bears throw themselves out the window. In the fall of 2008, those falling out of the windows were not bears; they were sacrificial investors splattered on the sidewalks of the world.

Galvin, discussing his investigation of UBS, said there was a "profound conflict of interest between UBS and its customers," and he pointed out "the devastating effect that this conflict had on those customers." UBS, he explained, propped up its auction rate market and manipulated the interest rate at which the auctions cleared. As the market became more risky, the banks stepped up their efforts to unload auction paper on clients.

He moved on to a July investigation of Merrill Lynch, then headed by the poster boy for self-absorption, John Thain. It was Thain, with the markets crumbling all around him, who whimsically decided to spend $1 million in shareholder money to redecorate his office. Galvin would not be forgiving in his description of Merrill Lynch. His investigation of the company led to the first recovery by a state regulator.

"In July [2008] . . . the firm was implementing a sales and marketing scheme which significantly misstated the nature of auction-rate securities and the overall stability of the auction market," Galvin told the committee.

He said his office had received complaints that Merrill had co-opted its supposedly independent research department to assist sales efforts designed to dump the company's inventory of auction bonds onto its customers.

As to the behavior of banks and brokerages, Galvin said, "It became apparent that the broker was controlling the interest rates at which most auctions were cleared." In doing so, the broker was beholden to its investment banking clients to whom Merrill and UBS has promised low-cost financing, "yet needed to raise interest rates just enough to be able to unload its own inventory onto unsuspecting clients."

Many of us who were stuck with ARS would never forgive their brokers. ARS destroyed broker-client trust nationwide. But did the brokers know what they were selling? This question hung in the air of the hearing room, and Galvin went straight at it.

"Two other points which arose starkly in our investigations were the *significant incentives* [emphasis mine] to financial advisors to move [ARS] and the profound lack of training those advisors received with respect to those products and their attendant risks."

Most investors assume their advisors will select appropriate products suited to an individual investor's circumstances. But Galvin was telling the committee that the brokers were receiving incentives to off-load ARS, while at the same time they were in effect the victims of improper training. This made little sense. If the brokers were getting, say, 25 to 50 basis points to sell ARS, but nothing to place cash in money market accounts, wouldn't they wonder why ARS rang the cash register when plain money market funds did not? Were the brokers criminally incurious or merely incompetent? Could they plead ignorance and claim their bosses kept them in the dark—despite the little tail of commission money that was suddenly made available to them?

"I believe the overnight disappearance of the $330 billion market for auction-rate securities should give pause to those who think that the markets can effectively police themselves," said Galvin. "If the free market is to be truly free," he added, "it must be saved from its own greed and its repeated willingness to deceive and dissemble in the name of higher profits."

I hit the TiVo button and sat back, a little breathless. There would be a time for questions and answers. I wanted to be ready for it. Galvin had inspired me to sit through the rest of the hearing, word-by-word. It seemed we were getting close to answering the big *how* and *why* of what was clearly an orchestrated rip-off.

* * *

Back at the hearing, discussion moved in a steadily heated tone to the write-down in auction paper value. Martha Coakley, Massachusetts attorney general, told the panel the banks were busy chipping away at par values and wringing money out of municipal organizations. Fortunately this little game went into litigation.

Six weeks after investigating ARS investments made by Springfield, Massachusetts, the Galvin team recovered, at par, $14 million. When UBS began letting its auctions fail, it took 10 weeks to stop the bleeding and the bilking of investors. "We recovered over $37 million for 18 Massachusetts municipalities and state entities," Coakley reported. She then added an ominous note: "We still need to consider the stability of the underlying assets that back these notes."

Chairman Frank had pointed questions for Susan Merrill. She had been involved in settlements against SunTrust, Robinson-Humphrey, SunTrust Investment Services, Comerica Securities, First Southwest Co., and Washington Mutual.

"The individual one-time investor or investor engaged in a one-time arbitration is at something of an institutional disadvantage," the chairman said.

Merrill said FINRA discussed pilot programs designed to cut through some of the red tape and restore balance to the arbitration process. There might be public and nonpublic panels, she said. A decision on which course to take was two years away.

What Chairman Frank knew at the time of the hearing, but wisely kept to himself, was that his committee would introduce a proposal in November 2009 titled, Investor Protection Act and Securities Arbitration, HR 3817. Section 201 of the proposal would mandate significant modifications to the arbitration practices and possibly eliminate the requirement for investors to sign up for mandatory, binding arbitration to settle disputes with their brokerages. Section 201 was one of my personal favorites. To have announced the proposal in September 2008 would have given the banks and their brokerages advanced warning to mount an all-out campaign against any proposal for regulatory reform.

I recalled the terror expressed to me by the blind physician. She had been hounded, she said, by her broker, her broker's boss, and lawyers from the brokerage firm. She said the attorneys had dumped hundreds of documents on her, which had to be read to the physician by a friend. Facing binding arbitration, she was warned that any publicity might not go down well for her. In other words, she was to keep her mouth shut. She had sent an e-mail that pleaded, "Will you please help me?" Nearly all of her savings were locked up in ARS, and being unable to work, she faced ruin.

I wrote back, telling her I wanted to write her story for Harry's site. Harry was all for it. I then telephoned the physician and took notes on her situation. Harry thought it would make a powerful story. But there was a problem: The physician refused to identify herself in print. "They warned me not to go public," she insisted. I pleaded with her to use her name. She was cautioned repeatedly that any such action, any publicity whatever, would prejudice the FINRA hearing panel. No, she told me, she couldn't afford a lawyer and she couldn't afford to buck the brokerage she said, tearfully.

Harry, the veteran journalist, refused to post the story without her direct attribution. I disagreed with him (I had written many strong "sources said" stories, a technique used by every major publication on a regular basis).

"Please, please," I said in a subsequent phone call to the physician. I said if she allowed her name to be used the entire ARS house of cards would come down. The story would be picked up by the major news organizations.

"This may be your best chance," I told her.

In the end, the story was never posted, and the physician never called me again.

My takeaway, as I listened to Chairman Frank's comments on arbitration, was that the process was a bear trap constructed by the financial services community, a pure sucker play in which investors were forced not only to sign away their rights, it was also a surefire slam dunk for the banks and brokerages fighting investor complaints.

Rep. Bachus tossed another curveball at Merrill.

"The current broker licensing examination doesn't have a single question on auction-rate securities," he said. "Is that an omission and should questions be asked of financial professionals?"

Merrill answered, "Well, I think your question highlights an issue with [ARS] that we are looking at internally at FINRA, and that is something that we look at on a risk-based basis."

What? Was I hearing right? *Risk-based basis?* I had no idea what she was getting at. Her answer was, at the least, obscurely phrased. She continued: "We saw the securities as relatively low risk. Certainly on an examination for registered representatives, you can't ask about every product, and so this may not have risen to that level." But FINRA, she said, now having discovered "risk," will go back and examine Bachus' question.

At this writing, there is no indication that the question was examined or that brokers would be tested on the risk posed by auction-rate or any other similar debt securities.

✳ ✳ ✳

The questions, answers, and statements were by now coming rapid fire as the committee members warmed to the subject.

Rep. Shays: "I am pretty convinced that those who were marketing these [ARS] in a way that didn't represent an accurate picture are going to pay a penalty, and I am pretty content that fact has been established."

Ms. Thomsen: "Yes, the individuals who have been involved in bad behavior will be pursued. We have not yet brought individual cases, but we can continue to pursue them."

(To date, individual brokers have not been penalized, but have been made aware of what they have claimed they were not aware of— that ARS, despite all the evidence, the rulings by financial accounting boards, and massive consumer complaints—were sold in a deceptive manner, as the regulators have alleged.)

Rep. Shays: "If this has been an instrument for 24 years, has false advertising occurred throughout all 24 years?

Sec. Galvin: "I can't answer you decisively, but I believe that it became a practice, and because these instruments were successful for so many years and they worked for different consumers, they worked for the institutions who were trying to get some advantage to their debt. . . . What we became involved in, and I think it has already been referred to here . . . is that at some point the market makers [became aware of market problems] and instead of dealing with it in an upfront way, they went ahead and deceived people."

Rep. Maloney: "I would like to ask Ms. Thomsen and the SEC, when you censured in 2006, why did you not impose transparency on the auctions then? As I understand it, there was an investigation in 2004. Why did you not require disclosure just like the U.S. Treasury does on all its auctions?"

Ms. Thomsen: "Thank you for that question, and indeed there was a disclosure requirement at that time."

Rep. Maloney: "Did it talk about fees and the fact that it is not cash and that it is really a hazard for people to get into?"

Ms. Thomsen: "The investigation that led up the cases in 2006 had to do with how the auctions were conducted . . . and in some cases [the ARS sellers] sort of gamed the system. . . . I think it is fair to say that as a result of this investigation and focusing on the sales practices, it is clear that investors were not told about the potential liquidity risk and—"

Rep. Maloney: "Are you telling them now?"

Ms. Thomsen: "Well, right now there is no requirement for paper disclosure or written disclosure with respect to this. Indeed, most of the—"

Rep. Maloney: "Why not? We know that millions and millions of dollars have been lost. I find this astonishing, really astonishing that going back to 2006, nearly 85 percent of the auctions would have failed or produced different results without . . . broker invention. So what are we doing to stop this conflict of interest? And the SEC, I have to tell you, I have constituents who have lost their jobs . . . because the SEC didn't act quickly enough to stop the naked shorts. I am glad that you have finally stopped it. Maybe it can save some other firms. But we know about this scandal now, and why are [you] not telling clients and individuals and investors and issuers about this horror that is not cash? They can lose all their money. They will not get their hands on the money, not to mention taxpayers who are supporting these institutions. . . . So I think a lot of people are losing in this, and I think they should be told. Why aren't we telling them?"

Ms. Thomsen: "The disclosure obligation is on those who are selling the product and it is a secondary sale, by and large—"

Rep. Maloney: "Why aren't you requiring them to tell the innocent people who are being lied to? Why don't we get an SEC rule in tomorrow that says don't lie to investors and to consumers? We are in a financial crisis. We cannot continue financial practices that lose money, hurt communities, hurt consumers, and hurt investors."

Ms. Thomsen: "We do have rules, and, in fact, the fact that we are able to bring the cases that we are bringing right now demonstrates that registered reps cannot lie to their clients, they cannot tell them false information, they cannot represent something to be liquid that isn't, and that is what we are doing with our law enforcement efforts here."

It was getting hotter by the second. The committee was digging in hard. The enforcement contingent was back-pedaling. It was obvious by now that enforcement and regulation had come apart under the administration's economic team. This was no accident. There is an old Mafia axiom: The fish rots from the head. No one in the room would be so crude as to utter Mafia jargon. These were, after all, ladies and gentleman, trusted public servants. They didn't resort to the language of mobsters or display the outrage of those who had been lied to—and who would continue to be lied to for at least another year. It was Rep. Melvin L. Watt, the North Carolina Democrat who said what few others had dared to say: "I mean we had regulators regulating all of this stuff, and if they had been competing to do their job rather than competing to protect their particular constituencies in their industries, we probably would have avoided a lot of this stuff."

He went on to challenge each of the witnesses to come up with some formula that would prevent another crisis in which lies and deception are commonly accepted practice.

Ms. Thomsen said, "I think we ought to do more of what we did in this particular case, which is to work together and bring swift law enforcement action to those who engaged in wrongdoing."

Mr. Watt shook his head. "Unresponsive," he said.

Ms. Merrill spoke of regulations already on the books, of ongoing investigations, and rounds of internal soul-searching.

"Ma'am, don't tell me what you have been doing. Tell me one thing that you would do to stop this from happening in the future, please," Rep. Watt pressed.

It was left to Secretary Galvin to put the problem into perspective.

"If I were to summarize in one idea," he began, "it would be to revisit the idea of whether the significant or substantial repeal of Glass-Steagall in the late 1990s was a good idea. I think by taking down the wall that existed between investing and banking, you open the door for many conflicts. And I think if we are going to be serious about regulation, you have to have rules that make some sense, and I think this one didn't, and it is time to change it again."

He was conjuring the portly image of Senator Phil Gramm and his sponsorship of the Financial Services Act of 1999, in which he was joined by House Republicans Jim Leach of Iowa and Thomas J. Bliley Jr. of Virginia. Together they pushed the Gramm-Leach-Bliley Act into law, destroying the firewall that had existed since the early 1930s between commercial and investment banking.

The move was severely criticized by leading economists, including Nobel Prize winner Paul Krugman, who told the *Wall Street Journal* on March 10, 2009, that Phil Gramm had become the "father of the financial crisis." Other economists have excoriated the Gramm-Leach-Bliley Act as corporate welfare. There can be little question it acted as a spark that ignited excessive leverage practices by banks and the subsequent meltdown of equity markets.

Big banks, Citigroup in particular, were allowed to review drafts of the legislation before it was passed. Perhaps the most troubling aspect involved then-Treasury Secretary Robert Rubin. Prior to resigning the Treasury post, Rubin was in secret negotiations to head Citigroup, one of the biggest backers of Gramm's gift to his banking buddies.

* * *

A line of questioning by Rep. Ed Perlmutter, a Democrat from Colorado, shone a light on a lingering controversy:

Rep. Perlmutter: "People started getting nervous. Now, were there any big blocks of purchasers? I want to know if there was a lot of foreign investment that stopped and really started this house of cards tumbling. So we have a fragile economy, a fragile market, but it was just generally everybody [that] stopped?" he asked trying to get at the *who* and *how* of the market implosion.

Ms. Thomsen: "I don't believe so. What happened was that increasingly, beginning in the summer of 2007, the underwriters were coming into the auctions to keep them from failing. So they would put in bids so there were no failures, which meant that they were only taking on more of these securities onto their books as they were becoming less liquid in a time when they were having a hard time carrying illiquid securities. And I think they hoped at some level that the market would recover and they wouldn't have to keep doing this, and by February, in combination with the monolines, the pressure became so great they simply stopped supporting the auctions."

But who was talking to whom about leaving the market to fail and allowing investors to be stuck with billions in frozen cash? The answer would come later, and when it did, much uncertainty would remain.

I wrote the hearing story for Harry's web site. There was a great deal of information to convey. The response was greater than I had anticipated. It was by now clear that the ARS implosion was scripted by a few major banks. But no one dared to name them at the hearing, and no one really dug into this scripting. In a sense, those behind the freeze—the banks that in effect said, "Okay, let's shut down the market!"—were not identified, not even by Secretary Galvin. More than anyone in the room, he was in a position to know the answer.

My computer screen filled with messages from angry e-mailers. On the first day, there were at least 50 fresh correspondents crying foul. The following day another 50 to 60 e-mails showed up. And this continued for about a week before tapering off. I urged all correspondents to send angry letters to their representatives in Congress. And from the feedback I got, it seemed many of them followed this path.

This was the beginning of the larger base of ARS investors who would assail their brokers and state attorneys general. The writers wanted action. Many assumed I knew infinitely more about the inside dealings of the auction market than I actually did.

More hardship stories poured in. Most of all the victims wanted to connect, to use cyberspace to form a lobby determined to get their money back and punish those who had lied to them.

Now I was facing a full-time job responding to these investors and, at the same time, digging around Washington looking for new story material. If a concerted effort against the banks was to succeed, it needed fresh information—some might say *provocation*.

After countless calls to House Financial Services Committee members and staff, I got lucky. One of the most influential economists decided to give me an interview, though he made me promise not to name him. (The source has since resigned from the committee.) I have always believed in naming sources, but sometimes it just isn't possible. The situation surrounding ARS was too volatile. It reached into so many corners. Practically no one wanted to put themselves in the crosshairs of the press.

I asked the source if the committee would issue a report, a set of recommendations.

"I doubt it," the source responded. "We've got the bailout to deal with. It's overwhelming. It's getting in the way of everything."

He said most committee members believed that the SEC might work with the Federal Reserve and Treasury to issue a security, or means of financing the ARS debt, that would allow investors to be made whole. He said that while Secretary Galvin and Andrew Cuomo had won ARS redemptions from Merrill Lynch, Wachovia, Citigroup, Morgan Stanley and other major broker-dealers, there remained something in the neighborhood of $110 billion to $160 billion in frozen ARS cash.

"We want the SEC to take whatever action it can," he went on. "SEC has got to create a new leverage mechanism for the closed-end fund issuers."

He explained that the closed-end funds were reluctant to redeem "because it reduced profits to common shareholders. So it's necessary to create other kinds of securities to bring back some leverage to replace the auction bonds."

Was this a scripted failure?

"No question," the economist replied. "But, well, it's all anecdotal evidence. I don't want to speculate on that."

Why didn't investors receive prospectuses?

"There were prospectuses, *sort of*," he said. "They weren't called that. They're called 'disclosure documents.' You probably could have found them online, but you'd first have to know what you were looking for. It wouldn't be easy. One thing is for sure. Almost no one we've talked with was offered any detailed information. The whole system, in this case, was the villain."

He spoke of restructuring the system, what remained of it. He also speculated on a rumored "Liquidity Facility"—a buyer of last resort run by the Fed and Treasury. This operation would presumably be part of the TARP program. "It would, theoretically, issue short-term bonds to create the needed liquidity. But, like I said, none of this is on paper yet."

Unexpectedly, a note of anger came into his voice. "Everyone was screwed in '08," he emphasized. The banks made plenty of money while the ARS auctions were working, "and they're still making money from fees—fees paid for auctions that aren't happening. People aren't going to be happy to hear this, I know, but it's true."

He said the committee has heard from hundreds of outraged investors.

"Yeah, they were let down. We didn't issue any new regulations or proposals, and they didn't care for that, either. We're not fiduciaries. That's not our role. The banks let everybody down. It's a bloody mess. Depressing!"

Chapter 14

Stretching to Meet the Man

If you get belted and see three fighters through the haze, go after the one in the middle.

—*former Heavyweight Champion Max Baer*

A s 2008 drew to a close, State Attorneys General William Galvin and Andrew Cuomo had wrestled nearly $61 billion in frozen funds from nine large banks and brokerages: Citigroup, Deutsche Bank, Fidelity, Goldman Sachs, Merrill Lynch, Morgan Stanley, UBS, Credit Suisse, and Wachovia. Wells Fargo Investments on November 18, 2009, redeemed $1.3 billion in a settlement by California Attorney General Jerry Brown. Wells Fargo agreed to pay $1.9 million in fines, virtually all of which presumably will be taken out of stockholder shares.

Taken together, the various buybacks focused on retail investors, nonprofits, and other noninstitutional investors, while some large

institutional sources were offered "delayed relief." That meant they'd
have to wait six months to a year or more to get back their money.

It would be an overstatement to claim that our burgeoning online
efforts were entirely responsible for the $61 billion in redemptions. But
the growing legion of ARS investors had a distinct role. They ginned
up the action in a letter-writing campaign and a series of telephone
complaints to the AG's offices. By now we had found moles who were
willing to offer advice and keep us in the loop. There were other
important players with whom we worked, such as Kathy Kane's always
lively arspfraud@Yahoo.com and an interactive site called Blogging
Stocks, which ran as a link on Harry's web site.

Harry's site, however, had built a vocal, retail investor constitu-
ency. We never knew for sure how many visitors came to the site,
although we were constantly surprised by inquiries from faraway
places. I had received e-mails from correspondents in the Canary
Islands, France, and Canada. It was clear from the feedback we received
from friendly bankers, as well as regulators, that a concerted letter-
writing campaign we had promoted had helped to fuel the speed of
the buybacks, and lit a fire under slow-moving regulators. I was focusing on the holdouts.

The smaller and midsized broker-dealers understood that they faced
possible hefty fines and court costs if they didn't clean up the ARS
mess. Some of them, such as Nuveen, began making "partial" buybacks, especially for favored clients. Others, such as Charles Schwab
and Oppenheimer, went on a campaign against any form of buyback.
Schwab, whose unctuous TV ads invited potential investors to "Talk
to Chuck," claimed their brokers never pushed ARS, and that investors bought them on their own bonds from the company's "cafeteria"
of investment products. This claim stood in sharp relief against investor howls to the contrary. Among the Schwab investors was Richard
Havunjian, MD. Dr. Havunjian wrote to us: "Schwab's position of
their clients researching and discovering ARPS (ARS) on their own
and just self-serving themselves to it through the 'Schwab Cafeteria' is
just not true, as far as my case is concerned. They were actively promoted to me." My impression was that Dr. Havunjian and thousands
of other investors were plenty eager to meet with Chuck in the cafeteria for a serious exchange of their illiquid paper for cash.

The more aggressive regulators did not take half-measures lightly. Important holdouts remained to be dealt with. These were the down-streamers that didn't underwrite the auction paper but nevertheless had no problem selling it to clients and then refusing to redeem when the market failed. Many claimed they couldn't afford buybacks. Some, like Oppenheimer, allegedly told state regulators a buyback of nearly $1 billion worth of auction paper would break the company, although the company's public face told another tale. Oppenheimer expanded offices, hired new talent, paid for an expensive new TV ad blitz, telling potential clients, "Oppenheimer Funds . . . the right way to invest!" We were making the opposite claim: Stay away from Wall Street products! At one point, Harry, writing in his column, "In Search of the Perfect Investment," confessed that if he had stayed away from hedge funds and other Wall Street inventions after the sale of his tech publications, "I'd be a lot richer today." He also would have avoided the considerable headache of having been caught up in the ARS meltdown.

Many correspondents echoed Harry's sentiment. Others believed that, despite the sufferings they had endured in the auction market, they had "good investment genes" and would continue to waltz with the jib-jabbering Jim Cramer types, whose mantra was, "Stay in the game!"

We were winning, slowly gaining ground. Still, the fight was far from over. There remained about $120 billion to $160 billion in frozen cash to be accounted for, fought over, and redeemed. Our focus shifted to a laser-like campaign against the holdouts.

In late 2008, the group of online commandoes, including the tough-minded Kathy Kane, began to gather itself into a select unit. Our weapons were anger, interaction, letter-writing, and posting stories and commentary on the Web. We were in effect a lobbying consortium using digital tools. Our basic business ethic was 10 percent inspiration and 90 percent perspiration. We continued to view ourselves as a determined gang of no-holds-barred fighters with unimpaired purpose. For those who had been made whole by the banks, there was a cutting edge of idealism. Even though they were off the hook, they stayed in the arena. "It's just the right thing to do," said Kane, whose view of Wall Street was as bleak as my own.

Harry was for now pleased by the increased action. Action and more action was the underlying theme of his web site. As long as there was a dustup, he was willing to play the role of field general. But not always. At times he lost patience with those who e-mailed or phoned him for advice, victims who seemed paralyzed by timidity and confusion, a combination often complicated by debilitating wrath. I had no idea how much of Harry's time was spent dealing with such people. I had my own share of them. They appeared to be hopelessly lost. "I don't know where to turn or who to talk to," was a common plea. It was understandable, this ragged edge of investors who were at their wits' end. I couldn't help empathizing, having experienced my own dark side. It was my policy *never* to lose patience. Harry's skin tended to be a little thinner.

✳ ✳ ✳

I had yet to meet Harry in person. I didn't know all that much about him. We maintained phone and e-mail correspondence. These tended to be brief exchanges—even abrupt at times. Harry was a busy man. Although I wasn't sure what it was that kept him so busy, I assumed he was playing the market and working on his column. He was also a fitness buff; tennis for an hour and a half most days, and bicycling around the city for an equal amount of time. This accounted for at least three hours a day worth of sweat equity. Busy, busy, busy was the ubiquitous Harry Newton, and getting in his way invited the chance of receiving one of his terse "Do I make myself understood?" commands.

Harry made a point of being a tough-love guy. When he felt himself being put upon, he flashed a temper that was very much of the Aussie variety. No nonsense! Straight to the point, mate! His was a sleeve not to be tugged by those who appeared otherwise hapless. I wasn't getting paid for my services and, now and again, I wasn't pleased with commands handed down from New York that sounded as if they'd been shouted from the quarterdeck by Wolf Larsen, the *ubermensch* and antihero of Jack London's famous novel, *The Sea Wolf*. Harry was no Wolf Larsen. London's famous character was driven by hatred and fear of anyone standing on two legs. Harry's occasional flares of temper made him intriguing, not threatening. Besides, I recognized something very special in him, something I could not quite identify. This enigmatic quality of personality drew my respect and my fascination. Here's a sample from the web site of Harry's occasional explosive frustration with presumably bewildered ARS investors:

I'm Stuck in ARPS (ARS). What Do I Do Now?

By Harry Newton

Frankly, I'm sick of hearing this question. Dear Folks Who Are Stuck, I am NOT your wet nurse, your babysitter, or your unpaid slave. I put up this web site to help get myself out of $4 million plus in ARPS. And I did. I got redeemed at 100 percent. I didn't lose a nickel.

But many of you are sitting today stuck in ARPS (ARS) earning a miserable 30 to 50 basis points. . . . You're sitting with your thumbs up your ass waiting for the Messiah or some other mythical creature to descend from the sky and save your sorry asses. I contemplated shutting this web site down when I got my money back. But Phil Trupp and others said, "Help these poor innocent souls who are stuck. Keep the site open a bit longer." So I did.

Let me be clear. I pay money to keep this site alive. The pennies I earn on the advertising don't put food on my family's table. And I don't see any of you readers—with one exception—sending me a thank-you bottle of wine. I'm not begging. Trust me. I'm simply commenting on the sorry state of America's apathetic investors.

So before I do shut this time-waster web site down, I'll answer your question: What do I do now?

You have two basic solutions:

1. Sell your ARPS (ARS) on the secondary market. You'll lose 10 to 15 percent or so. But you'll get cash for the rest and you can get on with your miserable life. I say "miserable" because the vast bulk of you have done nothing to get your money back. I'm sure you've made the mandatory two or three phone calls to your broker, who, like Schwab, has fobbed you off with bullshit. But basically, you've done nothing else. So go sell your ARS. Lose some money and get on with your life.

2. Hire a lawyer. Figure $50,000. There are good lawyers out there. They'll make a stink. That "stink" has a greater chance of getting your money back than what you're doing now—nothing. If you're not prepared to blow the $50,000, don't even think of calling a lawyer.

3. There is a third solution—namely, do nothing. Be my guest. Do nothing. But don't bitch to me or any financial advisor you meet through some nice friend. And, if you think this doesn't happen, well, go figure what caused me to write this column today. A friend called a friend, who knew me and then promptly wasted 30 minutes of my and his time discussing the idiocy and laziness of the man who has $2 million in BlackRock ARPS, is being paid 30 basis points a year—less than he can earn at the savings bank or his friendly money market fund—and is too lazy (or too rich) to take care of his own money.

The only thing missing was one of Harry's Wolf Larsen–like declarations: "Do I make myself understood?"

✳ ✳ ✳

Harry's outburst had the effect of bringing many disenchanted investors out of hiding. I don't know how many "please don't shut down the site" letters Harry received. But the next day, my computer screen was filled with new names and e-mail addresses, all of them lobbying to keep the site alive. From the look of it, our audience had a major silent-majority component, including many tort lawyers and securities attorneys. The response was loud enough to keep Harry from slamming shut the cyber portal. This surprised me. After his frustrated outburst, I had a queasy sensation that he'd follow through and close down the web site.

I confess my heart sank when contemplating the total loss of the site, although I accepted that his generosity had limits. He had done more than enough. Only a select, hang-tough group in the universe of victims possessed his grit. He could have taken his ARPS, all $4.5 million, and purred over the win. It turned out that Harry's rough exterior had a soft center. Aristotle Onassis had a similar personality. Onassis often remarked that the world was like an egg, with a hard shell and a delicate center, though it was said that he was, in truth, describing his own personality.

It was disturbing when it became clear that many victims chose to stay on the sidelines while a small, uncompensated group continued to fight. It seemed at times that I could never do enough to satisfy some of these outliers.

Not unusual was the e-mail that complained that we were focusing on "favorites" or that we were not pushing hard enough.

The Raymond James story caused a stir, most of it positive. Attorneys inundated me with requests for copies of the documents, and I sent them to anyone who was pursuing class-action or individual cases. This was done in the role of advocate. Never would I deny the advocacy role, even though the stories I wrote for the web site were as accurate and objective as I could make them. Some e-mail correspondents insisted I should have done more. Here's one example:

> Do you have friends at [Raymond James]? Or friends who do business with them? RJ is not the only holdout, but I don't see you writing about others or soliciting documents about other companies who won't redeem.

I did not send this e-mail, or others like it, to Harry. It was easy enough to predict his reaction. It would serve to underscore his contention that some investors leaned on a sense of entitlement. This would have ratcheted up Harry's impatience with those who, for whatever reason, either wouldn't or couldn't take action on their own. It might have caused him to rethink keeping the web site alive.

The reality was what every school kid knows: No matter how hard you try, you're never going to please everybody. For every dozen or so positive e-mails, there were a few from others who didn't like the tone of the text or the thrust of an argument or a story posted on the site. No one insisted that I quit the campaign or that I quit writing investigative stories. But I received mail critical of press coverage in general, and this criticism ricocheted against my journalistic fortifications with an unpleasant jolt. Here's an example of the media bashing:

> The press isn't paying one damned bit of attention. That is one of the main problems with this situation. Media is not interested

and is hanging us out to dry. Shithead media is in bed with the crooks. I should not be surprised. Keep up the good work.

This galling criticism ignored the hundreds of stories collected on Harry's site alone. To me, personally, it was amazing how much coverage we received in the face of a total economic meltdown and Henry Paulson's multibillion-dollar bailout of the cheats and reckless traders on Wall Street. Even at the height of the larger economic meltdown, our message was getting out to the regulators. We knew this from insiders and from a number of journalists. Harry's site was infamous— or famous, depending upon one's point of view.

It was clear enough that the Internet served as a locus of mainstream outreach. Every major financial news organization kept track of Harry's web site. It was by now a proven resource. I knew it and Harry knew it. Perhaps without intending to, he had created a vital, topical, and highly critical resource within the financial community.

It was, however, disappointing to find a lack of coverage by TV outlets. Maybe ARS wasn't sexy enough. Or perhaps it was judged to be overly complex. TV keeps it simple and visual. There was little, if anything, of substance on ARS that was broadcast by CNN, CNBC, MSNBC, CBS, ABC, or the Fox Business Channel, although by now Larry Doyle had become a part-time Fox commentator. One could only assume that the biggest fraud in memory just wasn't big enough for the tube. On the other hand, at least two dozen headlines had appeared in major dailies within days after the market shut down.

Harry was toughening his stance. On March 30, 2008, two weeks after the market imploded, he had written an article titled "My Present Position." It presented a detailed battle plan.

He started with the bleak forecast that the brokers "will probably never give us our money back, though it would be a great PR coup if one actually did." After this pessimistic beginning, he went for the jugular: "The issuers will eventually redeem our ARS—if and only if we bring sufficient pressure on them. They need to understand that no one will *ever* do business with them again if they abandon the thousands of investors who bought their ARS on *their* assurances that these . . . were equivalent to cash."

He added:

Pressure on the issuers needs to come from the brokers, from you and me, from the regulatory authorities, from the courts *and* from the press. . . . We can all put pressure on our brokers by threatening them with an SEC complaint. Everyone needs to write, e-mail, phone, boycott, picket their brokers' offices, and their issuers' offices. It's time for you and me to contact our equivalent regulators in our state, tell them we were *not* informed of the risks that our investment might become illiquid, and ask them to get involved.

On March 30, the same day Harry's initial call to arms appeared on his web site, Gretchen Morgenson of the *New York Times* wrote a scathing editorial, headlined "Fair Game: If You Can't Sell, Good Luck; Where's My Bailout?" Morgenson noted that the Federal Reserve took $29 billion in "malodorous assets" from the balance sheet of Bear Stearns (RIP). She then plunged her pen into the reptilian heart of Wall Street:

Everybody knows, she wrote, that only big guys get bailouts. Long-suffering small investors, unable to sell these supposedly liquid [ARS] securities, have to look elsewhere for satisfaction.

And again, on March 30, SECLaw.com flashed a digital headline: "Regulators Start Auction Rate Investigations," by Mark Astarita. He ended his article with a prophecy: "Hmmm, has the SEC and FINRA heard about this? Who reviewed those materials before they were distributed to investors? Stay tuned, this is going to be big."

It certainly was. Here was the biggest single scam in modern Wall Street history, and, as far as Harry was concerned, it was the biggest act of plunder since the Vandal hordes sacked Rome in 455, usurping Emperor Petronius Maximus. In today's dollars, Harry may well have had it right. As an example of how vicious the ARS scammers were, UBS, which finally settled at par, cut 5 percent of its clients' ARS valuation on March 28, according to a story by Adam L. Cataldo and Martin Z. Braun of Bloomberg News.

Everyone, it seemed, jumped on the case. But Harry was first, and by the time I got on board with his AuctionRatesPreferred.org, his efforts were getting real results and plenty of attention.

*** * ***

I had been writing for the web site for several months before I decided I had to meet Harry in person. This would prove to be a little messier than anticipated.

In trying to catch up with the hundreds of stories and letters on the web site, especially the early ones, I came across a letter to Harry from a woman named Angela Goodwin, whose unfortunate run-in with UBS had her fuming. She suggested that ARS victims band together and "start the attack."

Harry replied that Ms. Goodwin was on the right track. He gave her good advice, and added: "As to banding together? I'm asking for everyone stuck in these things to also send me their story, their name, and e-mail address. Right now, I don't have sufficient numbers to become a lobbying force. As this drags on, I hope that will change. Meantime, I'm trying, with this column, to keep everyone informed on each day's developments."

Yes, I had to meet this man who was willing to put his time and money on the line for the cause.

I phoned him from Washington. He was very gracious and thanked me for writing original stories. They had been quite informative, he said.

"Well, I'm writing a book, and you're part of it—a big part," I told him. "Can we meet? Lunch? On me? Or however is best for you."

The friendly voice on the other end made a sudden and unexpected shift.

There was a long pause. "Only an hour. At most," Harry said in an abrupt voice.

"It's a start," I said, off balance from his in-your-face, hurry up tone.

"I'm terribly busy. Just an hour. *Absolutely* no more," he repeated.

We set a date. I put down the phone and turned to Sandy. "So?" she asked.

"So I didn't like the tone of it. He—he made me feel, I don't know, like I wanted to take advantage. Like I'm some off-the-wall schmuck."

"That's absurd," said Sandy. "You've got a good working partnership."

She was a little frazzled. She'd been working hard at Planned TVArts, the Washington division of Ruder Finn's New York public relations company. She had her hands full of clients wanting to be seen and heard on *Oprah*. It was apparently hard for her to imagine Harry stuffing me into a single hour-long box, especially after months of my pro bono work for the web site. "Sleep on it," she advised. "Harry was probably in a hurry. You're too sensitive."

Maybe. But now I knew why sweaty palms sprouted whenever I considered calling Harry for an interview. It may have been a sixth sense. I call it ordinary survival instinct. It's a theory I've nursed most of my life. I truly believe we're born with a capacity to sense trouble from afar. By the time we're mature, however, the wise and worldly among us have stomped our innate prescience into the dust, dismissing it as paranoia or hypersensitivity.

After Sandy slipped into bed, I tried to watch TV. I wanted to decompress after my brief, troubling conversation with Harry. I was uneasy and a little weary. TV didn't help. It served up the same numbing menu of outrageous cop stories and sitcoms in which all the males are dorks and all the females rescue them with wisdom and common sense and cable news with talking heads talking politics, not news. The History Channel explored the not-so-mysterious ways of nomadic tribes, and the Military Channel showed off the latest killing machines and the incompetence of Hitler's military acumen. I hit the off button on the remote.

I poured a little Chianti and tiptoed downstairs into what Sandy called the family room but was in reality my private lair, shared mostly by our grandchildren during overnights.

The green carpet spread out peacefully to the walls. Indirect lamps cast little circles of light that reminded me of miniature tide pools. My drum set stood in a corner, silent, tempting, impatient for a little action. Those drums had been very good to me over the years, but now I couldn't coax a note out of them. The spirit was on hold. The music that had once been so much a part of my life had been dulled by encounters with Wall Street gamesmanship.

Slumped into my armchair, I scanned the art collected over many years, which now brightened the walls. The big yellow

"Sailor's Cat" (one of my favorite works) stared down at me with his wry, been-there-done-that grin. *You have none of my problems*, I thought, starting into the cat's luminous eyes. *But I suppose you live in a better world.* There was, of course, the seemingly sadistic game of cat-and-mouse that appears to be the way of nature and of all felines and also the way of humans who, by luck or by persistence, find themselves in a position of dominance. The Sailor's Cat played the game because he was born to it. Maybe the same was true of Wall Street types.

I wanted to sleep. Ever since the market collapse in February 2008, my usual sleeping pattern had been blown apart. Even after Wachovia made me whole, I found it hard to sleep and harder still to stay asleep. The experience had changed me in so many unexpected ways. The old French saying, *il faut d'abord durer*—"First, one must endure"—played in the channels of my mind. I finished the wine, put my feet up on the ottoman, and drifted into a kind of twilight dream.

In the dream, I found myself in a large, dun-colored room. Wine bottles were stacked neatly against the walls. There was a long community harvest table at the center. The room seemed vaguely like the basement of The 21 Club in Manhattan, where the bootleggers stored their hooch during Prohibition.

There were other people in the room. They were seated in an unnatural silence around the table. Someone invited me to join them. In the dim light I recognized my table mates: Lloyd C. Blankfein, of Goldman Sachs; Ken Lewis, formerly of Bank of America; Jamie Dimon, of JPMorgan Chase; Mary Schapiro, then-head of FINRA; Bill Gross of PIMCO; former Treasury Secretary Henry Paulson; Timothy Geithner, then-chairman of the New York Fed; one-time Senator Phil Gramm; TV jabberwocky Jim Cramer; SEC Chairman Christopher Cox; and at the far end of table sat none other than President George W. Bush.

How did I get here? These were not my friends, my golfing buddies, my political pen pals. Was this some vision out of Dante? I was there with them, although I was somehow entirely invisible; a ghost, a spirit disconnected yet in touch with a larger reality.

Bush was the first to speak. "Sit," he said, motioning to an empty chair at the far end of the table. I walked slowly to the chair and sat down. But in the dream the seat remained empty. "I understand you have a problem with us," the president said.

The others chimed in. They were howling at me and at one another. It was a cacophony of insults. The language was vulgar, boisterous, yet utterly random. It was like trying to isolate a single voice in a stadium jammed with tanked-up football fans. I was shouting above the noise. My voice was absorbed. As best I can recall, I was accusatory, enraged, and at some point in this mixed up Chianti vision I was the revolutionary, the disenchanted one speaking up on behalf of citizens who had been injured, whose lives had been torn apart, whose dreams had been shattered.

"What do we do now?" I growled. "Eat cake?"

I snapped awake. I looked up. Above my head floated the flying pig figurine I had purchased in Bali. His golden mouth laughed without making a sound. On top of a bookcase was the wooden flying frog, red and fierce as an African wasp. *You're losing it, boy*, my inner voice scolded.

On the far wall the Sailor's Cat grinned.

In the morning, I told Sandy, "I don't like Harry's attitude—the way he talked to me. You know, in such a rush-rush way. Like I was some unpleasant pest."

Sandy laughed. "You'll get over it."

But not right away. I phoned Harry again.

"I can't make it," I said. "You're rushing me. I'm taking the plane up to New York and back, and you're rushing me."

"What?"

"I don't want to be pushed. Or rushed. Can't work that way. Sorry."

"You're not coming?" he asked softly, apparently taken a little aback by my annoyance.

Did this turn of events surprise him? Surely, he was not used to being stood up. No. Not Harry. My phone call canceling our appointment must have struck him as absurd and willful. But Harry was smart, and perhaps between the lines he read a secret message.

"Not now," I told him. "We'll do it later . . . the meeting."

"As you wish," he said.

"I'm still onboard, Harry. We'll set up another time, okay?"

"Fine, as you wish."

I hung up the phone. And, yes, I would call again.

Chapter 15

State of Play 2009

History needs data, details, portraits, information, and it needs
eyewitnesses.

—Peggy Noonan, Wall Street Journal *columnist*

To investors still stranded in the frozen zone, January 2009
appeared to be new era of hope—the beginning of a cleanup campaign in which the economy found a passage out of
the depths.

Democrats imagined the new White House eager to take on the
ARS scandal as an easy populist mark. "Obama's looking to make
waves," one observer remarked. There was hardly a ripple. Looking
for action ended in dashed hope.

President Obama has yet to denounce the debacle or to take advantage of the job-creating possibilities that might grow from the unleashing
of wealth that remains illiquid. You can buy quite a few jobs with the
$100 billion-plus frozen in institutional and corporate accounts.

Two economics professors at the University of Delaware put a human face on the possibilities. James Butkiewicz and William Latham worked with a group of 25 companies stuck with approximately $8 billion in frozen ARS backed by student loans. These companies wanted Butkiewicz and Latham to figure out what might flow to the economy if all student loan-backed ARS were made liquid. This would include not only the $8 billion held by the companies that commissioned the study, but also the $70 billion still frozen in auction-rate student loans.

The professors concluded that for every $1 billion redeemed, 15,000 jobs and $2.3 billion in spending would be generated by new corporate projects.

Michael J. Beyer, CEO of Foresight Energy, a privately held mining company located in Palm Beach Gardens, Florida, is a member of the group that sought the study from Butkiewicz and Latham. Foresight has $146 million in ARS it still can't redeem. Beyer is trying hard to finance mining projects begun earlier in Illinois. The company had raised capital for the projects two years earlier and placed the money on a temporary hold in ARS only weeks before the market collapsed.

Dunstan McNichol, writing in the October 21 edition of *Bloomberg News*, reported that Beyer and his corporate coalition are trying to reach out to the Obama administration and its economic team. "Our goal is to show the administration that this money could be creating jobs in a high-unemployment area," said Beyer. The result of his efforts thus far: silence. For the administration, the problem created by punching a 2 percent hole in the nation's GDP appears to be off the radar.

The president's economic team, notably Larry Summers and Treasury Secretary Timothy Geithner, remained focused on the last administration's bank/AIG/auto industry bailout scenarios, along with Obama's signature multibillion-dollar stimulus package—the brave new initiative that was supposed to create millions of shovel-ready jobs. At least some money for these jobs might have come from ARS redemptions. Summers and Geithner, however, are creatures of Wall Street. Their apparent indifference to the auction market implosion remains discouraging, although it surprises no one familiar with the Washington-Wall Street nexus.

The good news during early 2009 was that many of the big banks and brokerages have been forced to settle major ARS complaints on the retail level. Andrew Cuomo, who had been an early mover taking on the big banks, displayed courage and risk with his gubernatorial ambitions—perhaps turning off a number of campaign contributors. Cuomo had succeeded in recouping billions worth of ARS money. Even Goldman Sachs, the "giant squid wrapped around the face of anything that smells of money" (thank you, Matt Taibbi) had returned $1 billion to its hapless investors.

But a year later, many investors were unhappy with Cuomo's actions. In an April 15, 2010, e-mail, one of my correspondents spoke up for those who wonder why the New York AG apparently turned down the heat:

> "Please keep in mind there are many retail investors still stuck in ARS," the correspondent wrote. "Oppenheimer & Company, Raymond James, and Charles Schwab all owe investors about a billion each. There has been no equality in justice, especially by AGs like Cuomo in New York. . . . I agree with you that institutional investors have gotten totally screwed by regulators in this ARS mess. Thousands of us continue not only to be victimized by the likes of companies like Oppenheimer but also by the SEC, FINRA, and AGs like Cuomo."

At the end of 2009, there was considerable frustration over the lack of redemptions by various funds. The one hero was Nuveen, which said it would redeem all taxable ARS and expected to do the same for tax-free municipals by the end of 2010. A correspondent, praising Nuveen, reflected the discontent of investors stuck in other funds:

> Why is it that Nuveen has simply done the right thing by ARS investors? Why have BlackRock, Eaton Vance, Neuberger, Van Kampen, and Pimco not lifted a finger to rectify this terrible situation? Are they not as capable as Nuveen?

Seeing no sign of relief from the new administration, investors and regulators began to focus on the holdout firms. Among them was Credit Suisse, which, in late 2009, finally redeemed millions in ARS dollars.

I was busy sending documents to various tort lawyers who had requested them and who followed my work on Harry's web site. I was in touch with attorneys in San Francisco, Florida, Massachusetts, and Kansas.

This interchange made me a bit queasy. Advocacy journalism covers a multitude of options. You make your choices as they arise. In the end, I took the position that information that might be of assistance to investors was one of the coins of the journalistic realm that was meant to be shared.

I was amazed to find a few outraged brokers willing to send internal documents my way but who ducked for cover when I asked them for quotes. There appears to be an inordinate amount of fear in the brokerage industry. One false move or any deviation from the company line can instantly end a career. Think mob psychology, mob-think. Corporate lawyers are no less ruthless than the money-making schemes hatched by the financial industry that employs them to enforce silence and find legal loopholes. I had to wonder if the lawyers secretly cheered every scandal, since billable hours mushroom in the fertile soil of fraud and duplicitous behavior.

I was dismayed to find so many class-action suits failing. Gretchen Morgenson reported in the November 8, 2009, edition of the *New York Times* that judges overseeing at least 23 auction-rate cases had dismissed them. One judge said the plaintiff wasn't specific enough in his allegations. Another judge, ruling in an individual case with $10.7 million at stake, said the plaintiff was a "sophisticated investor" who had purchased the securities through his accountant. Translation: The investor's accountant should have known the risks.

The sophisticated investor argument was used time and time again by FINRA panels to deny claims in arbitration. It doesn't take much to be a sophisticate; if you have high net worth, you fit the arbitration definition. If you've traded stocks for a few years, you fit the category of sophisticated investor. If you ask for a prospectus, read it carefully, but miss something in the unintelligible small print, you're considered sophisticated, even if you are a little careless. Finding a fair FINRA panel is akin to finding a petunia in a cabbage patch.

In the January 22, 2010, online edition of *Investment News*, Darla Mercado reported that new arbitrations filed with FINRA surged in 2009 with a reported 7,137 cases, almost double the 2008 total. The complaints went up in nearly every category. "The most common complaint . . . involved—surprisingly—breach of fiduciary duty, racking up 4,206 arbitration claims last year," Mercado reported. Misrepresentation and negligence claims were second and third on the list. Not all of these cases involved ARS. Still, it was obvious that the investing community was shaking free of its former passivity. The blogo-sphere and our ARS sites had set a fire under a lot of investors who felt helpless in the past.

The Obama administration appointed Mary Schapiro to head the SEC, a move that has drawn much criticism, such as the following commentary titled, "A Failure of Leadership at the SEC," in the November 30, 2009, *Baltimore Sun* by Marta Mossburg:

> Senators [confirming the appointment] did not seem to care that Ms. Schapiro was incompetent when confirming her to her position. Under her stewardship, the Financial Industry Regulatory Authority . . . missed serious fraud. Those scandals include Bernard Madoff's bilking of billions from clients, members securitizing "no document" and other fraudulent mortgages while reaping billions, and the meltdown of the . . . auction-rate securities market . . . in no small part caused by [FINRA] member firms . . . even when the market for [ARS] was failing.

Mossburg is a senior fellow at the Maryland Public Policy Institute, and a columnist for the *Washington Examiner* where her article first appeared.

Many legal questions remain about Schapiro's role at FINRA, where arbitration continues to live up to its reputation as the place where ARS cases go to die.

According to Herb Perone, FINRA's spokesman, nearly 500 ARS cases have been filed. Nearly half are pending, and about an equal number have been closed. As of December 2009, fewer than 20 claims had made it all the way through the agonizing process. Investors came out on top in only four of these disputes. About 150 of the closed cases were settled.

Perone said terms of the settlements remain confidential, although it is understood that most, if not all, ARS money was returned to investors in those cases that were successful. Those who filed for con-sequential damages—about 32 investors—handled their complaints through regulatory enforcement.

FINRA is currently on a major PR campaign. The basic theme is that this registered front for the banking system is really a touchy-feely consumer advocate whose seasoned staff is doing all in its power to keep the greed and treachery out of banking. FINRA is looking out for you—which gives Congress an excuse to stay out of its way.

The TV ads imply the self-regulatory organization will see to it that those nasty money-sucking squids will get their tentacles slapped and fined if they attack ordinary investors. It's a fine sounding pitch, I admit. But you'd have to be living under a rock to believe it. What is omitted in these ads is FINRA's joined-at-the-hip relationship to the banks. Also unspoken is the whispered truth that Wall Street has never figured out how to make money except by sucker-punching unwary prey—and you surely know who you are!

* * *

I recognize the mass of numbers and facts presented in these pages are hard to digest. Economic calamity, like war, produces the infamous "fog" that overtakes clarity and perspective. A skirmish here, another there. Some reported. Others neglected or misreported. The result is confusing even to the most clear-eyed observer.

One reason for the FINRA ads is to defuse, or at least dampen, public outrage and give the appearance of transparency. Wall Street knows it is held in low esteem and that trust has been broken. The broken trust and a bonfire of greed spelled out in huge headlines means only one thing to the Street: lost business.

The industry loathes populist anger and has only a vague idea of how to deal with it. Viewing themselves as the best and the brightest, the denizens of Wall Street are not at ease on Main Street. Number crunchers, MBAs, and the likes of Bernie Madoff hate bad publicity in the same way the Old Confederacy hated the idea of public education. An informed public, especially one that is both financially savvy and angry, represents a mortal threat to the financiers. This is one of the gambits behind financial complexity. Ordinary mortals, it is assumed, can never comprehend, say, the securitization of derivatives.

Yet, despite the scary financial crisis of 2008–2009, the same old forces remain in vogue. The ARS debacle isn't over. So, for the sake of the narrative, it may be instructive once again to imagine yourself fighting for money that can make or break your future—money the financial industry will hold in a death grip until you can find a legal means to pry it loose.

Sandy's constant question, "Who's got all that money?" comes up over and over again among investors. Add to this the complication of finding the best and most affordable means of getting your cash—and your future—back, and you will find yourself slogging through the current state of play.

I chose FINRA arbitration as a way to get my money back. Thankfully, Andrew Cuomo saved me the humiliation of playing a fixed game. In hindsight, I probably would have lost. The panel would have been against me from the start, and the fact of my experience in the markets would have been a scarlet letter hung around my neck. But then, I didn't expect to be duped by those in whom I placed so much trust.

Presumed sophistication in all its permutations would have been my downfall, despite the deception that made me believe (foolishly) that an investment in a student loan municipal bond was a cash equivalent and completely liquid, or that the bond was actually worthy of its Triple-A rating, a better bet than Treasuries, and as safe as money stuffed into my mattress. In hindsight, it's hard to accept the fact that I took the bait for a little extra yield.

Had I taken another route of defense, a class-action lawsuit, the lawyers would need to prove that the brokers involved in the case fully understood just how risky these investments were. This is a hard case to prove.

There are other problems, none of which favor the investor. It may take years to get a judge to hear a complaint, and all the while you know your bank, the opponent you are up against, can delay indefinitely with its team of high-priced attorneys. One attorney gave me the following warning: "They [the banks and brokers] hire the best money can buy. They are experts at sniffing out ways to nullify your complaint. Loopholes—that's their game. Most of the time, it works."

✳ ✳ ✳

Harry was still very much on top of the action, posting dozens of stories on the web site—though he didn't let this get in the way of his strenuous routine of tennis or bicycling. That he is a competitive athlete (he beat an opponent half his age at tennis) brought him closer to me. At my age, I always cheer for the senior athlete in any sport.

Harry was never far from the ARS scene. "I travel everywhere with my laptop," he told me. He remained an active investor and columnist. I continued to read his "In Search of the Perfect Investment" column, though I didn't always agree with his choice of investments. Once in a while, I'd send cryptic e-mails: "Gold always ends in a pool of tears." He never responded to my comments on his stock picks.

I was gaining confidence in my dealings with him. My intention was a face-to-face interview. I was getting there slowly, carefully.

Harry, being deeply involved in tech, is a computer wiz. Then something happened that indicated Harry was truly viewing me with increased trust. Once, when my computer nearly crashed, he guided me, via phone, and talked me through various fixes. He even offered to lend me one of his laptops with Windows Office XP software installed, the software of choice for both of us.

Small, non-business-related things drew me closer to him. He had taken time out to attend his son's graduation from Harvard. Later, he enjoyed a father-son action adventure on a visit to the Grand Canyon. A European family trip was planned and executed. Harry kept a running diary in his "In Search of the Perfect Investment" column, and I got to know more about him through these personal columns, which he invariably ended with a series of jokes and cartoons scanned from *The New Yorker*.

I sent jokes to him, although he never used them. At least we both were hooked on *The New Yorker*. The magazine served as a kind of literary meeting of the minds. After a while, I could make a 99-percent bet on the cartoons he'd display at the end of his columns. To know someone's sense of humor is to know them on a very basic level.

In September 2009, after JPMorgan Chase returned $28 million in frozen ARS to investors, Harry posted the news with a lead-in cheer: "Thank God for Missouri's Secretary of State!!!!!" (Robin Carnahan).

I was delighted to discover that he shared my admiration for Carnahan. It was Carnahan who swooped in on Wachovia and untangled the bank's auction-rate scheme.

Later, Harry posted on the web site an *Investment News* story I had sent him. It was headlined, "Bill Banning Mandatory Arbitration Picks up Support." Dated September 1, the article cheered me. I was cheering on a bill to do away with this sucker trap.

The bill, HR 1020, was gaining support. Eighty-nine House members had signed on to efforts to nullify predispute mandatory arbitration agreements between brokers and their clients. The related Senate bill, S 931, was gaining ground.

This was one of my most cherished projects. Harry knew I was pushing the issue, despite the lack of a direct ARS angle. Apparently he thought the measure didn't stand much of a chance, but he understood my personal involvement. He posted the story on the web site, and for this I was grateful.

* * *

The more I connected with Harry the more relaxed I felt about the face-to-face interview. The sweaty-palm syndrome was gone. He might be the $130-million man. Still, he remained close to the woes of ARS victims. I had to admire his persistence and dedication, despite his occasional outbursts of frustration with those investors either too timid or too lazy to pitch in. Harry presented a tough, no-nonsense exterior, and this was good for morale for those who followed the web site. But I was beginning to see another side of him, and the urge to meet was becoming irresistible.

"I think it's time," I told Sandy.

"Don't even think about his money," advised Sandy. "You know plenty of successful people—really wealthy types. They seem to have a thing for you."

She knew I was wrestling with the interview idea in a slightly muddled fashion. Sandy, whose business involves gaining publicity for big-name personalities, is well aware that anything can happen in an interview. Say the wrong thing, or say the right thing in the wrong way, and the connection can turn you into someone like Lott's wife. It's not easy to recover from a slipup, the wrong tone of voice, an unfortunate word, or even the wrong haircut. Sandy understood the delicate balance.

"You're a pro," she said. "Get over this worry about the Harry thing."

Despite her cheerleading, there remained a lingering hesitancy; an inexplicable anxiety. Would an aggressive former journalist and publisher like Harry sit still as I tossed lots of questions his way? I had the feeling that he'd be conscious of the smallest details, perhaps looking for weaknesses or wrong-headedness. I recalled my youthful boxing mantra: *How will I start? Who's going to land the first punch? It's not how much you give. It's how much can you take.* Our meeting might turn into an intellectual sparring match, like the old *Mad* magazine cartoon, "Spy vs. Spy." I had to be prepared to see around corners!

"You two will get on just fine," Sandy said. "You've been corresponding forever." I reminded her that I had broken the first interview date when I thought Harry was being too pushy. "Like you don't get moody?" she laughed. "Come on, get with it."

And then fate stepped in and settled the matter.

✳ ✳ ✳

It was the beginning of June 2009 when I received word from my agent that John Wiley & Sons, the respected publishing house, was interested in my ARS book proposal. This was great news. It had come a lot sooner than I expected. Most book proposals take forever to find a home. But $336 billion worth of lost cash has a way of making people sit up and pay attention.

Though I was involved with the ARS mess and had written a detailed book proposal and a couple of sample chapters, I was in no great hurry to take on the work of writing something like 100,000 words. I was living my normal life and working out frequently at the gym, where I swam and taught boxing. I wrote occasional short pieces for various venues. But it was impossible to ignore the scale of the ARS story.

I knew the job of writing the book would turn me into a desk potato. I'd be forced into a sedentary routine, which was not exactly my idea of living it up in semi-retirement. Sandy had a blunt take on the matter: "So what else would you be doing?"

Any number of things, I replied. But writing was the most exciting prospect.

Besides, a really big story doesn't come along everyday, especially one that might make a difference to tens of thousands of investors. I wanted to remind them of the kinds of deceptive snares Wall Street invents to lift your money. Wiley presented the perfect opportunity to expose a complex financial issue to a wide, mainstream audience— expose it not in the gobbledygook of Wall Street but in plain every- day language. I would do my best to "KISS" the narrative: *Keep it simple, stupid!*

A discussion of the project with a John Wiley editor would bring me from Washington, D.C., to my home-away-from-home, the Upper West Side of Manhattan, just a short cab ride away from Harry Newton's Central Park West apartment. Sandy had business in the city at about the same time, and we could have a little fun later on.

At last, the stars were aligned.

Chapter 16

Kathy's War

I do not admit that one can turn away: One has no right to ignorance.

—Martha Gellhorn

A few weeks after California Attorney General Jerry Brown brought his ARS complaint against Wells Fargo, I received a news item from Kathy Kane, one of the more tenacious fighters in the ARS wars. The headline, published in the Orange County Register and dated April 24, 2009, was a prime example of the suffering experienced by ARS victims. Yet it also shows that while this war continues, ordinary people who are willing to stand and fight can make a big difference in the outcome.

"O.C. Woman's Complaint Fueled $1.5 Billion Suit" was the headline of the story Kathy had picked up in her daily scan of ARS events. The article was written by John Gittelsohn. Kathy sent a note along with the story. "My heart goes out to her," she said.

The article profiled the troubling saga of Johannah Markley. Ms. Markley had been diagnosed with lung cancer two years earlier and had sold her home, knowing she needed a great deal of cash for medical bills. Her banker, in this case Wells Fargo, recommended that the cancer-stricken real estate agent place her savings in ARS, according to the news article.

"They said they were 100 percent safe," Ms. Markley recalled. "I was single. I had stage three cancer. I had no money," Ms. Markley told the Register.

Informed by her broker that her savings had run into a "little issue," that the $400,000 she received from the sale of her home in Newport Coast was now frozen, she realized she was broke—and worse. Broke in America is bad. Broke and sick often spells doom.

"I fought my lung cancer and I fought Wells Fargo," she told the Register. "I'm a survivor and so I'm happy to see something being done."

That story appeared a day after AG Brown filed a $1.5 billion complaint against the bank's affiliates. Brown's office released a statement citing, among other things, Markley's medical situation, along with numerous allegations in the complaint alleging deceptive sales pitches related to the risks inherent in auction-rate securities.

Brown said the bank's affiliates "ignored clear industry and internal warnings about risk and previous auctions failures." He said Wells Fargo had to have been aware that as far back as 2005 the SEC, along with major accounting firms and the Financial Accounting Standards Board (FASB), had warned that ARS could not be considered "cash equivalents." Wells Fargo brokers, however, apparently failed to mention this little detail to Ms. Markley.

This distressing news story was typical of the items Kathy shared with me and other ARS watchers and victims. An ARS victim whose money was returned in late 2008, the ARS crisis has transformed her into an official activist. For nearly two years, she has worked on the Internet with fellow activists in an effort to make all ARS victims whole. Like Harry Newton, she is driven not by personal gain but by a sense of principle and decency, qualities hard to find in today's undisciplined financial arena.

I've included Kathy's story here, in her own words. Her perceptive and insightful tale of bankers gone bad, and what ordinary investors can do to fight back, is the stuff of classic consumer activism. Ralph Nader, listen up!

What follows is Kathy's story.

* * *

In November 2007, my husband and I took most of our investments out of the stock market. As middle-aged, middle-class people, we've saved for retirement, and we could not afford to lose money. We also needed to keep savings liquid; my husband works in an industry that had already lost 20 percent of its jobs in recent years, and we needed cash available in case he lost his employment.

We were very specific with our UBS financial advisor about needing a safe, liquid place for our cash. He even chided us for being overly cautious. He put us into auction-rate securities—in our case, Calamos, Duff & Phelps, and Kayne Anderson closed-end auction-rate preferreds. He had put our money into ARS before for interim savings, and he reiterated that these were just like cash, retrievable on a week's notice.

It was never disclosed to us that we stood a risk of not getting our money out dollar-for-dollar, which was our explicit request. We were never told that these were complicated, long-term financial instruments. We never received a prospectus or statement of risk. There was no mention of any risk of illiquidity—certainly no hint that UBS had propped up these auctions and might one day stop doing so without warning.

It is important to note here that we never wanted or intended to buy a long-term instrument. We *never, ever* would have agreed to buy perpetual bonds.

On March 6, 2008—a full three weeks after the auctions failed—I got a call from our broker, saying that it was urgent my husband call him. So I asked him to talk with me, even though I was not financially sophisticated. He said: "Your money is safe. You just can't have it now. There is nothing you can do about it. Just wait." He said he had faith that it would all be worked out. UBS *had* to get this worked out—for their reputation.

The next day, he faxed us a letter that he had composed on March 5 for his clients. He explained that UBS had supported the auctions previously, but to protect its own position, had decided to stop.

I began to study the issue. I asked the FA increasingly specific questions but got no specific answers. He could or would not tell me why this was happening. He could or would not tell me what solutions UBS might attempt. When I asked what UBS was doing to resolve the problem, his response was, "They don't tell us that."

I got the message: You're on your own.

A frightening reality began to take shape. We thought we had done all the right things. We had been careful. We had been risk-averse. We had trusted a major institution and chosen someone we thought to be a reputable professional who would steer us to a deliberately planned goal. And now our "perfectly safe" investment was about to be wiped out.

It was a sickening, terrifying feeling. It kept me up every night, and it woke me up in the morning.

✳ ✳ ✳

Those days shattered everything we thought we knew about our financial system. I had thought UBS provided investment advisors; I began to think that we'd had a salesman. Investment banks suddenly appeared to us no more honest or trustworthy than a huckster with a shell game in a subway station. That realization was devastating, and it will never go away. In retrospect, it is the one good thing to have come of this disaster. We got wise.

I began searching the Internet to educate myself—and I had so much to learn. I had no idea what a closed-end fund really was. Within weeks, it seemed I knew more about the crisis than our FA did. I was sending *him* articles from the Web.

The more I knew, the more I realized he was not telling us the whole truth. That meant his assurances that we would get our money back were empty.

I was damned if I was going to sit around while we lost our future and accept that there was nothing I could do. Within two weeks, I found an online column by Babson University business professor Peter Cohan on BloggingStocks.com, a financial blog that allows interactive comments from readers. [Author's note: This web site became an unofficial meeting exchange used by ARS victims on a daily basis.]

Cohan condemned the ARS freeze, and there were comments from others in the same boat we were. There was total confusion. People were afraid the investment banks themselves would go bankrupt, and we would lose everything. No one was sure whether to leave the ARS where they were, or to move them to protect them somehow, but we didn't know who, if anyone, was trustworthy.

We began to respond to each other, filling out the picture with information about how our different investment banks were treating us and what we were learning from the various funds. A spontaneous online grassroots coalition had begun.

* * *

Leaders emerged and provided information. One of them, a West Coast attorney named Lisa, had done research on which regulatory bodies were in charge. She found names and addresses at the SEC and the individual states and encouraged everyone to get busy filing formal complaints with the government, their states, and their individual banks. Another was Serge, a Russian immigrant who set up a discussion forum on his personal web site that allowed us to share information by topic.

One outstanding group member was Lily, the queen of give-'em-hell on the telephone. There was no one she was afraid to call. She called fund presidents at home. She called reporters. She called regulators in every agency at every level. I am glad I never had to be on the receiving end of one of those calls.

I tried to be useful in the ways I knew how, by sharing and helping to organize information. I posted the URLs for articles and helped refine an action list, things everyone needed to do.

This is one of my BloggingStocks.com posts from March 31, 2008, just six weeks after the freeze:

Another organizing possibility:

Serge, your site lists ways to take action concentrated into one space, as opposed to the 50+ pages of this blog. Even on your site, though, there's a fair amount of content to search through.

What do you think about having a page or section on your site exclusively dedicated to how to act? You can list, in one easily accessible place, all of the links that someone new to this list can follow to take action, for example:

- SEC complaint and link.
- Links to class-action lawsuits.
- Links to the group of California investors looking for others.

- Any state-level regulators listed; reporters and columnists who want to hear from people.
- The Massachusetts regulatory system.
- Links to find your own Congressional representatives, etc.
- Links to FINRA and any other agencies we should be writing to.
- Links and e-mail addresses of funds and brokerages.

If we are going to follow multiple avenues of action, it might be helpful to have a central list.

There were also efforts to organize ourselves as a group. Here's another post from April 2:

I'm sure a lot of us are willing to commit to a concerted plan of action, if we can figure out what will be useful.

What is the best way to organize ourselves? We have all engaged individually in action, and I know from the conversations I've had with funds that we're making them nervous. That's good.

Beyond individual action is organized action. What can we achieve as a group? We have several leaders on this board. How can we generate ideas for group action, discuss them, and then commit to one or two that seem most effective?

Let's take steps to do that. One option is a meeting—a conference call, or a virtual meeting in a chat room—of leaders/volunteers to generate ideas for effective group action. We could meet in Washington and do some group lobbying. We could appear as a group at fund board meetings.

* * *

Everything I did, many others did as well. We taught each other; we shared information about how to protect ourselves; we looked for alternatives for the money that was left.

Letters, letters. I wrote rescission letters and demand letters to UBS. I wrote multiple letters to the three funds I was stuck in. I wrote to reporters—everyone who covered ARS. I wrote to thank them and urge them to keep it up. I spent the entire spring of 2008 learning, writing, and calling.

I'd had no idea what the SEC really did, but with the help of fellow victims on the BloggingStocks blog, by now our unofficial community, I figured out how to work with it. On April 2, I called the SEC and actually got a return call. I was heartened: they were "collecting information." On April 11, I filed my formal complaint with the SEC. That complaint shows how much I was learning in those early weeks.

I have learned more than our broker ever told us about auction-rate securities. I learned that in mid-2007, before these three funds were sold to us, accounting regulators told corporations that ARS are not cash equivalents. This resulted in corporate flight from the market, but UBS continued and still continues to list them as such. I learned that UBS knew auctions were failing in December and January, but kept that information from its clients and continued to sell ARS. I learned that UBS had been artificially supporting the auctions, and that the company decided to stop supporting auctions to protect its own balance sheet, damaged by subprime excess, at the expense of clients it had misled.

Our contacts at the SEC were in both the Investment Management Department and the Enforcement Department. But in the end, the SEC was not encouraging; they would not be working to have our money returned.

I had filed my FINRA complaint on April 8, 2008. On April 23, I received a letter saying that they were forwarding it to the SEC. Since the SEC had already told me they couldn't help, this wasn't promising.

On June 13, I received an e-mail from the SEC, asking me to fill out a form. They wanted to know how they were doing! Lousy.

* * *

My first experience with state securities regulators in my home state wasn't encouraging. It took weeks to determine that I should file where I lived, not where the broker's office was located.

The agent at my state securities department told me that mine was the first complaint she had received. I found that shocking—a $336 billion fraud and no one else cared? But a few days later, she called back to say that her boss had heard more about the issue, and they were supposed to collect all the information.

It turned out that NASAA, the North American Securities Administrators Association, had organized a multistate task force to investigate ARS. Karen Tyler, the North Dakota securities commissioner, was head of this task force. She let it be known that she wanted to hear from all of us, no matter where we lived. While she could make no promises, the goal was to get our money back based on the brokerages' fraud at the point of sale. The states had the power to order rescission, and that was their intention.

Tyler told us that they needed our information. How were ARS characterized on our statements? How did the investment banks describe ARS on their marketing brochures? What risk statements had we received? Our group set about sending our personal information to regulators in the various states, as different states had been assigned to take the lead on investigating individual banks.

On April 11, I filed my formal complaint with Christopher Mulvihill in New York Attorney General Andrew Cuomo's office. On April 23, I filed a formal complaint in Massachusetts, writing to Joshua Grinspoon in Secretary William Galvin's office. I wrote to Missouri's Secretary Robin Carnahan, as well.

In the end, these three state regulators turned out to be ARS victims' most effective advocates. After four long months of unrelenting worry, we finally got a major breakthrough: Galvin filed a formal complaint against UBS in June 2008, alleging fraud. This was the first moment that I thought we might, just might, get our money back— though I knew I would not believe it until the dollars were in a bank account. I finally breathed.

✳ ✳ ✳

One of the primary fronts in the ARS battle was with the funds. Instead of a cash investment, I had discovered that we owned perpetual bonds held by closed-end funds. I felt ill when I learned what perpetual bonds were. These funds could keep my cash forever!

ARS victims had begun to realize that we were pawns. The investment banks wanted the funds to pay, and the funds wanted the banks to pay. They actually characterized the ARS crisis as a game of "Old Maid."

Neither of them intended to be left holding the bag; they would let their clients do that.

In statements to the media, the leadership at Duff & Phelps and Calamos were offensive to victims. One fund executive reputedly told an ARS victim that he should feel proud to be able to hand his ARS down to his children. DNP Select Income Fund representatives suggested that if we didn't like the situation, we should sue UBS! (Of course, UBS had that covered. Investors were not allowed to sue in court.)

With the help of those on the BloggingStocks.com blog, I used the SEC web site to track down the board members and executives of my funds. Needless to say, they didn't want to hear from us. I wrote desperate letters and got stock responses. They referred us to non-committal, uninformative "alerts" on their web sites and obfuscated the issue when someone managed to get through to them by phone. In my "action" diary, I noted on March 26: "Third call to Duff & Phelps. Spoke with Eden Levenson, who wouldn't even volunteer her last name." I remember how grudgingly she yielded that pearl of information.

I called Levenson again in early April, but our sparring got me nowhere. Then Nathan Partain, the head of DNP, made particularly insulting statements in a press release. I called DNP again and spoke with Joy Brown, vice president and analyst. She was more forthcoming about what was happening at the fund. But she added that from their perspective, they were not in default. They were therefore under no legal requirement to do anything, and they wouldn't do anything that would lower their payouts to common shareholders (and, I concluded, themselves and their profit). So much for being a "preferred" shareholder!

I asked to speak with Mr. Partain, but he refused to take my call. So I concluded by telling Brown that it was insane to tell us to go sue UBS. It was their product. We never agreed to a long-term investment. DNP was holding "hot" money, and they needed to give it back.

In frustration, I ultimately called the Phoenix Companies, the parent company of DNP, and spoke with John Flores, chief compliance officer. And lo and behold, the next time I called DNP, I reached the head of client relations, Brooks Beittel. In a very stressful conversation, I tried to convey our desperation about DNP's deliberately opaque position. He expressed compassion, but left me with no insight and no answers.

In all of these months, I can identify exactly one person for praise: a young, recently hired public affairs professional at Kayne Anderson named Monique Vo. She always took or returned my calls with courtesy and the best information she could offer. She often couldn't offer much: All the funds insisted they were legally restricted from sharing information with one client that was not available to all. But she tried her best to tell me the truth and to treat me as someone who deserved the truth.

* * *

While DNP and Calamos stonewalled, Kayne Anderson indicated early on that they would prefer to refinance and make all ARS-holders whole. But the economy was worsening, and they said they were having a hard time finding the funding to do so.

By mid-May, other funds had begun to say that they, too, wanted to refinance. They claimed that the requirement for 300 percent collateral was a barrier. The law needed to be changed, requiring less collateral. For better or worse, that initiative stalled.

But gradually, refinancing began, at least for some of us, and with that came a new source of anxiety. Funds were refinancing in a piece-meal fashion, as alternate financing vehicles opened up, and investment banks were using a lottery to apportion these returns to their clients. We feared the firms would favor some customers over others—and why wouldn't we? They had done nothing but stonewall us to that point.

Once again, our group went back to our respective banks. We demanded a written policy for distribution of partial refinancing. I was one of the lucky ones; I got my first shares back during the summer of 2008. Some of the other vocal victims, however, seemed to come up empty in repeated lotteries. Was it chance, or were the lotteries fixed? We'll never know, but the fact that we could believe such a thing demonstrated the catastrophic loss of confidence we'd experienced.

* * *

Our online group continued to dig for information, trying to understand who was at fault, and how this disaster had happened. The investment banks had argued that they had no idea these auctions would fail. My own broker told me that, since ARS had been a successful cash-parking tool for 20 years, they couldn't possibly expect massive failure.

But it became apparent that the financial industry *had* been warned, as early as 2006. We learned that auctions had failed in 2007. And corporations had begun to bail out in the summer of 2007, responding to the FASB ruling that ARS could not be listed as a cash instrument. Yet UBS and other supposedly reputable banks had continued to claim on statements and in marketing materials that ARS were "cash alternatives" and "money markets."

Was the U.S. government going to allow this? If so, how could we trust them again? No one, neither in the industry nor the federal government, seemed to be telling the whole truth. More than $300 billion had fallen through the cracks of our economy, and no one wanted to talk.

✳ ✳ ✳

A secondary market emerged. I was offered about 85 to 89 percent for my ARS. Others were being offered less. Each victim was trying to decide whether to lock in a devastating loss, or count on someone to do right and return the money. In my own case, both Cuomo and Galvin were by now chasing UBS, so I decided to wait. My internal clock was set for the end of 2008. If there was no substantial progress, I planned to take my losses and get out.

Another wrinkle: Some banks were actively interfering with clients who wanted to sell. On June 20, the *New York Times* discussed why firms had to allow secondary sales: to maintain "high standards of commercial honor." It turned out even investment banks could be embarrassed. They backed down and cooperated with sales on the secondary.

Another line of discussion among victims on the blog was whether to file for arbitration or to join a class-action lawsuit. One of the lasting blows of the ARS crisis was my realization that UBS had required me to sign away my rights to sue in court in favor of arbitration—and that arbitration was managed by FINRA, which I saw as the trade association of the investment industry, a fox guarding the henhouse. We all worried that the arbitration panels would be biased against us, and clearly it would be expensive and burdensome to take on the process. Small investors like us were at an enormous disadvantage.

The only lawsuit that might succeed was class-action, and that, too, was a poor option. It would take years, and the return to members of the class was likely to be pennies on the dollar.

In late April, I spoke with an attorney at Cotchett, Pitre & McCarthy to discuss the possibility of a class-action arbitration. It didn't pan out, though, and the attorney was candid: Because I was out of state, I couldn't afford the process.

Thus I had no viable legal alternatives.

To me, this was perhaps worse than the original fraud behind propped-up auctions and mislabeled financial instruments. This was the moment I saw that the entire industry had been organized to protect itself from responsibility for fraud, theft, and any other kind of unethical, criminal behavior. And worse, the government had allowed this self-dealing.

* * *

UBS began talking about a 100-percent loan program in April, but having been victimized by them once, everyone was suspicious of their motives and their fine print—in particular, the need to let them off the hook legally before taking the loan.

In retrospect, they may have been trying to do a good thing, but at the time, it seemed they were looking for another way to cheat us. The feeling was exacerbated when they devalued ARS by varying percents. No one knew what it meant. Certainly all we got from UBS was more sanitized, meaningless PR.

Everything we learned about the financial industry showed us how deceitful it could be. Banks were continuing to scrape fees off auctions that were not going to be held. There was evidence that the ratings agencies had taken what were essentially bribes for positive ratings. [Author's note: Finance professor Ed Kane, a Brookings Institution scholar, wrote a September 6, 2009, Washington blog that provides such evidence. He says: "One has to remember these [rating agencies] are profit-making institutions. Issuers will pay more money for a good rating than a bad one. . . . This is a straightforward way to pay *bribes* without ever violating the law, it appears, and the credit rating organizations do not take formal responsibility for their incompetence or negligence."]

We also learned that brokers had been offered higher fees for pushing ARS onto retail clients—us—as the market collapsed, and as top banking executives bailed out of their own ARS holdings. We'd always felt that we had been defrauded. Now there was solid evidence of it.

Naturally, our community of activists sought congressional action. Early on, I called my representatives, but I got no help. My senator referred me to the SEC.

I turned to Senator Christopher Dodd, the Connecticut Democrat in charge of the Senate Banking Committee. I reached his staffer Aaron Kline, and was pleased to see that he was informed and understood the issue. But in the end, Senator Dodd has done nothing for ARS victims.

We waited anxiously for House hearings set for September 2008. We e-mailed the House Financial Services Committee in advance, telling our stories and providing documentation. And then the day of the hearings arrived. I sat at my computer, listening to the audio stream, taking notes on . . . nothing. It was worthless. Barney Frank barely showed up. There was a lot of empty testimony, some of it shockingly self-serving. It was an enormous disappointment. [Author's note: See Chapter 12 for complete coverage of the House hearing.]

Through it all, hopes rose and fell. On the BloggingStocks.com blog, we continued to brainstorm ways to attract attention. One proposal was to create a huge, inflatable rat and parade on Wall Street in front of the outlaw firms. I wish we had done it; it certainly expressed how we were feeling about the way banks and funds were treating us.

It also expressed how hard it was to get attention. The issue would get an article or editorial here or there, but it repeatedly dropped from view. No one seemed to care that $336 billion had just dropped out of the economy—to this day, I don't understand why—and our frustration was intense. A post on the blog in mid-June talked about the "feeling of helplessness and victimization." It seemed to us that firms were establishing a clear pattern: Steal, lie, delay, deny.

There were some who thought we'd all be made whole in the end. But with the economy collapsing, how would that happen? Was there enough money in the system? On July 3, I commented, "Let's suppose GM goes bankrupt. Banks fail. Stock market dives." It was my worst imagining. And of course it came to pass.

✳ ✳ ✳

Inch by inch, victims did gain ground. Refinancings trickled in. Finally, in the fall of 2008, Cuomo and Galvin won settlements with UBS, Citi, and other major institutions. But even as some of us rejoiced, it was clear that others were going to be left behind.

That was when I committed to stick with this issue. Was it any less a crime and a national disgrace if I got my money back but others didn't? I can never forget the sick feeling in my stomach when I realized all we had worked to preserve might disappear. And I knew how abandoned I would feel if other victims got their money back and walked away.

So here I am, in late 2009, still working with others online to fight back. We're focused in particular on so-called midstream dealers that still refuse to give back to clients the cash they took, waiting for someone else to do what's right and let them off the hook.

It is criminal that thousands of people are still waiting for their investment banks—those same institutions that are paying huge bonuses and buying expensive, touchy-feely "trust us" marketing campaigns—to make good on cash investments. They should have been forced by the government to give it all back.

I was one of the lucky ones. I got my money back simply because UBS decided to cut its losses for the sake of future profit. Pure luck, pure chance. And that's not acceptable.

I lost a great deal. I lost months of sleep. I've experienced a profound loss of faith in banks, one that has permanently changed my view of this country's economic system.

I had other things to do with my life. But I will not walk away from this fight, because something really wrong happened here. This isn't supposed to happen. Banks defrauded thousands of us of hundreds of billions of dollars in broad daylight, and the federal government has still not made them give the money back. How do you believe in the U.S. economic system ever again? And what happens to us all if we can't trust them?

[Author's note: All of Kathy Kane's official contacts and ways to fight back are included in the Appendix. The information represents a strategy hard-won and weapons that will serve any ARS victims and investors generally.]

Chapter 17

Hopeful Signs from the Hill

They alone were alive, and they sought for other things that were alive in order that they might devour them and continue to live.

— *Jack London,* White Fang, *1906*

Often painfully, sometimes furiously, the auction-rate debacle appeared to have turned a corner.

There were lingering cases in July 2009, puzzling and complex cases, still much debate, but a significant number of settlements had been accomplished. The question remained: How much frozen cash had yet to be thawed? As of July 2009, estimates from the secondary market, where ARS investors go to redeem their bonds at a discount, were as follows: approximately $200 billion had been redeemed. This left about $120 billion to $160 billion still floating about, mostly tied up in student loans, municipal bonds, collateralized debt obligations, and the secondary market itself. "They're spread all over," a secondary market guru said. "A vibrant secondary market has emerged."

"So more than half the money has gotten back to investors," Sandy said, checking my figures. "You must feel pretty good about it."

"It sure looks better than it did a year ago," I replied.

On the ride into Manhattan from LaGuardia Airport, I flipped through the recently printed pages of Harry's web site. It was a sizeable sheaf of paper, nearly 200 pages.

I noticed that Harry had posted stories I had sent to him on a $456 million settlement by TD Ameritrade. Another story spoke of an ex-Credit Suisse broker, Julian Tzolov, having been arrested in Spain on charges of fraudulently selling subprime mortgages linked to auction-rate securities. Tzolov's partner, Eric Butler, was awaiting trial in Brooklyn.

Regions Financial Corp.'s Morgan Keegan & Co. was being sued by regulators on claims it stranded clients with $1.2 billion in frozen cash. So many loose ends. I wondered if they could be settled in a neat bundle of rulings, although I had serious doubts this would happen in my lifetime. How many billions would go unchallenged? It was a question that eluded even the most careful observers.

Other headlines indicated that a lot of action was still taking place, that both large and small portions of the swamp were waiting to be drained. Even FINRA put on what amounted to a sideshow with its proposal to ding the records of any brokers who sold auction-rate securities, received hostile letters from their clients, and whose clients were later redeemed in global settlements. The organization also was conducting an investor-friendly PR campaign designed to tell its audience about the indispensable role of banking institutions. Most of us saw it for what it was: fluff!

"Typical FINRA flimflam," I said to Sandy as the taxi made its way along the East River.

"Makes no sense," Sandy replied. "Did you write that story?"

"Yep. There's this outfit called the Securities Industry and Financial Markets Association [SIFMA]. They're screaming bloody murder, complaining FINRA wants to make selling this crap a sin. It's just noise. No one takes FINRA seriously."

Before the year ended, *Investment News* ran the following headline: "FINRA Execs Pocketed Millions in '08 while SRO Was in the Red."

The story, dated December 2, 2009, and written by Jed Horowitz, charged 13 current and former FINRA executives made more than $1 million apiece in 2008, a year when the self-regulatory organization (SRO) lost $693.6 million. Mary Schapiro, who served as head of the organization that year, allegedly walked off with $3.3 million. Earlier in 2008, before taking over as head of the SEC, she pocketed $7.2 million as part of her "accumulated retirement plan benefits," according to *Investment News*.

I wrote the SIFMA story before these numbers were made public. It was the last investigative piece I submitted to Harry's web site. At this point in time, FINRA was the object of so much scandal and perceived insider trading of ARS that the December salary flap, when it finally broke, was taken for granted as merely another ho-hum story of Wall Street greed. The public was focused on the big name banks, especially Goldman Sachs, and published reports that it was betting against the very products it was selling to its clients.

Still, writing the story of the SIFMA complaint against FINRA was, for me, a poignant last journalistic act. It wasn't exciting news, although you don't find much comic relief on the finance beat.

By July 2009, I was scanning the Internet in my diminishing spare time and forwarding stories written by other reporters. It wasn't very satisfying, but at least AuctionRatePreferreds.org was keeping abreast of the news.

I signed the contract to write this book on short deadline. I had only six months to round up the entire scandal. It was like attempting to condense Operation Iraqi Freedom while the war was still in progress. Could I do it? It was going to be a hard push to the finish line. In the circumstances, it was no longer practical to make time for the usual phone calls or to arrange meetings to gather the information necessary to file original copy. The new routine was 24/7 on the book.

In truth, I missed the daily reportage routine, the shifting back and forth, the dredging up of skeletons from the rivers of muck where dirty deals are dumped out of sight. It was a nasty job, but satisfying. The book project was a greater challenge. I was turning out 1,000-plus words a day to keep pace.

"Well," Sandy grinned. "Maybe it is a sin, selling ARS, like they say. Yeah, maybe it's a no-no. Let's check it out in the Bible when we get to the hotel," she laughed.

I tried to recall how many stories I had written for Harry's web site. A half-dozen? A dozen? Maybe more. There were, however, countless e-mails shared with victims. This daily e-mailing took up hours each day and went late into the night. And there were those items I picked up off the Web and forwarded to Harry. I had long ago lost count of the numbers of odds and ends. Harry never rejected any of my original stories, with one exception: the sad tale of the blind physician. This was the story that would continue to haunt me.

"She's got to put her name to it," Harry insisted at the time. No contrary argument could sway him. "How do you know she's telling the truth if she won't put her name to it?" he persisted.

I argued that important stories were often attributed only to "sources," especially when the reporter was sure the sources were telling the truth. Watergate was the most recognizable example of this journalistic technique. Deep Throat was anonymous. His name never appeared in print until 30 years after President Nixon's resignation.

I implored the blind physician over and over to come out of hiding. Her terror of being exposed at arbitration kept her in a frozen silence. It was the one story I wanted to write that Harry refused. Should I bring this up at our interview? No, probably not. I disagreed with him on this call and there was no use bringing it up. We never did find out how the physician made out in arbitration.

As the TV monitor in the rear of the taxi babbled on about everything I didn't want to know or hear, like how to prepare proper eggs Benedict on a low-fat diet, I continued browsing the thick printout of stories, scanning each of our headlines. They represented virtually all the action that had taken place in the auction market since February 2008.

"Nuveen, Merrill, and Citi Slapped with Suit over Auction-Rate Losses." "FINRA Settles with Northwestern, Two Others, on Auction-Rate Securities," according to the Associated Press. And this from *Investment News*: "Bill Banning Mandatory Arbitration Picks up Support."

The headlines went on and on, covering many pages. Put them all together and they were the size of small town phone book.

✳ ✳ ✳

The arbitration story was especially pleasing. I had been bugging the hell out of various House members about this proposal, pushing, cajoling, writing e-mails, getting nasty on occasion, being turned down more times than I could recall.

Nothing ever gets done on Capitol Hill without a lot of shoving and pushing, coupled with almost superhuman anger management. Being polite and, on occasion, obsequious in the face of a twenty-something congressional aide's wrath, or kowtowing to an intern who tells you plainly to get lost—permanently—requires special restraint. So, often I whispered under my breath, "Ah, the corruption of power that comes of being a congressional aide. Exactly how much sucking up must one do to reach these dizzying heights?"

The FINRA headline was worth all the grief. This pet project, for which I had taken so much crap, was gaining traction. It occurred to me to start a faux movement to place Barney Frank's image on Mount Rushmore, as he might have done on his own, given the chance and resources.

A lot of people in Washington admire Frank, and just as many (mostly Republicans) wish he'd go away. My experience with him revealed a cooperative and candid legislator.

I had a chance to question him while attending a conference at the Reagan Building in November 2009. The group, which had invited a bright cast of speakers, including Secretary of State Hillary Clinton, was called "No Limits." Frank spoke on the economy, regulation, and his view of what caused the greater financial meltdown. He took questions that morning. I asked him about the ARS situation.

"Oh my God," he said, rolling his eyes. "What a mess. It was something cooked up by Wall Street to make money. That's all it was." It was clear from his tone of voice that he believed the freeze to be a sucker trap.

He patiently explained the details of the situation to the audience, taking his time to simplify the basic outlines of ARS madness. I was impressed by his patient approach, though not so pleased with the outcome of the earlier hearings by his committee in September 2008. I asked why no rules or new legislation issued from the hearings.

"It was the bailout," he said. "We were snowed."

He said the House Financial Services Committee was moving as fast as it could, "moving from the Bush recession to, we hope, an Obama recovery." He paused to measure his next remark, an unusual act for a man whose mind seems to be powered by Intel.

"You have to remember that the recession actually began in December 2007," he continued. "Every single bailout started with Bush. When Clinton left office, [then-Fed Chairman Alan] Greenspan was worried he couldn't operate without some debt. Bush, you know, he didn't believe in government, this movement to discredit *all* of government."

Frank moved a little closer to the audience, stepping forward with a funny rolling gait that reminded me of the way animated characters moved.

"The public," he went on, "must come up with rules to control these 'innovations' Wall Street comes up with. Remember, auction-rate securities weren't regulated." He chuckled with grim humor. "Wall Street says government will destroy innovation. *They are wrong*! But look, we don't have a silver bullet to fix the problem. Systemic risk counselors have to come into play here. But let's face it. No president since [Franklin Delano Roosevelt] entered office with so many problems. Still, I think things are going to get better."

As for the ARS scandal, Frank called it "a terrible trap. A serious problem." He said municipalities shouldn't be involved in such quirky transactions.

"We're going to regulate muni advisors," he added. "For now, [Fed Chairman] Bernanke should keep interest rates low. Greenspan!" he exclaimed. "That guy wouldn't regulate. Greenspan wouldn't even step into the dot-com bubble to regulate. Greenspan wasn't interested in regulating mortgages or auction-rate bonds. So," he concluded, "you can see the mess we're in now."

He said the Hank Paulson money express rolled over just about every other issue in town. Besides, Frank added, the ARS market had managed to kill itself off. One couldn't waste time making rules to cover a market that no longer existed.

When Frank walked off stage that day, I noticed that his shirt tail was dangling below his jacket. A woman seated beside me leaned over and asked, "Where do you think he was before he got here?" I could have given her a cruelly amusing response, but kept my mouth shut. Frank had treated me with respect.

"Those Hill people, they really protect each other like wolves," Sandy said, switching off the annoying TV in the rear of the taxi. "Glad I don't make a living pumping them for information."

I told her about a particularly off-putting aide to Congressman Paul E. Kanjorski, the Pennsylvania Democrat, who served with Barney Frank on the House Financial Services Committee.

No way would Kanjorski's aide allow me interview his boss.

No matter what editorial opportunity I might offer his eminence, this young man seemed determined to keep Kanjorski off-limits. He was as tenacious as Cerberus, the three-headed dog of Greek mythology who guards the gates of Hell and prevents those who have crossed the River Styx from ever escaping. Finally, I just lost it with this guy. I sent him an e-mail telling him how I had once covered Capitol Hill, the White House, the Pentagon—all the I-know-what-I'm-doing CV material. I tried to convince him that I liked what Kanjorski was doing in the regulatory arena and that I would take no more than 15 minutes of his time, and so forth.

Nothing worked. Unfortunately, the result is that no interview of Kanjorski appears in this text.

All of a sudden it seemed very funny, a little vain. I burst out laughing.

"What did Kanjorski's person say?" Sandy asked.

"Said his boss was too busy with regulation. Just too, too busy. Had a conference with God—maybe God's rabbi."

Sandy shrugged. The taxi swung right and headed away from the river and into the narrow, busy streets that lead to Central Park.

✳ ✳ ✳

I wanted to concentrate on Harry. But the headlines kept reminding me that there were game changing ARS holdouts. In my opinion, these stood out as icons of the whole auction-rate mess. I looked at them as cleanup cases with sufficient legal clout to set precedent for negotiations with the remaining holdouts.

A central figure among this group of possible game changers was Oppenheimer, which refused to redeem nearly $1 billion in auction bonds. And there was Charles Schwab and Raymond James. Like Oppenheimer, these downstream/midstream outfits were fighting the tide.

The firms were objects of investigation by state regulators. Raymond James had class-action suits hanging over it like pilot fish clinging to sharks with their suction heads. These pilot fish existed to consume the scraps left behind by the shark. As it turned out, Raymond James beat the rap in 2010.

I was focusing in on the details of these trailing cases with special intensity. Both Andrew Cuomo and William Galvin were on Oppenheimer's case. The outcome, I believed, would signal either the end or a continuing heartache for investors. But in 2010, Cuomo reached a partial settlement with Oppenheimer in which the firm would redeem its auction paper in small bites over a period of time. The outcome was especially distressing to New York investors. There was talk of forming a group called "Former Oppenheimer Clients Against Cuomo." They would make their dissatisfaction known with a media blitz and in the voting booth if Cuomo made an expected run for governor. One of the organizers explained the group's strategy this way: "It looks like he [Cuomo] favors big Wall Street firms over the little guy. And don't kid yourself. Sure, Cuomo would like Wall Street's support. But there are a lot more voters in New York who would be extremely turned off by his actions."

This book is being written ahead of the November 2010 elections. It will be interesting to see if the anti-Cuomo forces can convince voters that the Oppenheimer settlement was indeed anticonsumer.

"So, at last, you're going to meet Harry today," Sandy said as we turned into the park.

"Finally."

"Check your palms."

I did. They were dry.

Chapter 18

Going to Meet the Man

What a person does is what he is, not what he says.

—*Syd Field*

I was delighted to be back in New York. The meeting with Harry marked a turning point. Something was about to change. But the blur of events, coming rapid-fire, had me slightly off balance. Again I checked my palms. They were dry. Maybe too dry? A little stage fright, after all, is the best warm-up for a good performance.

I had been talking to a few friends on Wall Street. They were gloomy. Some were fearful. Populist outrage had gotten under their skin. There was talk of executives buying weapons to protect themselves. The Goldman Sachs gang was especially paranoid. There was palpable fear that an angry mob might storm the fortresses of lower Manhattan.

This glimpse of fear was counterintuitive. Goldman's Lloyd Blankfein and other bank executives liked to imagine themselves as "Dirty Harry" Clint Eastwood types: MBAs with vast intelligence and the toughness of Navy SEALs. Paper-pushers, it seems, like to imagine themselves as tough guys. But beneath the cocky exterior lurks an uneasiness that the proletariat might be out for blood, not only in lower Manhattan, but in the gated communities of Connecticut—hedge fund country. It may never have occurred to the bank executives that one day they would be seen as pirates, loathed and hunted by those whose fortunes and lives they had plundered.

I didn't take this talk seriously until months later. It was confirmed by Alice Schroeder in a December 2009 commentary for *Bloomberg News*. She wrote of rampant fear and loathing among the elite. It was crazy but apparently true. Of all the hated players on Wall Street, none generated more enmity than "Golden Slacks" (Goldman Sachs). Schroeder's column carried the following tale of real-life hunkering down:

> "I just wrote my first reference for a gun permit," said a friend, who told me of swearing to the good character of a Goldman Sachs Group Inc. banker who applied to the local police for a permit to buy a pistol. The banker had told this friend of mine that senior Goldman people have loaded up on firearms and are now equipped to defend themselves if there is a populist uprising against the bank.

Surely Harry was privy to these rumors; they must have amused him. He had once said that Wall Street is "a place where dumb people go to make a lot of money." At the time, Harry's "dumb people" comment seemed a particularly harsh characterization of the Wall Street archetype. In the months that followed, however, I came to share his view. I have a few good friends in the industry. I can count them on one hand. So many others I had known turned out to be narrow, insecure people. When they weren't into pack behavior, they preyed on each other. Harry made his fortune as a businessman, a publisher who had to meet a payroll and churn out magazines, which added tangible substance to the technology revolution. He wasn't part of what he called Wall Street's "product-making machinery." The things Harry made were real. You could hold them in your hand, read them, learn from them. Little wonder he harbored such low regard for the products of Wall Street. Economic Rube Goldberg derivatives, he said, were crafted to make money for the banks—period! They were not created to benefit the consumer or add anything of significance to our culture.

"The only thing you're good for is fees," Harry complained. For the most part, it was true. Wall Street innovation did not have investors' best interests in mind. "Just who the hell do you think those people are looking out for?" Harry asked rhetorically during one of our phone conversations. The best way to play the Street was to practice saying no!

It was amazing. Here was a man whose existential view of the financial industry was dismal, and yet he stayed in the market, a player in the casino. His caveat: "Cash is King." This attitude, I presumed, was partially a byproduct of his career as a journalist in Australia and later in the United States. It is a business where skepticism is a necessary and constant mind-set. I think Harry, with his contentious outlook, enjoyed trying to beat cons on their own turf. "I'm a lousy stock picker," he confessed. But this didn't deter him from staying in the game.

Almost every reporter I knew looked upon the financial industry as a swamp, a news beat in which most of the characters were as slippery as any Washington politician. To cover Wall Street certainly is better than chasing police cars and fire engines, but it is no less peopled by crooks. We need more media attention, not less. The mainstream media would do the public a service by *intense* coverage of the financial-services industry. It would be educational, and it would go a long way toward curbing the cons. In the end, plain language reportage might help us at least mitigate the boom-and-bust economic cycle. This was a point both Harry and I agreed upon.

To a great extent, Americans have been left in the dark. Seldom will you read in the popular press just how the casino operates. Editorials on the business page are useful, and there are some great writers. Robert Samuelson, Stephen Pearlstein, Andrew Ross Sorkin, Daisy Maxey, Gretchen Morgenson, and Paul Krugman, among others, do wonderful work. Too often, though, you will find their ideas squirreled away in the business pages or in financial magazines. Many of the ARS victims harbored a savage anger toward the press. They complained bitterly that the mainstream media had let them down, that somewhere along the line investigative journalism had tossed them under the bus. The media, they fumed, neither educated the public nor advocated on its behalf. They looked to the blogosphere, the specialized web sites and blogs, to launch a ruthless war against ruthless opponents. In the end, the blogosphere proved more powerful than the mainstream in the ARS wars. I confess to being skeptical at first. As a long-time professional in print media, I was a believer in banner headlines printed on paper. It took Wall Street's biggest modern heist to convince me that in our digital twenty-first-century era, print cannot compete with the blogosphere for audience reach and universal access. The Internet was—and remains—the most potent news forum of our time.

The blogosphere has no bias. It is open country. Unlike mainstream media, the Internet has few restrictions on tone or content. We can rage. We can vent. We can speculate. In the tangle of digitized rumors and wild guesses, we can always find some grain of truth. The Internet also made it possible to intimidate and force the truth out of those who make a practice of obscuring it.

Wall Street executives and many corporate chieftains are prolific when it comes to bending the truth. It's part of the business model. I had served as a reporter in what used to be called "trade journalism" and was bombarded daily by great steaming heaps of corporate deception. The executives I interviewed were hell-bent on *selling* their stories. *Telling* the truth was less than an afterthought. Anyone who has studied the interviews of traders and other financial-service workers will notice the rush to make the hard sell or to skew those stubborn things called "facts." There is a difference between fact and truth, and that difference is often exploited. In my trade journalism days, I had to know a great deal about the industry I was covering in order to avoid playing the shill. Harry might be blunt, but he was an advocate of truth. No matter how wrenching the truth might be, he would never try to bullshit you.

Sandy and I walked across 77th Street to our favorite 24-hour-a-day hangout, the Manhattan Diner. The air was warm and sticky. I loosened my tie. The diner was cool and only half full. The little Art Deco cafe was a familiar part of our neighborhood-away-from-home, situated in an area of the city where we had encamped for years. I looked at my watch. It was only nine o'clock. My interview with Harry was at noon.

"Are you going to ask him about Oppenheimer and those other holdouts?" Sandy asked when we had slipped into a booth.

"I don't know if I'll have the time."

"You said it was important."

"I'm concentrating on personality today. I don't want to get bogged down."

Harry believed all auction-rate investors deserved to get their money back. A discussion of the holdouts would tilt the focus of the interview.

Our waitress, Barbara from Warsaw, placed big steaming mugs of coffee on the table. We chatted about her children, her husband, and how the economic downturn was affecting business.

"Business . . . well, it is hurting," Barbara sighed. "Maybe they'll have to let me go." She stood straight, confident, determined. "I'll be fine," she said. "I can always wash floors and windows for somebody."

It was the first time Barbara appeared to be worried about the economic downturn. There was a time not long ago when getting a seat in the diner required standing in line on Broadway. Now the line was gone, half the booths were empty, and Barbara was showing a stiff upper lip.

Sandy and Barbara chatted. I went over my notes. I was eager to see where Harry lived. It is one of the great areas of the city. Central Park West is a lively swath of green space in which our family had spent many happy hours. Harry's building was across the street and only a short walk to Tavern on the Green, a New York landmark, which, unfortunately, has gone out of business. Still, the area maintains its magic. *Central Park West*—the great saxophonist John Coltrane had written a melody to suit the feel of the area. He wrote a simple but elegant series of chords, played with a kind of breezy nonchalance.

Again I looked at my watch. Time had slowed. I was becoming impatient.

Don't be in a hurry, boy, the inner voice soothed. *If time slows, there's a good reason. Settle down.*

✳ ✳ ✳

The Prasada doesn't shout at the passersby on Central Park West. It sort of croons, "Wouldn't you enjoy living here?"

The building where Harry lives with his wife, Susan, is faux French, one of those grand Second Empire-style apartment buildings at the southwest corner of West 65th Street. I love old buildings and had done a quick study of the Prasada. I liked the big arched windows and the two-story-high banded columns supporting a cartouche with the name of the building emblazoned on it. A forest green canopy shaded the entrance.

The doorman greeted me coolly. Did I have an appointment? He looked me over with suspicious eyes in the style of Larry David's character in the HBO comedy series, *Curb Your Enthusiasm*. It was one of those eyeball-to-eyeball confrontations in which both parties look for signs of disingenuousness, like flashing red lights behind the irises.

The doorman checked with someone inside the building, nodded, and gave me yet a second eyeballing before ushering me inside. He stood there for a moment, saying nothing. I wondered: *Is he waiting for a tip*? Nothing much gets done in New York without a tip.

"Mr. Newton will be another 10 minutes," he said. "Have a seat."

For some reason, it felt like waiting to see the doctor. I was there at the appointed time. Why the wait? I recalled a repeated phrase in Harry's In Search of the Perfect Investment (ISPI) column: "I'm notoriously cheap," he wrote. He saves money buying lightbulbs online. He watches every penny but doesn't seem flustered when one of his fund managers goes belly up. He makes it up with savings on the lightbulbs. But he certainly wasn't pinching pennies living at the Prasada.

"It was Susan," he once told me when I asked him when he had moved to Central Park West. Susan is Harry's politically astute wife who has enjoyed a successful marketing career. The couple lived in a loft while he was building the magazine business. But the loft grew to four stories as the business prospered. "She wanted a *real* apartment," Harry said. "So I figured okay, she deserves it."

Our culture maintains that where one lives is a statement of one's identity. It was only natural that I research the Prasada as part of finding the real Harry Newton—the ARS field general, the organizer who created AuctionRatePreferreds.org. This collection of $4 million-plus apartments reflected Harry's cultural stamp: success with plenty of style. He later told me the penthouse sold for $12 million.

The architecture of the Palm Room—the Prasada's lobby—is impressive. A barrel-vaulted, leaded glass skylight roof supported four carved classical caryatids and issued soft sunlight. A stone fountain is back-lighted by a wall of stained glass. With its marble benches, potted palms and Oriental rug, the Palm Room could rival the public spaces of some of the city's better hotels, only on a smaller scale. Still, it's the little things that make a big statement, like the tapestry hanging from the rear wall with a fierce-looking creature and the words *Et Vivum Detulim Aprum Terribilem.* "And he took away the terrible wild boar by force." Was this a message that no "terrible wild boars" were allowed inside? Harry had no idea what *Et Vivum Detulim Aprum Terribilem* meant. Just as well. He might think of it as a bit of an overstatement. My take was that it was an ironic symbol for the ARS scandal—an unintended credo. Yes, let's take away those terrible wild Wall Street boars, by force if necessary.

My quaint thoughts were interrupted by a dour woman who seemed to appear out of nowhere. She was tall and lean and had the expression of someone whose important mission had been interrupted by a petty inconvenience.

"Mr. Trupp?"

"Yes." I stood and extended my hand. She ignored the gesture.

"This way," she said, leading me in a kind of stiff march to an old-fashioned elevator. Once inside, the woman gave me the once-over. I wondered if she had been trained by the doorman. She didn't do the eyeball-to-eyeball bit; instead, she swept me up and down with a sloe-eyed scan, the kind you get at CIA headquarters when the guards notice your shoes aren't shined. This was getting to be just a little too much. I thought: *What? Do I look like an encyclopedia pusher? Or maybe a vacuum cleaner salesman? Do you think I'm here to fix the plumbing? And even if I do look like any of those things, what's the big deal?*

I don't enjoy being treated like an interloper. So I just smiled at the woman and talked of the warm weather. She nodded with faint approval at my awkward attempt at conversation.

The elevator was creaky but solid. An absurd recollection crossed my mind, and it instantly took my thoughts away from my escort. It was a recollection of something I had read about a superficially prudish ruler who counseled her daughter fearful of having sex on her wedding night to "Close your eyes and think of England."

The woman opened the gate and led me into Harry's apartment. I walked behind her trying to absorb the details of the place. The walls were lined with books—a library big enough for a small community in the mid-West. There was an aroma of paper and leather hanging in the stillness that is a hallmark of elegant New York dwellings. There was a hush, an absence of traffic noise, no jumble of cell phone chatter or other distractions. It was as if this long, book-lined hallway existed as a world within a world, unique and sufficient unto itself, like a state-room onboard a cruise ship.

We passed the kitchen. It was sleek and modern. A woman I took to be a housekeeper stood beside an ample sink. She gave me a chilly look. She asked if I wanted something to drink. "Water's good," I said cheerfully. She nodded. "This way," she said.

A few more steps and I was face-to-face with Harry Newton.

✳ ✳ ✳

He stood flush in the doorway of his office. Tall, slender, slightly stooped, clad in jeans and white polo shirt, he reminded me of a twenty-first-century urban cowboy whose inquisitive gaze created a short-lived degree of separation. This was a man whose bearing might have given pause to the security goons in the Palm Room. We shook hands. Harry had a quick, firm grip; there was no condescension in it, and his smile was genuine.

"Ah, so you've pinned me down," he said, the Aussie accent more pronounced than the voice I was used to over the phone. I think he found my presence mildly amusing. I had been persistent, had captured his attention—this despite his usual impatience. From the very beginning of our acquaintance, he somehow knew I'd eventually be standing there in the doorway of his office, the embodiment of *The Thing that Wouldn't Take No for an Answer.* As a former financial newsman, someone who was well-trained in the art of asking necessarily rude questions, I sensed that Harry was mildly amused at having been tracked down by a distant voice at the other end of a telephone line.

He put me at ease right away. Maybe it was a contrast to the supercilious arrival ceremony in the Palm Room. But, no, there was something else: a genuine welcoming spirit.

Harry invited me to be seated at one end of a long wooden table—a conference table, perhaps suitable for eight. The walls were covered floor-to-ceiling with bookcases; yet another small town library—mostly business titles: *Net Worth*, *Rules of the Trade*, *Growing Rich*, and so forth. This was Harry's office library. I had yet to scan the titles in the long hallway beyond the door, but I already sensed those bookcases contained intimate and more telling titles. Like most writers he liked being around all kinds of books.

Harry sat facing me at the far end of the table, his back against a large picture window; it didn't face Central Park or the busy avenue below, but instead revealed the back walls of other buildings, which jutted at puzzling angles like a Picasso painting in his Cubist period. Behind him, on a long, wide desk rested Harry's computers: a big three-screen number and 11 laptops. I suspected he had others tucked away. The man is a computer guru who once scolded me about my ineptitude with most matters having to do with technology. I had phoned him with news that my computer had crashed.

"You're a carpenter, a workman," he growled. "You've got to learn to take care of your toolbox." He was right, of course. Patiently, and with moments of humor, he walked me through the crash, scolding mildly along the way. "My God, man. When's the last time you defragged the damned thing?"

Now the sharp attitude was gone. He smiled his expensive smile.

"You sure don't want my teeth," he said when I brought up his frequent mention of dental problems in his ISPI column. We traded a bit of information known mostly to dental freaks. I had mentioned that Carly Simon might feel at home in our group.

"That's rich," he laughed. "Carly Simon."

Always conscious of time, I got down to the subject.

"How did you get hung up in the ARS mess?" I asked. "What motivated you to become an activist?"

"Well, it was mid-2007. Market's going down, down, down. And I'm *sell, sell, sell!* I was dealing with Smith Barney, not that it really matters. Anyway, after all the selling, I wound up with $4.5 million in cash. Then later that year, I put the cash in ARPS at Deutsche Bank." He sighed. It was the sound of a man who had won, lost, and won again. "You know the rest." Pause. "You're whole, right?"

"Right."

"Cuomo?"

"Yep. And Carnahan in Missouri. I was with Wachovia."

"Carnahan. Yes, she's a good one."

Slowly, Harry was feeling more at ease. It was happening faster than I had anticipated. It was clear to him that I was not going to be a wiseass, a bit of friction, but no third degree. We shared much in common, and he appeared to recognize this hint of commonality.

He is a complex personality. He can be abrupt, and then instantly show a milder side, as if he understood the personal pain that he and other experienced when it comes to being ripped off. He understands that this pain was not exclusively his. He was mild-mannered, yet beneath the surface I sensed his anger at having been caught in the auction trap. It must have been an arrant insult to his businessman side, his professional judgment, and his critical integrity.

I asked why he started the ARS site.

"I needed to make a noise. A stink. No one had created that kind of web site, you know, to raise hell about it." And there was another motive. In Harry's view, the ARS situation needed a *community* in order to be effective and to put things right. And he was to be the four-star general leading the charge. This fit his activist personality. It was going to be a bloody fight and Harry had the energy to keep up the pressure.

"You're at the center of this fight," I once told him. To this day, I don't know if his silence in the face of my remark was modesty or indifference. It didn't matter. The site was the *New York Times* of the ARS crusade, and I was proud to be part of it.

The web site was born March 27, 2008, a little more than a month after the auctions imploded, and it was obvious the banks and broker-ages were determined to hold on to all that "free cash."

"It's no big investment on my part," he said. The expense of main-taining the site was about $100 a month. To date, he's spent about $5,000 running it. And its creation, he said, had hard-edged, practical goals:

"I started the web site AuctionRatePreferreds.org because I wanted to put pressure on my broker—the one who sold me $4.5 million of ARPS," he explained. "I wouldn't have gotten my money back, with full interest, without the pressure. I figured the last thing he wanted was bad press. The advantage of a web site is that all the search engines—from Google through Yahoo through Bing—quickly find your site. And

I mean all of them. If someone searches for the name of that broker—let's say they're debating whether to use the broker or not—the search engine will find the web site and the bad mention of the broker. If the item is well-written and believable, because it looks true, then the person searching will have pause. The broker may lose the business. Since the web site is long-term, that damage to his reputation and business-winning skills could be long-term and serious. Nobody wants that."

Apparently Harry's broker had no illusions about his client's determined and clever ways.

"The good news is they knew from my background that I had the skills and temperament to hit them with bad press," Harry said. "Despite getting my money back in full, I've kept the web site going because many readers have asked me to. I hear from people all over the world. They say the web site is critical to their sanity—and to getting their money back. Fortunately, more and more are." He grinned and tapped the desktop with a pen. "You want to mention my philosophy when it comes to dealing with naughty vendors—especially ones that sold you a bill of goods. The squeaky wheel gets the most attention. It's your money. Go get it.

"That's my message—Go get it!" Harry repeated. The way he said it, with understated force, brought up images of him on the tennis court. This man is competitive, he is smart, and he will do what it takes to win. "Tennis is a game of force," he once told me. It was an emblematic comment. This was obvious from the joy he took in beating younger players. "I beat this guy half my age," he told me during one of our phone conversations. Harry was 67 at the time. He asked how old I was. I told him.

"Ha! I guess we're both limping to oblivion," he groaned.

I had to smile thinking about his relentless drive. It's not hard to grasp. It is the near universal compulsion to defeat age, to knock the odds, to keep oblivion at bay. Harry put high energy into virtually every aspect of his life.

"The web site created momentum," Harry told me. "The Internet is a powerful force. We've been stronger than anyone in the media. We've given everyone a voice—and put plenty of pressure on the issuers and brokers. And the site created a path for people who were stuck. I think it's been a success. Everyone says it's been helpful."

✳ ✳ ✳

Not many web sites receive the kind of attention Harry has attracted. The site was, and remains, where the action is. Its level of success is astonishing when compared with big-name, pricey sites like the one launched for $4 million by *Newsday*. A January 25, 2010, story by John Koblin in *The New York Observer* reported the *Newsday* site has attracted only 35 subscribers and grossed only $9,000. The difference is that Harry understands laser-like focus and the specific needs of his audience, and they get the information free.

Harry said the site has become a routine fixture in the offices of attorneys general all around the country.

"I posted pictures of these guys, the AGs, those who were going after the auction-rate issuers and those who didn't. Let's just say that those who didn't all of a sudden got *motivated*."

He spoke of doing a guest interview on CNBC in July 2008, a few months after the crash.

"They didn't do much with it," he said. "I was on a few minutes, I guess. They didn't do any follow-up that I can recall."

Harry informed me that the bosses of print media had warned their reporters not to cite the web site or attribute any of their stories to it. This was the standard print media protocol: The only sources you can trust are those who directly engage with you. These sources may or may not be reliable; they may be selling a bill of goods, but they are speaking to you and are responsible for their own words. Nevertheless, the print media watched Harry's site for tips and breaking news. It was a useful tool. The site reproduced virtually every ARS development published by countless news outlets, from the *New York Times* to more obscure sources such as Courthouse News Service. Plus, my investigative reports drew calls from reporters and securities attorneys all around the country.

"But the journalists *do* read the site," Harry told me. "They all do. We're making a noise. We keep people on the top of the situation."

Will he keep the blog going? It was a nostalgic question, really. The daily routine had become so much a part of my life. The thought of possibly losing it was unpleasant.

"Sure," Harry replied. "As long as there's a need I'll keep it going."

I wanted to tell him that soon after the crash I had written to Jim Cramer about the ARS debacle. Cramer never replied. Not even a perfunctory acknowledgment of having received my e-mail. I had gone sour on Cramer since that time, but Harry still quoted him as an authority—to my amazement!—in his ISPI column. It was hard to put this irony together: Harry, the tough-minded, hugely success-ful publisher, and Cramer, the self-absorbed TV personality, stock picker, and name-dropping alumnus of Goldman Sachs. It was strange to image the two of them in the same universe.

"What really surprised me," Harry went on, "was how apathetic some people can be about their money—the money they've lost. Really, it's disappointing. I don't get it. Why aren't they more proactive?"

"Maybe they're scared. Maybe they're intimidated. I hear plenty of ugly rumors from investors who've been told to shut up or they're never getting their money back. Others are in the fight to win. But you can't discount the fear factor. They're just unlucky to be stuck with one or another of the holdout brokerages." I'm not sure Harry empathized.

"Intimidated? What the hell, it's their money!" he insisted, again. He glanced out the window at the bare walls of the adjoining build-ings. "I'll tell you this. At the rate some of these brokers are going their clients will never get their money back." A streak of anger flashed. "It's only the regulators, the AGs that really make the redemp-tions. The SEC is doing practically nothing. I think maybe the web site, all of us together, have lit a fire under them." The holdout broker-dealers, he added, needed a bigger fire—one of those California-sized mountain-blasters.

"A lot of those people stuck with holdouts are prepared to fight to the end," I said.

"Yes, yes. If their clients don't stand up to them, well . . ." A sudden burst of laughter. "You know what's really funny? The whole damned auction-rate mess actually protected me from myself. You know, it kept me out of the market."

This was gallows humor. Harry had written that the ARS debacle "saved me from myself." That message appeared on the blog. The comment caused some of our crew of unseen warriors to criticize him as being arrogant and above the fray. They apparently didn't get the irony. What Harry meant was that the ARS freeze kept his $4.5 million out of a swooning stock market. When the market began to recover,

Harry gingerly stepped back into the casino, jumping in and out like one who knows well the feel of ground shifting underfoot. He was not to be outwitted. He remains invested in hedge funds, some good, some not so good. He has various money managers, one of whom recently declared bankruptcy. "Without the slightest word to anyone in advance," Harry scowled. "Not a damned word!"

Harry has often belittled his own market acumen. It's refreshing to let others know of one's own foibles, especially in the tricky business of stock picking. He is not ashamed in the least to tell his ISPI readers when he's made a bad call. He was a successful publisher of magazines, a shrewd businessman, and a prize-winning reporter for his native *Australian Financial Review* in his youth—but Wall Street is a game in which the rules of Harry's Harvard MBA don't always apply. "I'm a terrible stock picker," he often complains. It's a confession that brings a modicum of comfort to those of us who have made our own stumbles along the way.

Not long ago he wrote that the "biggest part of investing is saying *no*." I might have suggested that the biggest part of investing is asking, "How much can I lose?"

Despite everything, Harry stays reasonably close to the casino, even if he does get to say no a lot. "Perhaps I'm older and wiser," he wrote in mid-December 2009. "Perhaps more skeptical. Perhaps it's because Warren Buffett sees all the good deals and I get to see the leftover dreck. Perhaps it's because I'm late. It's not March 2009. Perhaps it's because good deals simply come along not very often." This is Harry Newton's mild lament. "Patience is a virtue," he said, "despite ultralow returns on cash today." Harry knows when to step back from the cliff; it's never far from his line of vision.

At one point he wondered, in print, what his life might have been like had he taken his millions and purchased municipal bonds and stayed out of the stock market altogether. He imagined that he would have spent his time clipping coupons and playing tennis and traveling and biking and never so much as dipping a toe into the muck of the stock market. But he stayed in. It's not as if he needs more money. It's the competitor in him, the action junky, the odds-beater side of his personality that draws him to the game.

"I like owning land, too," he said. "Land to develop. And beautiful land. Yes, beautiful land is best."

He and Susan own a home upstate and often spend weekends there. "Commercial real estate sucks," he told me. "Right now it's really bad. Even here in Manhattan we've got big problems. I have friends who've lost plenty on Manhattan real estate. They buy a property, wait for the rise . . . it goes up. They wait. It goes down, down . . . I tell you, commercial real estate has turned to dreck."

Will Wall Street ever be reformed and made to play straight? I asked.

"No," he said flatly. "Wall Street will never be reformed because it buys protection from Washington by donating huge amounts of money to politicians." The populist outrage doesn't surprise him; and though he didn't say as much, I had the distinct feeling that he empathizes with it.

Wall Street, however, was getting the message. Goldman Sachs, the object of so much anger, told the *New York Times* on December 10, 2009, that it would pay the top 30 members of its executive committee bonuses in the form of restricted stock with a claw-back option if their areas of business faltered.

"Look, the whole damned auction market thing isn't that unusual," Harry said turning back to our primary subject. "Think of all the people who are holding onto dead shit—stocks and property that's going nowhere. Hell, man, it's all a crapshoot."

Harry suddenly recalled something he had been meaning to tell me. Had I read Matt Taibbi's article "The Great American Bubble Machine," which appeared in the July 2009 edition of *Rolling Stone* magazine?

"No? Well, you must read it," Harry insisted. He gathered up a copy of the article and urged me to read the story's subtitle: "From tech stocks to high gas prices, Goldman Sachs has engineered every major market manipulation since the Great Depression—and they're about to do it again."

It was as if Taibbi's story had confirmed Harry's theories of boom and bust.

"Beginning in the 1990s, things changed," he said. "There was more money floating around and more opportunities. There also was pressure on Wall Street to make new products. Everyone was desperate for products." His use of the word *products* is translatable into *stuff you can invest in*. ARS, which had been around since 1984, was just another product being offered to investors, another pony that would allow the Street to cash in.

"You had some big banks supporting the auction market," he went on. "Then one day the trading desks said, 'We're not getting enough out of this. Let's drop out and see what happens.' Demand was dropping off. Bank inventories built up too much, and so they dropped out." He paused to see if I was following this scenario. Harry was keen on one's paying close attention. "Wall Street is no different than Hershey," he went on. "Inventory builds. You stop buying chocolate."

✳ ✳ ✳

As he spoke, I checked out some of the framed photographs on the walls. His daughter Claire and son Michael held prominent positions among many other photographs. Unlike their Australian parents, they were thoroughly American, graduates of Ivy League schools. Michael now lived in Oregon with his bride-to-be.

Harry is a devoted family man, taking every appropriate opportunity to show pictures of his kids on the ISPI site. During the summer of 2009 he toured Grand Canyon with his son Michael, making the long hike to the bottom and posting a father-son picture on the ISPI web site. He appeared so happy, free, hardy, and perhaps proud of having kept up with his son, "the genius," according to his father who let his readers know his son was a Harvard man.

In the fall of 2009, Harry and Susan toured his ancestral Romania, then Poland, and then on to Auschwitz, the Nazi death camp at Oswiecim, Poland. Harry didn't talk about that visit, but he had good fun posting online photographs of chubby Germans.

Harry had come to the United States from Sydney in 1967, graduated from business school (he paid his way through by working as a professional photographer) and found an advocate in the late William G. McGowan, chairman and CEO of MCI. Harry was writing for a technology newsletter at the time, and McGowan had invited him to Washington, D.C., where Harry was to interview him. They became good friends.

Not long afterward, he took the dive into the tech magazine business, publishing seven monthlies with his partner, Gerry Friesen. They branched out to found two successful convention/trade show forums—Call Center Demo and Computer Telephony Conference and Exposition. The shows attracted more than 26,000 visitors. The Newton-Friesen team also managed to publish more than 40 books on networking, imaging, telecom, and computer telephony. The business was run out of a drafty loft in Chelsea that grew into four stories of frenetic activity.

In September 1997, they sold the publications to Miller Freeman for $130 million. Susan wanted out of the now-overgrown loft. "She wanted a real apartment," Harry said. "So we moved up here."

He remains the persistent writer, publishing *Newton's Telecom Dictionary*—more than 1,200 pages containing nearly 25,000 tech terms. The dictionary, which rivals the heft of the Washington, D.C., telephone directory, has sold more than 770,000 copies and is sailing into its 25th edition.

I pondered Harry as a kid. His parents were wine growers in Romania, but wisely headed for Australia in 1939, when it was clear Hitler was on the move in Europe. His father went from wine to opening a hamburger store in Sydney.

"He then got into frocks," Harry said. "He opened a frock shop. 'The ladies always need frocks,' my father used to say."

He snapped out of the flashback. He was quick to get back to the point of our mutual distrust of Wall Street.

"If an investor makes money it's a fluke," he insisted. "Really, there's so much we don't know, so much uncertainty."

He remained frustrated over fruitless threats by ARS victims that never came to pass.

"Whatever happened to that hunger strike idea?" Harry wanted to know, referring to an idea floated by a few California-based ARS investors. "That was a *great* idea. You need to bleed," he said. "Bleeding would be sure to get their attention."

The hour went by quickly. I was conscious of time. Harry was a busy man. He escorted me into the living space. I complimented him on the wonderful art—especially the big earthy Australian piece hanging above the mantel. There were other works—one by a former and now-deceased assistant to the late Andy Warhol: "They became too close, I'm afraid," said Harry said of the assistant. We stood there for a while looking at the art. "Susan's the one who picks it."

We passed a small antique serving table upon which stood an assortment of liquor bottles, including a fifth of London Bombay Sapphire gin. I mentioned that it was one of my favorites.

"I hate the stuff," said Harry, with genuine disgust. His tastes tend to exotic wines, which he only rarely imbibes.

"You know," he grinned, "I got only one bottle of wine out of all this blogging. Don't get me wrong. It was great wine. I wasn't begging for wine, that's awful. I simply mentioned it and someone sent me this bottle. It was very good."

✳ ✳ ✳

When I got back to Washington, I checked on the price of the bottle of wine Harry had received from one of our blog readers.

"Oh, that one," Fernando, my wine guy laughed. "Here, let me show you." He opened a big book of wines. "There it is," he said. "You want it? It's only $1,700."

I shook my head. "Forget it. I hate the stuff!"

Chapter 19

The View from Here

Standing absolutely still in the center of the casino, I looked
for a lucky table on which to begin.

—Mario Puzo, Fools Die

December 21, 2009.

What have we learned in this season of banks robbing people? Have
we learned too little? Or is it just the opposite? Did we learn more than
we ever wanted to know? Have we become what *New York Times* writer
and author Thomas Friedman calls "suboptimal," a country with leadership unable or unwilling to respond in smart ways to financial crises?

What we know for sure is that the biggest scheme devised by Wall
Street to rob you of your money might have succeeded had it not
been for the sheer audacity of a determined band of focused, angry,
and financially literate bloggers and motivated state regulators. Wall
Street clearly believed it had the upper hand; it almost always does.

Left unchallenged, the banks and brokerages would have walked away with our "free money." And not just chump change. Unchallenged, the banks would have expropriated $336 billion dollars—2 percent of the United States' GDP—enough to create millions of jobs and keep people in their homes. Too bad the only well-being Wall Street cares about is its own.

Will this greedier-than-thou culture ever change? Washington is attempting to craft regulatory reform. Unfortunately, this effort has become a supermajority political game. The Democrats are proposing new financial safeguards. With exceptions, most Republicans are resisting change as the party of "no." Congress, Treasury, and the Fed have managed to bring some health back to Wall Street—with regulatory strings attached. But on Main Street, where the remaining one-third of ARS investors live, progress remains glacial. The banks and brokerage holdouts continue to cling to their ill-gotten spoils. Over time, and with continued pressure, most of them will be forced to redeem these ARS holdings. So the fight continues.

Ask 100 ordinary citizens what they want by way of economic and political change and you'll get as many answers. Ask a group of Wall Street bankers, and it's likely they will say the status quo is just fine. Ask them about auction-rate securities and the bankers will say victims should have known better. I can't count how many times this phrase has been flung in my face—without embarrassment. Well, if I *should* have known better, what about the broker who sold the junk? He was a pro. He had the inside track. And if he didn't, he *should* have. It was part of his professional responsibility.

To date, no one I know in the financial services industry is able to produce an auction-rate securities prospectus. I have asked at least a dozen brokers to send me one. One former CFO said the best bet is to go online, where anyone can find definitions of the product. The problem with that seemingly sensible approach is that the risk component appeared only *after* the market collapsed and trust was destroyed.

The Internet is a powerful force, but it can't assess risk or forecast the future. Prior to the market collapse, most online materials discussing auction-rate securities and the auction market in general lacked the necessary depth to help people make informed judgments about risk.

Ultimately the lesson is about trust. Every investor must weigh the limits of his personal trust profile. You'll find good advice from professionals and laypersons in the Appendix of this book. Trust, however, remains a very personal and intangible matter. It is a factor beyond the professional filter. It exists almost as a form of survival instinct—gut wisdom—and usually it is more accurate than market prognostications.

As to the auction market collapse, here's what we know for sure: Investor gut wisdom failed on a massive scale. It failed to penetrate the sham description by broker-dealers of a safe, liquid market. Trust was violated on the most basic level. Without constant public and regulatory pressure and confrontation, the bankers and their traders would have patted themselves on the back and pocketed a fat chunk of GDP. Another slick deal and no one's the wiser. Easy money. More proof-positive that P.T. Barnum was right when he said, "There's a sucker born every minute." Absent investor push back, the bankers would have celebrated their takedown of the "sucker money" with more $2,000 lunches and obscene bonuses.

Wall Street counted on Barnum's informal census to pull off its sleight of hand in the auction-rate securities market. It almost worked. And, according to the North American Securities Administrators Association (NASAA), there remains approximately $120 billion to $160 billion still outstanding. This is mostly institutional capital that might be put to work to help revive the economy and inject life into the jobs market. Until the attorneys general in every state force the issue and demand redemption, that lingering cache of money will serve only to enhance the lifestyle of the con artists.

There are, however, thousands of retail investors, the "guppies," who are still waiting for justice and a chance to get on with their lives, cash-in-hand. Their grievances are many. You can hear them shouted in all the capitals of the world. As one French investor lamented, "The banks of the U.S. and Europe, they have brought us to tears."

As to feats of strength, no one doubts Wall Street's ability to manipulate and dissemble. Wall Street has no shame. Mention ethics to an investment banker and you've dropped the equivalent of the F-bomb. Yes, I know the official excuse for the ARS problem. It was brought on by an "unforeseen credit crunch." This is a convenient talking point. It is also a half-truth at best. Yes, there were severe credit problems in 2007 and 2008. We even managed to "break the buck." And no one was more responsible for these problems than the financial industry. Wall Street created the ARS deception. As far as the financiers were concerned the auction market had lost its glow; it wasn't bringing in enough cash. Solution: make sure that broker-dealers dump excess auction paper off their balance sheets and into the portfolios of their unsuspecting and trusting clients. The banks decided it was no longer sufficiently profitable to support the market, and so the plug was yanked. This was a central theme of the "scripted failure."

The final arrogance was to slip into a cone of silence and tell investors nothing. We have determined that the scheme was illegal. I wasn't the only one caught in that cone of silence; tens of thousands of other investors were refused basic market information from the point of sale to the final collapse. Billions of investor dollars were in the possession of the banks and no one was giving the owners of that money the information they needed. It was quite a heist. No point confusing clients with details—or telling them anything at all. Telling the truth might make for legal trouble. When investors cried foul, the banks essentially responded, "The monkey's dead. The show's over. Sue us!" (Thank you, Lionel.)

Thus the banks and investors are still, at this writing, engaged in a battle to hold over billions of ill-gotten gain. The investors are facing financial companies that refuse to accept responsibility or to admit they knew the market was showing signs of failing as early as 2004. When confronted by regulators, they called in their lawyers and vowed to defend themselves "vigorously." Yet despite the tenacity of the holdout firms, many retail and institutional investors are being made whole—but not without a furious, investor-led push.

The blogosphere got to the regulators and the regulators got going. The institutional accounts, unfortunately, still have a long way to go before resolution. Institutional investors are by definition considered "sophisticated." Their chances of winning in arbitration are sketchy. It seems a pity that business acumen stands as a negative in the arbitration arena. There's something perverse in this logic. Something chilling.

About those firms refusing to redeem the auction-rate paper they sold as cash equivalents: Depending on the actions brought by state regulators and the SEC against the "sophistication" argument, the holdouts may yet win. Among the prominent holdouts at this writing (April 2010) are Raymond James, Charles Schwab, and E*Trade. All are under challenge and all are fighting back.

These firms are clinging to questionable legal logic. They argue that, unlike the major banks, they did not underwrite auction-rate paper for municipal entities nor did they manage the auctions. Still, they sold billions of dollars worth of ARS to their clients, calling them by various names such as "cash management tools" and "floaters." Wall Street is very imaginative in its use of the language. Its forte is deception; its strong suit is obfuscation.

Raymond James management described legal demands to redeem ARS acts of "extortion." Does this fall into the category of overstatement or desperation? When it comes to extortion, Raymond James is the one holding the money hostage. Who is extorting whom?

Oppenheimer is presently redeeming ARS in piecemeal fashion in a settlement with New York and Massachusetts regulators. But why so many delays, so many twists and turns?

Schwab's CEO, Charles "Chuck" Schwab, vows to fight to the end. He has said investors picked up ARS willy-nilly from the firm's "cafeteria" of financial products, that company brokers didn't push the product. In other words, we are supposed to believe that investors acted on their own without benefit of a sales pitch. Schwab's cafeteria apparently had no cooks and no servers. Schwab brokers have clean hands, CEO Schwab insists. How can a financial debacle of such magnitude fail to attract the attention of professional brokers? This is like asking people to believe in unicorns. It's like asking how one can avoid seeing a UFO landing on the roof of a neighbor's home.

The job of getting the remaining ARS cash thawed remains primarily in the hands of state attorneys general, urged on by unrelenting public pressure, especially from the blogosphere. AuctionRatePreferreds .org, among others, plays in the nightmares of those public officials who wish to be reelected, reappointed, or to move on with their dreams of higher political ambition. This much I can say without hesitation: If these regulators fail their constituencies, they will be forced into career changes. That is my grievance—and warning—to them.

Their feats of strength will be tested in the court of public opinion and in the voting booth. In the meantime, the blogosphere will keep up the pressure.

In fairness, there's plenty of blame to go around. The banks and brokers aren't the only problem. The federal government will not win any prizes for its sad performance in the regulation of the financial industry and investor protection. The future feats of congressional strength will be put to the test in the political arena. It's very simple. If the cops fail the investors, the cops will be looking for other work. If financial reform turns out to be yet another cover for the banks, the regulators can expect a political tsunami in 2010.

The House Financial Services Committee, headed by Barney Frank, put on a show in September 2008 when it held three hours worth of hearings on the ARS problem. Well and good. The hearings, however detailed, resulted in *nothing* of real substance. No federal intervention. No arm-twisting. No tangible solutions for frightened investors who were praying for relief or, at the least, some outward show of assistance. It didn't happen. That public grievance will show up at the polls. The committee deserves to be applauded for bringing some sunshine to the ARS fiasco, though in the end it left the dirty work to state officials, many of whom were fearful of taking on their own campaign contributors—the banks and Wall Street lobbyists.

FINRA settled a few complaints—not many, just enough to show a pulse. There was one small glitch. FINRA sold off millions of dollars worth of its own ARS in 2007 when it knew the auction market was at the edge of collapse. But, FINRA forgot to warn the rest of us of the market's fatal weakness. For this we can thank the new chairwoman of the SEC, Mary Schapiro, who was then-head of FINRA. This unsightly appearance of insider trading might never have come to light without the hard work of Wall Street expatriate Larry Doyle, who revealed the little FINRA "oversight" on his blog, Sense on Cents. His exposé caused a sensation. The news was later picked up by mainstream media outlets.

With it all, FINRA has yet to explain its actions. Who can blame it? FINRA is supported by the banks. It is an SRO—a self-regulatory organization, and it is careful not to bite the hand that both feeds and informs it. Its performance in the ARS matter has been disgraceful. Why didn't FINRA warn investors of the market weakness before it sold off its own stash of auction rate paper? Ms. Schapiro has a lot of explaining to do.

Doyle made his grievances known and shamed FINRA. He continues to press for transparency. He deserves a trophy, as does Harry Newton, as does Kathy Kane and all those who pitched into the fray. Doyle wrote on December 13, 2009, in his Sense on Cents blog that only in Washington could financial regulatory reform be passed without taking on FINRA— which is another way of saying Washington is afraid to take on the Wall Street political contributors.

"Congress intentionally overlooks the ineffective practitioners of financial regulation because it would expose the extensive incest amidst the financial industry, the regulatory authority, and Washington," Doyle wrote. "If Washington truly wanted to inspire confidence in financial regulatory reform and send a strong message to America that it is seriously motivated to clean up Wall Street, our leaders would publicly support the lawsuits pending against FINRA. . . . We need to promote transparency and integrity in our financial regulators before we can even think of achieving transparency and integrity in our financial regulations."

We need to take a hard look at the obvious. The Washington-Wall Street nexus is a danger not only to the soundness of the financial system and the rule of law, it spills over to into areas of economic growth and national security.

The SEC also settled some ARS complaints. Not nearly enough for an agency charged with such great responsibility. Like FINRA, it put on a show worthy of Machiavelli.

Christopher Cox's SEC did nothing to prevent the ARS debacle from occurring nor did he pursue a well-crafted solution in the face of the ongoing fraud. Former Chairman Cox failed to step in on behalf of the public. Like former President George W. Bush, Chairman Cox was a "market guy." An ideologue. Like Alan Greenspan, the one and only "Maestro" of the Fed (thank you, Bob Woodward), Chairman Cox assumed the Lotus position and sought guidance from above, bypassing the White House and the Treasury Department, which was putting together the Troubled Asset Relief Program (TARP) bailout.

Cox apparently took his cues from the late author Ayn Rand, who immersed herself in the nineteenth-century German philosopher Friedrich Wilhelm Nietzsche's concept of the "superman," the *ubermensch*, which inspired so many of the totalitarian regimes of the 1930s and 1940s. While my view may appear to be over the top intellectually, the truth is that the Randian philosophy persists like a chronic rash. Much of Wall Street and certain quarters of Washington are still driven philosophically by Rand's famous character, the superman John Galt. It's a nonsensical paradigm. Unfortunately it is still with us. If you doubt it, attend a State of the Union Speech after-party or any strategy session at Goldman Sachs, where they do "God's work." (Thank you, Prophet Blankfein.)

It may be years, and maybe never, before we get to the bottom of Chairman Cox's lack of action when it was most needed. His failure to address the obvious market forces that led to ARS and other fiscal disasters remains mysterious. This isn't the place to psychoanalyze those who believe that markets are self-correcting deities—abstract as any imagined god, wiser and more efficient than nature itself. SEC and FINRA showed themselves to be losers and cowards. But the biggest losses are suffered by the investing public and the cultural fabric of the United States.

✳ ✳ ✳

Denise Voigt Crawford, president of NASAA, could charm the most ruthless options trader in Chicago or New York. Her soft Southern accent, her perfect syntax, are echoes of a world of manners and graciousness that were once the quintessential marks of high culture. One would not expect to find her anywhere near the world of finance. Yet Denise Voigt Crawford, who is also the Texas securities commissioner, was the first regulator on the ARS scene. She settled the first complaint, gaining for 38,000 Citigroup investors a payback of $7.3 billion.

Crawford's polite-as-they-come manner, her halo of strawberry blond hair, and disarming smile, hide a tough-minded regulator who isn't afraid to pick political fights.

Barbara Roper, director of investment protection for the Consumer Federation of America, says of Crawford that she "never comes across as mean, but she is tough. And she has credibility with both political parties."

This is a rare quality in our era of polarization; it is the gift of transcendence. Washington can learn a lot from Crawford, and those who know her say she has tamed more than one stubborn congressman with her disarming manners.

Crawford told me she was appalled by the ARS meltdown. The collapse of the market put financial strains on individuals, towns, cities, hospitals, charities, and threatened to disrupt students' ability to finance higher education, she said during an interview in late 2009. Complaints flooded her office.

She understood the argument made by the financial industry that the severity of the credit crunch that began in August 2007 brought with it a number of unseen consequences. She also was aware of the argument put forth by Wall Street that placing "additional burdens" on the banks, deserved or not during chaotic economic times, might be like pouring gasoline on the fire of systemic recklessness. Despite the outrage that Wall Street and the regulators have brought down upon themselves, and in the face of all this tumult, Denise Voigt Crawford maintains a positive outlook.

"Yes," she admitted, "I am an optimist. We're going to get through this mess, which certainly takes into account the auction-rate problem. I truly believe we're going to work it out in a positive way."

Crawford praised state regulators, especially Andrew Cuomo of New York.

"He was very good at looking into things and getting the parties together," she said.

I asked her to speculate on the causes of the ARS market tumble. She apparently doesn't buy into the "scripted failure" talk that spread through the ranks in Washington. She was more focused on the regulatory aspects of the debacle.

"There was a gap in regulation. The SEC really should have handled the crisis. It was national in scope. That's SEC's business. But the commission didn't act, and so the state regulators stepped up to the plate," she said.

She is obviously not enamored of Washington's regulatory muscle. She finds it flabby and, to some extent, even atrophied. She appears to have a gimlet eye on the Obama administration's financial regulatory package. The failure of the feds to act in the auction market scandal has given her pause.

"It says something sad about regulation at the national level," said Crawford. "NASAA had to take it on. This proves how important it is to have a backstop at the state level. State regulators are an early warning sign. We hear about things first."

Does she believe investors have lost faith—and confidence—in the markets?

She didn't hesitate to jump on the question.

"Investor confidence? It's pretty low," she replied. "They're actually furious. They read about all these big bonuses, TARP, and all the rest. This leaves individual investors feeling a little helpless. Certainly they are fearful. I have friends who say they'll never invest again. That's worrisome to me."

One of the concerns dogging investors is the lack of fundamentals in the markets. Crawford believes the basics, the metrics by which we've measured and analyzed stocks and bonds over the years, have been reduced to prognostication, little of which is either smart or reliable. What's left over is technical analysis—a math exercise most investors shy away from, and for good reason. A substantial component of the economic meltdown that nearly brought the country to its knees was driven by a mindless faith in algorithms. Mathematical modeling has been a problem, especially in the volatile derivatives and swap markets. Math modeling produces projections that are too constrained to fit a chaotic reality. There is an old Chinese saying that says when a butterfly spreads its wings, the effects are realized in unpredictable ways in distant lands. This is to say that no mathematical projection can hold together against unseen and unpredictable variables—those scary black swans.

"One thing we're seeing is that mainstream investors are looking for really qualified advisors," said Crawford. With trust at its lowest levels in decades, the definition of a qualified advisor isn't easy to pin down. "We need investor education in the schools," Crawford believes. "We need to teach the basics very early on. Some policy makers are forcing the issue. I absolutely believe in financial education. On a state level, we're committed to making his happen. But we need support."

I had to wonder if education would have prevented the ARS calamity. Crawford said it might have helped. She gave me a definite maybe. There is no denying that legions of ordinary, trusting investors and institutional money managers were sucked into the ARS pit by seasoned advisors. And the institutional investors were not amateurs; many were sharp CFOs working in large corporations. When it came to the auction-rate market, it seems a leveling process, driven by deception, caught *everyone* in its snare. When the storm struck, the ordinary citizen investor and the CFO shared the same tiny life raft in a nasty sea where the sharks made all the rules.

"There are 'bad apple' advisors," said Crawford. "I'm not going to disagree with you there. But going it alone is risky. If you're going to invest, or have a professional do it for you, you still need to do your homework. There's no getting away from it."

As for trustworthy brokers, it's best to take the Ronald Reagan view: "Trust but verify," said Crawford.

Still, reading the business section of any major newspaper remains a discouraging task. ARS is a glaring example—a very big one. Each day there are thousands of smaller con games reported to various enforcement agencies. But what about those we never discover? We can track the peaks of the icebergs, but so much more remains below the surface.

Crawford wants Congress to expand the role of the states in financial-services regulation. She wants fiduciary responsibility to be shouldered by brokers and advisors. In addition, she'd like to end mandatory arbitration and wants a state role for any systemic risk regulator.

In a December 13, 2009, interview in *Investment News* by Dan Jamieson, Crawford said that if Congress arms itself with too many federal regulatory weapons, enforcement may suffer because it may make the process too cumbersome. But she has a rejoinder for those who argue that regulation is a bad thing: "Deregulation has swung so far that it could cause capitalism to destroy itself," she warns.

She is not a FINRA booster. SROs are accountable to their members, not the public. In essence, FINRA is bound to be conflicted. Crawford insists that the federal government must maintain its role as primary regulator. On the other hand, she believes the states can accomplish more frequent examination of economic booby traps than the SEC. She told *Investment News*: "It's healthy for there to be different types of regulators, multiple regulators, because you're likely to get a better result."

The volume of financial crime does not surprise her.

"If you think the media reports crime, you should see what state regulators see. The point, I guess, is to be very, very careful. Stay away from what you don't understand."

What's the message of the ARS meltdown?

"There are many," said Crawford. "One of them is that people can see the Wall Street-Washington connection. People wonder—and this is the big question—can Washington control Wall Street? People complain about Washington all the time, and I think that may be a mistake. We need good government. We need to be careful we don't allow things to get so far out of hand."

At the beginning of this interview, I said Denise Voigt Crawford is an optimist. The interview revealed that her optimism is tempered by a healthy caution born of experience.

"If we're careful, if we're diligent, we'll work our way out of this chaos. I really believe it. Yes, I remain optimistic," she concluded.

✳ ✳ ✳

About the blind physician mentioned earlier in these pages: We tried to contact her in early 2010. We wanted to know what happened to her in arbitration. We telephoned. The operator came on the line and said the phone was disconnected. We never heard from her again.

✳ ✳ ✳

As in war, you don't always know where the front is until it hits you in the face. The analogy applies to Wall Street. For ARS victims and other investors, the Wall Street juggernaut remains the front line, the point of attack that surrounds every spare dime in a classic *Kesselschlacht* maneuver.

The ARS collapse is only one of many economic assaults brought on by an out of control financial system stretching back to the early days of the Republic. Thomas Jefferson was right: Banks are more dangerous than armies. Americans have begun to heed Jefferson's warning. It's a late wake-up call. We hope it isn't too late.

Wall Street is perpetually on the attack. Many would deny this accusation, although who would question the unrelenting desire to relieve us of our wealth and to establish, in law, what some might call a *benevolent oligopoly*?

Wall Street also operates on a parasite-host paradigm. In the example of the ARS scandal, the symbiotic relationship is clear. Thousands of auction-rate investors hosted the parasites for 20 years. Wall Street banks made billions of dollars underwriting and manipulating the market before pulling the plug.

When the Wall Street-investor symbiosis is no longer bringing in sucker money, the Street moves on to its next toxic bag of tricks—swaps, collateralized debt obligations, bait-and-switch mortgages, perpetual mortgages, reverse mortgages, and a pandemic of derivative products timed to blow up in the faces of the gullible.

ARS victims didn't know they were on the front lines until February 2008, when the market imploded by virtue of the banks having shut down the auctions and hoarding investor cash. ARS investors walked into an economic ambush that has cheated them and the country out of a significant chunk of wealth at a time when every dollar is needed to create jobs and fund capital investment.

On a recent trip to New York, I had lunch with a successful business owner who expressed what I have heard from dozens of investors and business executives.

"I just want to get away from it all," he told me. "There's nothing in it for me."

We may never know how many tens of thousands, or even millions, of investors will no longer deal with Wall Street. The I-banks will continue to make deals. But the small investor—and in this group I include millionaires—may be gone from the scene for years, if not forever. They are disillusioned. They are bitter.

Attorneys representing ARS investors have warned their clients to stay away from reporters and other media. This is exactly the same advice I received from my attorney, Bill Heyman, at the beginning of this journey. And as the scandal slowly winds down, the same advice is in vogue. Wall Street attorneys have the power to subpoena information on your computers, financial records, even personal correspondence in search of investor "sophistication"—their ace-in-the-hole, the you-should-have-known-better killer argument that will sink any chance of financial justice. This is how the FBI treats racketeers. The FBI exposed

Al Capone's books. In the financial world an investor's private papers can be seized to prove a specious point. In a perverse way, the investor may be roughed up like a common criminal, and neither Washington nor state governments have done anything to protect against the right of Wall Street to invade one's privacy in the kangaroo court of mandatory arbitration.

None of this is fair or ethical. Such tactics serve as a poison pill to the wealth and health of the nation as a whole.

There will always be savvy and successful people, those whose success leads to the conceit that they can beat the market. It is a conceit only a handful of them can afford. They would do better, and have more fun, in Las Vegas where the fundamentals at the blackjack table are more substantial than today's stock market. Ask anyone whose 401(k) was shorted into near oblivion in 2008.

But the ARS investor was a different breed. Mostly middle-aged or older, they were risk-averse people at or near retirement. They desired safety above all else. Their mistake, like my own, was reaching for a little extra yield. We didn't believe that gaining an extra 25 or 50 basis points worth of interest implied much risk. We believed and trusted our brokers, and this was our second misjudgment. We pushed aside our deeper knowledge, our common sense, and a truth we could not admit: Our brokers are salesmen who operate as if they have little, if any, responsibility to look out for their clients. Insiders are still wrangling over this ethical point. If you have a broker without fiduciary responsibility, you may have problem.

The simple truth is that a majority of brokers are, in practice, responsible only to themselves. If their clients make money, well and good. But the bottom line is the broker's well-being. This will not change until a measure of fiduciary responsibility is imposed on them. In the meantime, brokers will remain self-serving middlemen. From the pathetic cold-caller to the strutting hedge fund manager, investors will remain a source of cash and will bear the greatest risk inherent in any investment.

The ARS scandal and TARP have left a stain on Wall Street and its band of executive cowboys. We have learned that the "best and the brightest" aren't so bright. We were foolish to give credit and trust where it was never due.

It is still hard for some investors to admit that Wall Street doesn't have all the answers. They blanch at the obvious: The financial industry is cagey and devious. It poses as objective and even scientific. It is this writer's opinion that if you believe algorithmic models reduce risk and provide a view of the future, then you might as well believe that immortality is an unshakable truth. This is no longer your father's or your grandfather's market. You are not Warren Buffett, the grandfatherly investor who buys railroads (railroads are considered strategic assets) and has enough money to make sweetheart deals with the likes of Goldman Sachs.

It was once an article of faith that investing in the United States was an act of patriotism. But now the world is flat. The engines that once created domestic wealth have been exported around the globe. Investors are now citizens of a larger and more complex universe. They would be wise to understand the implications.

President Obama has pressured the heads of the nation's largest TARP recipients to take "extraordinary" steps to kick-start lending for small businesses and homeowners. A dozen top executives from major financial institutions recently were summoned to the White House to hear the president demand more to help the economy create jobs. The presence of these executives at the White House would be a tip of the hat to U.S. taxpayers who funded the federal bailout that kept Wall Street and the banking system from drowning in its own bad decisions. But if the banks came hat-in-hand a year earlier, they now confronted the president—and the American people—with hubris.

In a December 14, 2009, *New York Times* article, Helene Cooper reported, "As they [the banks] scurry to repay the government and escape its influence over its operations, they have been fighting elements of the legislation to regulate the industry more tightly."

The banks also are seeking to restore executive pay to astronomical levels. They insist that government demands to hold healthier levels of reserves against losses makes it harder for them to issue more loans.

The heads of three of the biggest companies—Goldman Sachs, Citigroup, and Morgan Stanley—didn't bother to show up at the White House. They claimed they were stuck in New York and couldn't book commercial flights to Washington because of "inclement weather." I wonder if they considered coming to Washington 24 hours in advance or (heaven forbid!) hopping on Amtrak. I wonder if the no-shows realized how disrespectful they were, not only to the president, but also to the taxpayers who saved their companies. Wall Street, it seems, has a view of itself as an independent country, a sovereign entity responsible only to itself.

The president, obviously dismayed by this slight, nevertheless issued a strong statement after the meeting.

"I made very clear that I have no intention of letting their lobbyists thwart reforms necessary to protect the American people. If they wish to fight common sense consumer protection, that's a fight I'm more than willing to have."

Tough talk. Many wonder if the president can back it up or if Congress, which depends on the banks for campaign contributions, will have the courage to help the president make it stick.

* * *

Are we still capable of growing the United States in cooperation with the once-fertile fields of finance? Or has the world of finance dumped too much toxic waste into our gardens? I might have titled this book *Blood Is Green*. But *Ruthless* is the more fitting title for what we have witnessed and suffered at the hands of the financial community.

I would never dream of writing a book on how to invest. I could never offer up the kind of pap written by an endless stream of experts promising "systems" sure to make you filthy rich. Instead, this book is a cautionary tale. In it are many warning signs taken from real life— also hopeful truths. *Ruthless* demonstrates that ordinary investors can band together to beat Wall Street's bag of confiscatory tricks.

The battle isn't over. Some $200 billion in auction-rate cash has been returned—that's nearly two-thirds of the total. Those of us who fought are proud of our efforts. An estimated $120 billion to $160 billion in ARS remains under challenge. Investors continue to hang together and fight back using the power of the blogosphere, moral suasion, and all manner of noise-making instruments, including the courts. ARS investors educated each one another, pulled together, and became a force big enough, loud enough, and ruthless enough not to be robbed.

* * *

I admit I've been hard on Wall Street. In addition, I admit Wall Street is an easy target. It is a bully and its actions have made the world a more frightening place.

Is the criticism unfair?

I ask this because in the end the ARS scandal and Wall Street may be symptoms of something in us, perhaps an outgrowth of our own passion, fear, and greed.

We created Wall Street. Its sins are so big they are visible from outer space. We need to think seriously about our collective role in the creation of this financial cauldron. We overlooked much of what we now abhor when investors were full of "irrational exuberance" in the 1990s and the years between 2003 and 2007. We were making money. We were "geniuses." Jim Cramer was our populist guru. We didn't give a hoot how much bankers were paying themselves. We were happy to take our profits and spend more than we should have. We signed mortgages that advertised, "No job, no assets, no credit, no problem." We bought stocks on margin. When margin ran out, we borrowed more from banks to buy more bubble-inspired equity. We bought debt so bad that even a child could see trouble waiting down the road.

And we hated government. Oh, how we capitalists brayed in disapproval at any hint of financial regulation. We believed Alan Greenspan was a better economist than he was a saxophonist. We envied hedge fund managers. We didn't think twice about paying a 2 percent management fee and 20 percent of profits that these financial swamis demanded for their services. If they didn't deliver, the true believers paid these outrageous fees anyway.

It didn't bother us that hedge funds rode the big common bubble to outrageous profits—not because hedge fund managers were prophets, but rather because the bubble was being inflated by cagey bears. We didn't bother to anticipate collusive short selling as a consequence of phony rallies.

Where was our outrage in the fat years? Where was our wisdom? What happened to the hard-earned lessons of financial history?

None of this gloriously risky behavior meant anything as long as we were getting richer, fatter, dumber, and ripe for the takedown. There were voices of caution, visions of black swans. We failed to listen. We discounted what our eyes could see.

Foreclosures were ripping through Chicago's poorer neighborhoods in the spring of 2007 when the Chicago Fed convened on the bubble that was Michigan Avenue. Fed Chairman Ben Bernanke told the assembled businessmen and bankers that prosperity was in no way threatened by the subprime contagion. He said the banks faced no risk, that most weren't even involved in subprime. The economy was in fine shape, he said.

Bernanke then issued an uplifting statement, which was reprised in the pages of the December 21, 2009, *Washington Post* in a story by Binyamin Appelbaum and David Cho. It was a happy little note of confidence that has proven to be totally false:

> We see no serious broad spillover to banks or thrift institutions from the problems in the subprime market, Bernanke said after that Chicago gathering.

He was wrong, not that we cared to make a careful examination of his remarks. We were gleefully buying and selling stocks and reaching for yield, our eyes wide shut. Wall Street recognized our unrestrained optimism, ginned up the product-making machinery, and cranked up the short sellers for the coup de grace. Despite warnings, despite calls for sanity from those older and more experienced in the markets, we played into the trap.

It will be argued that all that followed was just business as usual. And much of it was. We, who created Wall Street, we who bought its products, we who believed auction-rate securities were good as cash and safe as Treasuries took the hit, and the rest of the country followed.

We've learned a great deal in the past two years. We may be wiser, more cautious, and less gullible. We may demand more from our government. The next time someone like Phil Gramm shows up with the brilliant idea of eliminating a proven market safety net like the Glass-Steagall Act of 1933, we may shout *no*! This safety net was destroyed in November 1999 by the Gramm-Leach-Bliley Act which, among other things, promoted the myth of the self-regulating "efficient market." Hopefully the days of wine and myth-making are over.

* * *

I wrote the broad outlines of the end of this book in a hotel room off Broadway in New York City. When I read my notes to Sandy, she said, "You have to leave your readers with a positive message—with hope."

So here it is.

Through cooperation, not mindless competition, we are winning the ARS battle. At the same time, we are slowly repairing the broader markets. We have learned that the new medium of the Internet allows us to reach deep into the realms of the markets and bring us face-to-face with federal and state regulators. Sheepish, trusting investors woke up in February 2008 and found powers they didn't know they had.

We have put Wall Street on notice. Shape up or those of us who are left will ship out. *We are no longer who you think we are.*

We say to Wall Street that the gunslinger days are over. Ignore this warning at your peril. What you have given us has too often been unethical and immoral and just plain crooked. We won't—*can't*—stand for it any longer. Investors now have those foolproof, shockproof shit detectors. Wall Street wise guys, take notice.

"That's better," said Sandy.

"I hope so."

"Well, was it worth it, all that writing?"

"Absolutely."

"Really? You're sure of it?"

"I am."

"It must make you feel pretty darned good."

"Oh yes, it does. That's the best thing about it."

Appendix

Lessons from an ARS Investor

Harry Newton

Background: After I got some cash in the fall of 2007, my broker put $4.5 million of my cash into auction-rate securities. He said it was a "cash equivalent." I could get my money every seven days. He also put in $800,000 of his own money. Many months later we all got our money back because our brokerage company—not the issuer—redeemed them. The company didn't need to. The company did it to win favor with its clients, like me. I'm guessing the company also worked some deal with the issuer. Here are some lessons I learned from the whole ghastly experience:

1. Don't believe anything your broker tells you. If he knew, he'd be rich. He wouldn't be wasting his time advising a pauper like you (and me).
2. Check everything three times. Remember it's your money. You worked hard for it. No one else cares about it.
3. When in the slightest doubt, say no.

4. Don't chase yield, also called "returns." Auction-rate securities offered us a trivial increase in return—less than a quarter of 1 percent. Yet the risks turned out to be gigantic. Many of us have lost our entire investment for a trivial potential increase in return.

5. Wall Street has no crystal ball and no conscience.

6. There is no way for a small investor (less than $50 million in assets) to ever win a fight with Wall Street. The odds are stacked against you. I could write a book.

7. If you ever do get into a fight with Wall Street, know that the squeaky wheel gets the most attention.

8. The worst thing you can do in your investing life is to lose your entire principal.

9. Reread this list, beginning at Point 1.

Words of Wisdom from a Former Wall Street Insider

Larry Doyle

The following was graciously contributed by Wall Street veteran and Sense on Cents blogger Larry Doyle. He was one of the active warriors—and still is— in the battle to gain fairness for investors.

There are a number of painful lessons embedded in the mass fraud known as auction-rate securities:

1. The importance of fully understanding the risks and intricacies of each and every financial product being promoted to you by brokers and financial planners. Do not think for a second that a particular financial product does not have a number of risks. Fully explore each and every one of them.

2. Realize that one of the greatest risks in the financial-services industry is counterparty risk. This risk addresses both the individual and the institution with whom you are engaging. Individuals and institutions generate revenues by selling products. Engage those with whom you have developed a personal rapport and relationship. Question them aggressively as to where risks are embedded in products. Ask for written details on products and their risks.

3. Do not think for a second that the industry or its regulators are looking out for you. From the SEC to FINRA to SIPC, our financial regulatory bodies failed investors miserably. Why? As much as they might like to project an image of protecting investors, the fact is these regulators have truly served at the behest of the financial industry.

4. Where is one to turn? What is one to do? Work at educating yourself via independent sites. Work at developing meaningful relationships with people who have your long-term interests at heart. When in doubt, simplify your financial life both in terms of assets and liabilities. Control your finances so that your finances do not control you.

How could a cash-like, cash surrogate product such as auction-rate securities cause so much pain and anguish? Very simply: Wall Street took advantage of clients in the process. Never allow yourself to be put in that position by a crowd that is focused on its bottom line and not yours.

Information for Use by ARS-ARP Investors Still Stuck with Illiquid Paper

Compiled by Kathy Kane

Comprehensive ARS Action List

1. File a complaint with the SEC.
   a. E-mail: ENF-ARScomplaints@sec.gov
   b. Phone: 202-551-4938 or 202-551-4824
   c. Write: SEC Complaint Center, 100 F Street NE, Washington, D.C. 20549-0213
   d. What to tell them:
      • Who your brokerage and financial advisor were.
      • When this happened.
      • Exactly what you were told and what you asked.
      • How these were described to you, that is, why and how you were led to believe this was always liquid and no risk to principal.
      • Whether you ever saw a prospectus or anything in writing regarding risk.

- Whether you received any verbal information regarding risk.
- How the account was described on your statement or application for account (cash equivalent, money market, seven-day paper, etc.).
- Any communication (or lack thereof) from your brokerage clarifying what your investment was subsequent to the opening of the account to the present, or any warning that it was "imperiled."
- Anything you think your brokerage might be relying on as a written defense, and why it didn't give you meaningful understanding of your investment given what the brokerage actually told you.

2. Call your Congressional representatives.

a. Ask your House Representative to ask Rep. Barney Frank, chairman of the House Finance Committee, to begin an investigation.

b. Ask your senators to ask Senator Max Baucus, chairman of the Senate Finance Committee, to begin an investigation.

c. If you don't get a response from your legislator, keep calling.

3. File a complaint with your state's securities regulator. Find your state securities office at the web site of the North American Securities Administrators Association (NASAA) www.nasaa.org.

a. **Florida residents**: To file an online complaint with the Florida Department of Regulation against your broker or brokerage: www.flofr.com/Securities/Complaints/Online/Comp.o_qt2.htm Tel: 850-410-9701

- Florida residents, Palm Beach County: The number to call and file the complaint is 561-837-5203.

b. **California residents**: Web site is www.corp.ca.gov/.

- In 2008, Wayne Strumpfer was Deputy Commissioner, Dept of Corporations 916-324-6912 WStrumpf@corp.ca.gov

c. **New York residents**: Contact office of Attorney General Andrew Cuomo (see more following).

d. **Illinois residents**: The Illinois Secretary of State's Department of Securities will take your complaint and open an investigation for you. They will then appoint an attorney/investigator to help you with your case. Their contact information:

Toll-free within Illinois: 800-628-7937

Chicago Office:
69 W. Washington Street
Suite 1220
Chicago, IL 60602
Phone: 312-793-3384 / Fax: 312-793-1202

Springfield Office:
Jefferson Terrace
Suite 300 A
300 West Jefferson Street
Springfield, IL 62702
Phone: 217-782-2256 / Fax: 217-782-8876

Web address, Illinois SEC: www.cyberdriveillinois.com/departments/securities/home.html

  e. **Washington State residents**: www.dfi.wa.gov/sd/ or http://dfi.wa.gov/sd/investor_online_complaint.htm
4. Contact your own state Attorney General.
  a. **In California**: AG Jerry Brown has prosecuted cases. PIU@DOJ.CA.GOV. Fax: 916-323-5341. Also: www.corp.ca.gov/about/complaint.asp

5. Residents of all states: Contact the multistate securities investigation. The state regulators want to compel the brokers to rescind our fraudulent ARS transactions, based on point of sale. That is what the multistate investigation of the NASAA is all about.

NASAA www.nasaa.org. Leaders on ARS at NASAA:

Denise Vogt Crawford
Texas State Securities Board
www.ssb.state.tx.us/

Karen Tyler North Dakota Securities Commissioner
State Capitol, 5th Floor
600 East Boulevard Avenue
Bismarck, ND 58505
701-328-2910

They want to talk to you no matter what state you are in.

The principal objective of the multistate task force is to get us our money back, based on brokerage fraud at point of sale. The states have the power to order rescission.

The multistate task force organized itself brokerage by brokerage. (One state is assigned to investigate each brokerage.) The original task force chair, in Massachusetts:

Bryan Lantagne
Director, Securities Division
ARS Task Force Chair
617-727-3548
Bryan.lantagne@sec.state.ma.us

Mr. Lantagne's assistant prosecutor in Massachusetts is concentrating on UBS:

Joshua S. Grinspoon, staff attorney
Enforcement Section
Massachusetts Securities Division
One Ashburton Place, Room 1701
Boston, MA 02108
Telephone: 617-727-3548
Fax: 617-248-0177

Mr. Grinspoon has stated that the principal goal of the investigation is to obtain rescission of the ARS transactions from the brokerages to the investors. Mr. Grinspoon said, "All I can tell you is that we are pursuing this with as much energy and dedication as we have ever applied to any matter."

California victims should contact the Department of Corporations directly to organize California action:

Wayne Strumpfer [has since moved to the SEC]
Deputy Commissioner, Department of Corporations
916-324-6912
wstrumpf@corp.ca.gov

The original Texas securities regulator in charge of the Citi/SB investigation: TX (lead on Citi/Smith Barney)

Benette Zivley, director, Inspections & Compliance Division
512-305-8300
bzivley@ssb.state.tx.us

6. Residents of all states, contact the New York State Attorney General.

    a. The New York State Attorney General's office is investigating, and they want to hear from you no matter where you live. Contact Christopher Mulvihill, assistant attorney general (to Andrew Cuomo).

        Telephone: 212-416-6563

        christopher.mulvihill@oag.state.ny.us

        Mailing address:
        State of New York Office of the Attorney General
        120 Broadway, New York, New York 10271

    b. Contact Massachusetts Secretary of State William Galvin. His office is investigating and has taken action against multiple firms. Let him hear from all of us. www.sec.state.ma.us/ or the Securities page: www.sec.state.ma.us/sct/sctidx.htm

7. Write the media.

8. Complain to the funds that sold you this junk.

    a. Call regularly. Ask them what they are doing to get you your money.

    b. Write letters to the president of the company.

    c. Find out who sits on the board of directors of the fund, and write and call them. Here's how to find these names:

- Go to www.sec.gov/edgar/searchedgar/companysearch.html
- Type in the name of the closed-end fund family in the "Company name" field (i.e. Van Kampen)
- Click on the link on the left side of the page that corresponds to your particular fund (i.e. Van Kampen Advantage Municipal Income Trust)
- Click on the text link on the left side of the page next to "DEF 14A."
- Scroll down the page until you come to the section called "Information Regarding Trustees and Nominees for Election as Trustee."
- Once you have the name, you might want to use Switchboard (http://switchboard.intelius.com) to look up the names of all of the trustees to get their home phone numbers.

- You may choose to call the trustee at home. Tell the trustee your problem, politely but directly.
- Post information you receive on the Bloggingstocks blog: www.bloggingstocks.com/2008/02/27/when-the-collapsed-auction-rate-securities-ars-market-gets-per/435#comments.

9. Other government representatives to complain to:

   a. Timothy Geithner
     The Department of the Treasury
     Office of the Treasurer
     1500 Pennsylvania Avenue, NW, Room 2134
     Washington, DC 20220
     Fax: 202-622-6464

   b. Write and call Senator Baucus and Congressman Frank yourself:

     Honorable Senator Max Baucus
     U.S. Senate Committee on Finance, chairman
     511 Hart Senate Office Bldg.
     Washington, DC 20510
     202-224-2651 (Office)
     202-224-0515 (Fax)

     Honorable Congressman Barney Frank
     House Committee on Financial Services, chairman
     2252 Rayburn H.O.B.
     Washington, DC 20515
     202-225-5931

   c. Write Senator Chris Dodd, chairman of the Senate Banking Committee. His e-mail: http://dodd.senate.gov/ Be sure to check "Banking" as the subject on your e-mail.

   d. Write to Erik R. Sirri, director, Division of Trading and Markets, U.S. Securities and Exchange Commission. He is an important player in all of this. Do not assume each division of the SEC is working together to find a solution. His e-mail is SirriE@sec.gov; phone: 202-551-5500.

10. Other regulatory bodies to complain to:

   a. Financial Industry Regulatory Authority

     FINRA Arbitration
     FINRA Dispute Resolution

One Liberty Plaza

165 Broadway, 27th Floor

New York, NY 10006

Phone: 212-858-4200

Fax: 301-527-4873

FINRA Dispute Resolution

55 West Monroe Street, Suite 2600

Chicago, IL 60603-1002

Phone: 312-899-4440, 240-386-4357

Fax: 312-236-9239

FINRA handles general complaints against brokerage houses and/or dealers: www.finra.org. Complaint form bottom right of home page.

   b. Better Business Bureau of the state your broker resides in: www .bbb.org

11. Complain regularly to your brokerage firm: your broker, the branch manager, and high level broker management. Tell them to pressure the fund companies for a solution, and tell them that they have lost your trust and will lose the rest of your money, too.

   a. Consider filing an SEC complaint against the national president of the brokerage firm.

12. Other agencies to complain to:

   a. National Fraud Information Center: www.fraud.org

   b. Investor Protection Trust: www.investorprotection.org/iec/ question_scams.html

   c. Alliance for Investor Education: www.investoreducation.org

   d. Your state securities agency: www.nasaa.org/QuickLinks/ ContactYourRegulator.cfm

   e. Securities Industry and Financial Markets Association: www .sifma.org

   f. Federal Reserve: www.federalreserveconsumerhelp.gov/contact.cfm

13. Consider legal action: Read up and decide whether you want to join a class-action suit or class-action arbitration against the investment banks and the funds, or perhaps sue/arbitrate individually.

14. Check your own nest: Read the fine print in your agreement with your brokerage firm. Figure out the statute of limitations for filing grievances and whether you must agree to arbitration to resolve disputes.

Acknowledgments

O ne of the lessons learned in writing this book is that people are ultrasensitive about their money, especially these days. Because they pitched into the fight and disclosed sensitive financial information, some who are acknowledged here insist on confidentiality, and I have identified some of them by their aliases.

The following persons and organizations offered invaluable advice and information and have the author's deepest respect:

Brad; Aaron Sheanin; GRJ; Alan L; Ed; AG; Lily; DM; Bill Heyman; Harwood Nichols; Bonnie Krosin; Ann Purcell; Sam; Janell Cannon (RAHR!!); Professor Bruce Freeman; Helen Thomas; Howard Kastel; Mike Perks; Rep. Barney Frank; the late Peter Panerites; raccoon; National Association of State Securities Administrators; Jim Weber; Daisy Maxey; jaylisa; Jay Haley; Denise Voigt; Kevin M. Carroll; Robert A. Buhlman; Jerry; Liqal; John Rausch; Yves Geniaux; Jason Coles; Lisa Shenkle; Paula S; Richard J. Busman; Gregg McNelley; Al G; Sam Edwards; Laura Edgerdall; Americas Watchdog; Patricia Murphy; Robert Greene; Leah Manzari; Marty Lobel; Rod and Beth; June Hoidal; Bob Webster; Yves Boulliet; Neil and Kathleen Hughes; Sharon Hoefler; Jay and Eva Jagoe; Marc Trupp.

With special appreciation to Harry Newton, Kathy Kane, and Larry Doyle.

I also wish to thank Debra Englander of John Wiley & Sons for taking a chance on this book. Her courage is a rare gift. Others at Wiley to whom I am greatly indebted are Kelly O'Connor and Adrianna Johnston. To the entire John Wiley team—thank you.

Much respect and gratitude to Cindy Zigmund, whose critical eye and sage advice were invaluable. She was always there for me. Cindy and John Willig are superagents. Without them, this book would not be.

I take a deep bow to the talented publicists and friends at Planned TV Arts: especially Rick Frishman, David Hahn, Jeff Nordstedt, Deborah Kohan, Amy Hess, Hillary Buckholtz, and Dee Donavanik.

My family was especially supportive in trying times, of which there were more than a few. My ever-patient wife Sandy lived through this book and many sleepless nights with me, and I have dedicated this work to her. Also, much love to Rebecca Saron Trupp; John and Kathy Trupp; Zack and Amy Price; Julian and Sophie Trupp. Together you are the gravity that keeps me from flying off the planet.

About the Author

Phil Trupp was a reporter at the *Washington Evening Star* and the *Baltimore News-American*. He spent seven years covering Washington, D.C., politics for Fairchild Publications and ABC/Cap Cities radio news. He has won commendation for stories on mob influence in the trucking industry. His articles on coal miners' black lung disease appeared in *Reader's Digest* and were reprinted in the *Congressional Record*. His fascination with the sea led him to become the first journalist to work in the United States' only undersea habitat, Hydrolab, earning him the title of NOAA Aquanaut. He wrote of his ocean adventures in the 1998 book *Sea of Dreamers*. He is a fellow of the Explorers Club. His interest in economics and finance led him into day-trading. His commentary appears on financial blogs such as the *New York Times* DealBook, Seeking Alpha, Sense on Cents, and In Search of the Perfect Investment. Trupp is a graduate of the University of Maryland. He lives with his wife, Sandy, in Washington, D.C.

Index